On Terrorism and Combating Terrorism

On Terrorism and Combating Terrorism

Edited by
Ariel Merari

Proceedings of an International Seminar, Tel-Aviv, 1979

University Publications of America, Inc.

JCSS Publications

Publications of the Jaffee Center for Strategic Studies present the findings and assessments of the center's research staff. Each paper represents the work of a single investigator or a team. Such teams may also include research fellows who are not members of the center's staff. Views expressed in the center's publications are those of the authors and do not necessarily reflect the views of the center, its trustees, officers, or other staff members, or the organizations and individuals that support its research. Thus, the publication of a work by the JCSS signifies that it is deemed worthy of public consideration but does not imply endorsement of conclusions or recommendations.

Copyright © 1985 by University Publications of America, Inc.
44 North Market Street, Frederick, Maryland 21701

On Terrorism and Combating Terrorism is published by University Publications of America in association with the Jaffee Center for Strategic Studies.

Library of Congress Cataloging in Publication Data

On terrorism and combating terrorism.

    1. Terrorism—Congresses.   2. Terrorism—Prevention—
Congresses.   I. Merari, Ariel.   II. Merkaz le-mehkarim
estrategiyim al shem Yafeh.   III. International
Seminar on Political Terrorism (1979 : Tel-Aviv)
HV6431.06   1985   363.3´2   84-22037
ISBN 0-89093-652-8
ISBN 0-89093-651-X (pbk.)

Printed in the United States of America

JCSS Publications

Editor
Aharon Yariv

Executive Editor
Joseph Alpher

The Jaffee Center for Strategic Studies publishes books, papers, memoranda, and digests in Hebrew and English. JCSS Papers (in English) are distributed on a subscription basis. Recent JCSS books in English include:

Feldman, Shai. *Israeli Nuclear Deterrence: A Strategy for the 1980s*. New York: Columbia University Press, 1983.

Heller, Mark. *A Palestinian State: The Implications for Israel*. Cambridge, Massachusetts: Harvard University Press, 1983.

Heller, Mark, ed., Dov Tamari, and Zeev Eytan. *The Middle East Military Balance 1983*. Tel-Aviv: Jaffee Center for Strategic Studies, 1983.

Lanir, Zvi, ed. *Israeli Defense Planning in the 1980s*. New York: Praeger, 1984.

Jaffee Center for Strategic Studies
Tel-Aviv University
Ramat-Aviv, P.O.B. 39012
69978 Tel-Aviv
ISRAEL

Contents

Introduction

The 1979 International Seminar on Political Terrorism brought together top academic experts on the subject of terrorism and key public officials from several countries who are involved in combating it. This book contains lectures and discussions that took place during that conference, held in Tel-Aviv. Publication has been delayed for several reasons, in themselves unimportant. Yet, it is astonishing to realize that the material in this book remains so highly relevant several years after it was written. The very same questions which occupied the participants' attention then remain at the center of public interest and decision makers' concerns today.

Consider, for instance, the problem of the impact of the media on terrorists, their supporters, and the public at large, addressed by Hillel Nossek; the problem of state support for terrorism and the possibility of combating terrorism by retaliating against such states, broached by M. Asa; or problems involved in hostage incidents, which were the subject of papers by Frank Ochberg and myself. Not only basic issues have remained relevant. Even area-specific topics, such as terrorism in the Federal Republic of Germany, have not disappeared from news headlines: a new generation of the Red Army Faction has recently started a new wave of terrorism, similar to this organization's activity in the mid-1970s.

The book's continued relevancy is a good reason for contributor satisfaction. However, anyone with a responsible outlook must find it worrisome that the same issues remain on the public agenda five years later. For during this period, the problem of political terrorism has not diminished. On the contrary, the incidence of terrorism has increased not only numerically, but in lethality and severity as well, making the threat terrorism poses to world security greater now than five years ago. A recent Rand Corporation report shows that compared to terrorist violence in 1979, a larger proportion of today's terrorism is directed against people rather than property, and the average terrorist act claims more lives. Terrorists have become more sophisticated technologically and use more powerful bombs. The use of terrorism by states as a tool of foreign policy has become a common occurrence. Yet, despite some impressive declarations and rhetoric, very little progress has been made in achieving international cooperation in the fight against terrorism. On the whole, one cannot avoid the conclusion that the West has generally failed in responding to the challenge of political terrorism, some local successes notwithstanding.

Another point raised by the continuing relevance of the conference's proceedings concerns the role of this kind of meeting. The international brain trust assembled at the conference deliberated the problem at hand over several intensive working days and came up with a number of conclusions and recommendations. Yet, several years later, nothing seems to have changed as far as coping with terrorism is concerned. Hence, one may justly ask: What is the purpose of conferences of this sort? They raise questions. Granted, they raise more questions than they can answer. But problems need to be articulated before solutions can be developed. So seminars like this are an essential early step in combating terrorism.

To illustrate the relevance of this question of purpose, it may be noted that several months after the conclusion of the seminar, American diplomats were taken hostage by Iranian revolutionaries in a case of blatant international terrorism exercised by a state. Despite its long-standing declared policy of no negotiations with and no concessions to extortionate terrorists, the United States both negotiated with and conceded to the Iranians in this test of wills and steadfastness. Public debates and official confusion marked the handling of this incident, as if the issues of hostage taking and international terrorism by states were novelties. In fact, not only were these topics discussed at the Tel-Aviv conference (as well as in several other seminars), but a situation of American hostages being held in Iran by the Khomeini regime was actually the subject of a two-and-a-half-day simulation exercise at the conference. What have we learned, then?

There are several possible answers to this question. The basic truth, however, is that the free world has not yet found the way to cope with political terrorism. All it has managed to do so far, and with only partial success, is limit the physical damage done by terrorists. Apparently, there are no simple remedies to a problem which is innately very complex. Democracies are just beginning to learn what it takes to combat terrorism— or to live with it. Obviously, there is still a very long way to go. A case in point may be provided by the history of Israel's relatively lengthy struggle against terrorism.

Despite its international reputation and possibly its self-image as well, Israel has not fared better than any other nation in the struggle against terrorism, nor has it been more consistent. Over the years, Israel has faced several periods of intense terrorism and has tried a number of coping modes. Typically, these have included a varying mixture of defensive and offensive measures. The former, consisting of physical barriers such as electronic fences and mine fields as well as patrols and ambushes, have been mainly intended to reduce the physical damage of terrorist activity. The latter have included occasional surgical raids, which were based on solid intelligence and designed to thwart planned terrorist attacks; more often, however, Israel's offensive measures have consisted of retaliatory assaults, the declared purpose of which was primarily deterrence through punishment.

These measures have not been uniformly successful. From a historical perspective, one cannot avoid the conclusion that, while the defensive means have been highly effective in limiting the damage incurred by terrorism, retaliatory attacks have failed to deter the terrorist organizations, nor have they been successful in convincing the terrorists' sponsor states to refrain from aiding and abetting them. In the early 1950s, about four years of repeated Israeli reprisal raids on Egyptian and Jordanian military camps and police stations failed to compel these countries' rulers to cease their support and encouragement for *fedayeen* terrorist attacks on civilian targets in Israel. These attacks stopped only after the 1956 Sinai Campaign, a war which was waged, inter alia, to terminate the terrorist assaults on Israel. Terrorist attacks against Israel were resumed in 1965, largely without the support of Arab countries, but were considerably augmented after the 1967 Six-Day War, when these countries decided to replace their obviously unsuccessful conventional war effort with low-level warfare by proxy.

Having learned little from her previous experience, Israel resorted again to a policy of retaliation with an eye to deterrence, achieving the same degree of success as before. From 1967 to September 1970, Israel conducted a series of reprisal attacks on Palestine Liberation Organization strongholds and on Jordanian targets. These reprisals were intended to punish the terrorists and to convey the message that there would be no peace for Jordan as long as she was an accomplice to terrorist attacks on Israel. But either Israel failed to get its point across, or perhaps Jordan refused to listen, for despite painful Israeli strikes over several years, Jordan continued to grant the terrorists free reign. Only after the PLO became an undeniable internal threat to King Hussein did the Jordanian army crush it in a series of clashes in September 1970 and July 1971.

The PLO's subsequent entrenchment in Lebanon left Israel with no clear address to which to direct its retaliation policy. Since the Lebanese government had practically no power in the area controlled by the PLO, the only target for deterrence was the terrorists themselves. Recognizing this fact, Israel aimed its effort almost exclusively at the PLO. Initially, it adopted a policy of response contingent upon terrorist activity; that is, following every major terrorist attack, Israel would launch a retaliatory strike in the form of an air, artillery, or ground forces raid. In April 1979, after a particularly atrocious terrorist attack that resulted in the deaths of a father and his two little daughters, Israel turned to a new policy of continuous assaults on PLO strongholds in southern Lebanon. The idea was to take the initiative and harass the terrorists constantly, so as to keep them preoccupied with defense and, hopefully, to undermine their morale by attrition, thus achieving a deterrence effect. This policy was maintained for six months in 1979, with no clear result. It was resumed in April 1980 following another shocking incident in which Palestinian terrorists took children hostage in a kibbutz nursery. For more than a year, the impact of this policy on the PLO was a subject for debate. But in July 1981, the PLO demonstrated that it was far from attrited or deterred: in the course of ten days, it poured hundreds of rockets and artillery shells on Israel's northern border towns and villages, forcing many people to flee. This episode ended in an apparent draw: an indirect, vague cease-fire agreement between Israel and the PLO, which was in fact the beginning of the inevitable countdown to the 1982 war, in which the PLO was driven from Lebanon.

In political terms, the dust has not yet settled from that war, and any attempt to weigh its consequences would be premature. It is clear, however, that the 1982 war has not solved the problem of Palestinian terrorism, nor is there an alternative solution in sight. As suggested by Aharon Yariv, the problem should perhaps be defined in terms of containment rather than victory, at least for the foreseeable future. Indeed, this lesson appears to be applicable to the phenomenon of terrorism in general.

Editing the conference's records, particularly the discussion sections, was not an easy task. The assistance of several persons, which at times seemed Sisyphean, was truly invaluable. Ms. Orit Har'el helped screen out illegible parts of the discussions, and Ms. Barbara Karni contributed much to turning them into proper English. Most of all, however, I am indebted to the Jaffee Center's executive editor, Mr. Joseph Alpher. Had it not been for his highly professional work on the manuscript and his tolerance of my shortcomings, which attests to his abundantly good nature, this book would have never been published.

Tel-Aviv   Ariel Merari
February 1985

Participants

Prof. YONAH ALEXANDER, director of the Institute for Studies in International Terrorism, the State University of New York; the Center for Strategic and International Studies, Georgetown University, Washington, D.C.

Dr. ISRAEL ALTMAN, the Shiloah Institute, Tel-Aviv University.

G. AMOS, the government of Israel.

M. ASA, the government of Israel.

Prof. GABRIEL BEN-DOR, the Department of Political Science, Haifa University.

Prof. YEHEZKEL DROR, the Department of Political Science, the Hebrew University, Jerusalem.

Col. ELKANA EFRATI, the Israeli Police.

RAFI EITAN, the Prime Minister's Advisor on Combating Terrorism, the government of Israel.

Ms. T. FABER-de HEER, the Ministry of Justice, the Netherlands.

Dr. SHAI FELDMAN, the Center for Strategic Studies, Tel-Aviv University.

Dr. NEHEMIA FRIEDLAND, the Department of Psychology, Tel-Aviv University.

Dr. J. BOWYER BELL, the Institute of War and Peace Studies, Columbia University, New York.

Prof. SHLOMO BREZNITZ, director of the Institute of Study of Stress, Haifa University.

B. DAVID, the Institute for Technological Forecasting, Tel-Aviv University.

Mr. Z. GAD, the government of Israel.

Dr. EITAN GILBOA, the Department of Political Science, the Hebrew University, Jerusalem.

Prof. GALIA GOLAN, the Department of Political Science, the Hebrew University, Jerusalem.

Col. YEHUDA GUY, deputy director, the Ministry of Transportation, the government of Israel.

Prof. YEHOSHAFAT HARKABI, the Department of International Relations, the Hebrew University, Jerusalem.

Col. YA'AKOV HEICHAL, the Israeli Defense Forces (IDF).

Dr. HANS-JOSEF HORCHEM, director of the Department for the Defense of the Constitution, Hamburg, the Federal Republic of Germany.

Dr. ZEEV IVIANSKI, the Department of Political Science, the Hebrew University, Jerusalem.

Mr. BRIAN M. JENKINS, director, the Security and Subnational Conflict Program, the Rand Corporation, Santa Monica, California.

Col. (Res.) YIGAL KARMON, the Israel Defense Forces (IDF).

Dr. JAKOV KATWAN, Dipl. Psych., director, the Institute for International Scientific Exchange, Berlin, the Federal Republic of Germany.

Dr. ROBERT H. KUPPERMAN, chief scientist, the U.S. Arms Control and Disarmament Agency.

Mr. ASA LEVEN, the government of Israel.

Maj. R. MALADOWITZ, U.S. Army.

Mr. GERNOT MAYER, Bundeskriminalamt, the Federal Republic of Germany.

Dr. ARIEL MERARI, the Center for Strategic Studies and the Department of Psychology, Tel-Aviv University.

Capt. P. VAN DER MOLEN, Police Headquarters, the Hague, the Netherlands.

Mr. ROBERT MOSS, editor, *The Economist Foreign Report*, London.

Prof. TAKESHI MURAMATSU, Tokyo, Japan.

Mr. HILLEL NOSSEK, the Institute for the Study of Communication, the Hebrew University, Jerusalem.

Dr. FRANK M. OCHBERG, associate director for crisis management, the National Institute of Mental Health, U.S.A.

Mr. ARYE OFRI, the Department of Political Science, the Hebrew University, Jerusalem.

Ambassador ANTHONY C.E. QUAINTON, director, the Office for Combating Terrorism, U.S. Department of State.

Col. RICHARD H. ROBERTS, U.S. Military Attaché, Israel.

Col. REINHARD RUPPRECHT, the Ministry of the Interior, the Federal Republic of Germany.

Brig. Gen. (Res.) ARYEH SHALEV, the Center for Strategic Studies, Tel-Aviv University.

Col. ADAM SHEFI, the Israel Defense Forces (IDF).

Dr. ARYE SHMUELEVITZ, the Shiloah Institute, Tel-Aviv University.

Col. ULRICH U. WEGENER, commander, G.S.G.-9, the Federal Republic of Germany.

Prof. PAUL WILKINSON, the Department of Politics, University of Aberdeen, Scotland.

Mr. CHARLES D. WISE, the Department of Political Science, University of Oklahoma.

Maj. Gen. (Res.) AHARON YARIV, head of the Center for Strategic Studies, Tel-Aviv University.

A Strategy to Counter Palestinian Terrorism

Aharon Yariv

For more than fourteen years, Israel has been combating Palestinian terrorism in its Fatah mold; it is reasonable to assume that at least in the near future, it will have to continue to do so. During these fourteen years there were over eleven thousand terrorist incidents of varying scope and character. Over six hundred Israelis lost their lives and over three thousand were wounded. This level of physical damage could be deemed acceptable in terms of what one could rightfully call a war—more Israelis are killed or wounded in traffic accidents in a single year than were in all of the terrorist incidents in the last fourteen years. From the political perspective, however, these losses are unacceptable. The tenacity of Palestinian terrorist activity has not only given prominence to but has also gained world sympathy for the Palestinian cause and for the Palestine Liberation Organization. Moreover, this tenacity has contributed to the fact that over fifty governments have officially recognized the PLO, which has a permanent representative at the United Nations. Besides, Palestinian terrorist activity has strengthened the PLO's position in the Arab world at large; among the population in Judea, Samaria, and the Gaza Strip; and among Israeli Arabs. Palestinian terrorist activity may also serve as a catalyst for military escalation, escalation that could lead to war between Israel and Arab states. In addition, Palestinian terrorist activity has a marked impact upon public opinion in Israel. For all these reasons, then, Palestinian terrorist activity constitutes a threat which must be confronted.

The PLO and terrorist organizations included therein have a vowed political intention—the establishment of a Palestinian state in the confines of what was once the British mandated territory of Palestine. The first three articles of the Palestinian National Covenant state:

(1) Palestine is the homeland of the Palestinian people and an integral part of the Great Arab homeland, and the people of Palestine is a part of the Arab nation. (2) Palestine and its boundaries, which existed at the time of the British Mandate, are an integral territorial unit. (3) The Palestinian people possesses the legal right to its homeland and when the liberation of its homeland is completed it will determine itself, solely according to its own will and choice.

While there may be some doubt as to whether Jordan is perceived as part of Palestine, Israel's inclusion is clear. Speaking in Beirut on November 10, 1978, Yasir Arafat emphasized this point: "The PLO will not agree to partial settlement and autonomy. All it wants is the continuation of the revolution for the liquidation of Israel and [the] crushing [of] her by the force of arms."

The PLO seeks to achieve its goal through a so-called strategy of protracted struggle. This strategy is implemented by repeated terrorist acts against civilian targets. There have been very few incidents in which Palestinian terrorist organizations attacked military targets. In an interview in *Time* magazine in November 1977, George Habash declared: "This is the long struggle. In twenty years I can see us fighting in Haifa, Jerusalem, in all the occupied towns (i.e., within the lines held up to 1967). I don't see why we should not win the war." The cumulative psychological effect of Palestinian terrorist activity is intended primarily to attract attention and build up sympathy for the Palestinian problem in the Arab world as well as in the world at large. But it is also intended to undermine opposition, to establish the idea of a Palestinian state among Israelis and among Jews in the Diaspora. The clever use of mass media by the PLO ensures the maximization of psychological impact for Palestinian terrorist activity. In addition, terrorist activity is intended to provoke an Israeli response which will darken Israel's world image, thereby making further acts of terrorism by the PLO more palatable to world public opinion. That is, Israeli reprisals help justify continued acts of terrorism by the PLO. Without this continuous use of violence, Arab and non-Arab support for the PLO might weaken, sympathy might diminish, internal squabbles might increase, and the PLO's stature might decline.

In implementing its strategy of protracted struggle, the PLO enjoys a number of important advantages. First, a large reservoir of human resources is at their disposal in the refugee camps of Lebanon, Syria, and Jordan, in the administered territories, and in other Palestinian communities in the Middle East. This reservoir has so far easily met the PLO's demands with respect to quantity and quality of men recruited to the movement. Especially at the senior levels, there is an experienced and dedicated cadre of leaders capable of learning lessons and of applying them. Secondly, the various Palestinian terrorist organizations have bases in the Arab countries, especially in Lebanon, where they act in almost total freedom. These bases are actually sanctuaries, and many of them even double sanctuaries—a base serves as a sanctuary when it is provided by a host country, like Lebanon; it becomes a sanctuary within a sanctuary when it is located (as it very often is, on purpose) inside a civilian community, whether a refugee camp or a village or a school. Elimination of these large bases would require major military operations with all the political and military risks involved. Thirdly, the terrorist organizations enjoy support from the Arab states. This aid includes financial, political, and diplomatic aid, as well as the provision of military equipment and training installations and the instructing of PLO terrorists. The motivations of the supporting countries may vary, but the result is the strengthening of the terrorist organizations. A major role of support is also played, as is well known, by the Soviet Union and its satellites. Fourthly, there is cooperation between the Palestinian organizations and other terrorist groups all over the world, facilitating Palestinian terrorist activity overseas. Finally, the democratic nature of the Israeli regime, its moral character and accepted norms, and the liberal policy regarding the population in the administered territories constitute well-understood and accepted constraints on the war against Palestinian terrorism.

There is no foreseeable change in all these advantages that could weaken the threat posed by the Palestinian terrorist organizations. These organizations are doing and will continue to do everything in their power to step up their activities, in scope as well as in character. This applies to Palestinian terrorist activity within Israel and the administered territories, along the borders, and overseas. The stepping up of activity is also accompanied by significant improvements in organizational and conspiratory techniques.

What strategy should Israel adopt in the struggle against Palestinian terrorism? The desirable aim of the strategy would naturally be the complete cessation of terrorist activity. But when choosing a strategy, we must first remember that the roots of Palestinian terrorism and its aims are political. We must also remember the characteristics and advantages of Palestinian terrorists. First, let us examine a strategy of decisive destruction, that is, a strategy realized by a relatively quick series of devastating blows destined to resolve the terrorist problem once and for all. Such a strategy necessitates the annihilation of both the command and combat elements of the PLO, as well as the destruction of the main terrorist bases. Conquest and protracted occupation of large areas within certain Arab states, particularly Lebanon, in order to prevent reorganization are also required. Furthermore, a very hard line in the administered territories—closing the bridges, expelling and arresting large numbers of residents—would need to be adopted. Independent of the operational burden involved in implementation, such a strategy is impractical because of internal and external political and legal constraints. But we must note that this strategy did succeed in the early 1970s in the Gaza Strip. Success there was due not only to capable leadership and excellent tactics, but also to the special circumstances pertaining to the Gaza Strip.

A second possibility is a strategy of active deterrence. This means the application of severe punishment to the terrorist organizations. The punishment should be as painful as possible, so as to deter the terrorists from continuing terrorist activity. Fourteen years of experience, as well as a brief analysis of all the factors involved, however, will show clearly that no price we are able to set will be high enough to bring about the cessation of terrorist activities. Nonetheless, punishment that is appropriate in timing, scope, and character can, under certain conditions, bring about a temporary weakening of Palestinian terrorist activity at a given time and in a given area.

Still another possibility is a strategy of constraint, which means acting sharply against the powers supporting the terrorist organizations (or the powers refraining from stopping them), forcing them to pay a price they will be unwilling to pay. Such a strategy would aim at stopping their support and even making them take steps against the terrorist organizations. In order to achieve this aim we shall have to strike a number of consecutive and effective blows against several Arab states, both inside their territories where possible and against their interests overseas.

As far as terrorist activity in Israel is concerned, a number of serious problems arise in trying to apply a strategy of compellance. The severity of the regimes in the Arab countries concerned makes effective activity within them difficult. Directing efforts against the overseas interests of these Arab countries will not be accepted by the host countries and might severely strain Israel's international relations. The same would apply to operations against non-Palestinian terrorist groups who actively support Palestinian terrorism. Furthermore, a decisive effort to implement a strategy of compellance against the relevant Arab states may lead to war. In such a war, with all the attending risks, an Israeli victory is not at all certain to bring about a cessation of Palestinian terrorist activity in the postwar period.

Should we then consider a strategy of pure defense? Such a strategy suffers from a serious drawback: it leaves the initiative wholly in the hands of the terrorist organizations. Such a strategy obviously cannot put an end to Palestinian terrorism. One should remember, however, that experience has proven the value of defensive tactics and techniques. Such tactics often have a deterring and disruptive, albeit limited, influence both in time and scope.

I have examined here a number of strategies, offensive and defensive, and found that while in each there are useful elements, none of them can bring about an end to Palestinian terrorist activity or even a gradual dying out of it under prevailing circumstances. These circumstances will not change substantially in the near future, and Palestinian terrorist activity is certain to continue. As the roots of Palestinian terrorist activities are political and as the organizations benefit from a number of important advantages, cessation or even a gradual dying out cannot be achieved without a political solution of the problem acceptable to both sides. Unfortunately, such a solution is not at hand, although this should not discourage us from constantly looking for political solutions that might be acceptable to all. Meanwhile, the war against Palestinian terrorism must be carried on lest the terrorists achieve their avowed objective.

Since Israel is unable to achieve decisive results with respect to the terrorists, it must employ a strategy that brings about only partial results. The degree of success will depend largely on the exact nature of the tactical steps to be taken and the efficiency of their employment. This strategy of containment, as I call it, should incorporate both offensive and defensive elements in order to (1) prevent Palestinian terrorism from achieving its political aim; (2) prevent, or at least reduce, the political achievements of Palestinian terrorism; (3) hurt the terrorist organizations as much as possible without impairing Israel's overall defense posture and without weakening its political posture; and (4) maintain normal life in Israel and the administered territories and minimize damage and maintain morale in Israel. Although not defined as such, this is a strategy that Israel is actually practicing more or less. Defining the strategy formally may be important for psychological, educational, and public information reasons in Israel and in the rest of the world. The act of defining can reinforce the efforts for improving the fight against Palestinian terrorism. It can help convince the public that there is no definite, final, and full military answer.

Rather than analyze fully all elements of the strategy, I would like to emphasize a number of important points. First, let us consider organization. Inevitably a number of services participate in combating Palestinian terrorism. These include the Israel Defense Forces, the members of the intelligence community, and the Foreign Ministry, all of which are coordinated by the advisor to the prime minister. Naturally, clear delineation of responsibility and good coordination is of great importance. But that does not eliminate the necessity of having somebody at the cabinet level, other than the prime minister, who follows matters daily as far as the war against terrorism is concerned and has an overall view of the problem at the highest level.

Second, there is the need for continuity of policy. As the war against Palestinian terrorists has been going on for over fourteen years and will continue for the foreseeable future, it is vital that a long-range view be taken of matters at all levels. It is imperative to be rigorous in examining, improving, and reexamining everything that exists and everything that is being done in the realm of combating Palestinian terrorism. This will also eliminate the danger of resting on the laurels of past success and will ensure proper allocation of resources. Continuity also demands constant attention to the maintenance of public consciousness regarding the war against Palestinian terrorism. Here we have a paradoxical situation. On the one hand, we are interested in a high degree of alertness on the part of the citizen, and this measure has proven itself many times over. On the other hand, we want to desensitize the citizen vis-à-vis terrorist activities. I think this paradox can be overcome with good psychological advice. Not only psychologists but also all other relevant academicians should be recruited in the war, whether for research and development or for other purposes. Painful experience has shown us how vital it is for the government to be properly organized, prepared, and rehearsed for the management of crisis situations. What has happened in the past can surely happen in the future in a more difficult and complex context. The year-old bus hijacking incident in Israel can serve as a grave reminder to that effect. One last point I would like to raise concerning continuity is the necessity to tenaciously pursue cooperation and coordination with friendly states and to carry on persuasion efforts on the international front as a countermeasure to PLO propaganda.

Continuity brings us to the subject of selectivity. As we are forced to employ our resources over a long period of time, resources are selectively applied to both defensive and offensive usages. As far as defensive measures are concerned, selectivity is relatively easy, as the factor of resources will almost always be the dominant one. The problem is more complicated with regard to offensive measures. In the selection of targets, means, methods, and timing, it is vital to check thoroughly and carefully how much material, psychological, and political damage will be inflicted by any particular offensive operation. The political impact and the effect on world public opinion must also be considered. Special attention must be paid to Israeli public opinion. In connection with this point I would like to emphasize the danger of developing a conditioned reflex. The public in Israel automatically expects immediate reprisals for every terrorist act. This may impair the decision-making process. It is noteworthy that lately there has been a shift in Israeli policy which has decoupled offensive measures and reprisals.

Finally, as to the media: The vital, and sometimes fatal, importance of the mass media is well known, but sometimes forgotten. Therefore it must be emphasized that what is printed and broadcast, as well as the way in which it is presented, can be decisive in terms of the effect of a defensive or offensive act in combating Palestinian terrorist activity. Hence, the authorities must be geared to work with the media. A continuous dialogue with the media can be very helpful in fostering mutual understanding.

In conclusion, I recommend that the strategy for combating Palestinian terrorism be formally defined and it be called a strategy of containment. I believe that if properly implemented, there is a reasonable chance it will have the desired effect in diminishing the terrorists' faith in their tactics and in convincing them that their hope that Israel will accept their political objectives is false. Along with other developments in the area, especially progress in normalization between Egypt and Israel, the PLO might then change its tactics from a strategy of protracted struggle to one of true political negotiations.

2

On the Problem of Countering Population Support for the Terrorists in the Administered Territories

Yigal Karmon

I would like to begin with a very short description of the historical and political scene in Judea and Samaria in order to clarify the origins of population support of the terrorists. Jordanian rule over Judea and Samaria was initiated in 1948, when King Abdullah extended Jordanian authority to those territories. Before the Jordanian takeover, the territories had been ruled briefly by the people of the area and the congress known as the Jericho Congress of 1948. The Hashemite Kingdom of Jordan comprised a mixed population, including Palestinian Arabs and Bedouins, all of whom were loyal to the Hashemite monarchy. Indeed, the Palestinian part of the population was no less Jordanian than the original Jordanian part. The Palestinian population has played a central role in the government of the country. It has been part of the ruling administration and the army and has shared in the responsibility and power. It should be stressed that these facts were not altered by the crisis of 1970 between the terrorist organizations and the Jordanian authorities; they remain as valid today as they were in any other period in the past. More than 60 percent of the Jordanian population are Palestinians by origin and are considered by all as Jordanians. They are represented by the Jordanian authorities and not by the Palestine Liberation Organization. The PLO itself recognizes the legitimacy of this fact and does not deny Jordan's right to represent its citizens of Palestinian origin.

The Rabat resolutions taken at the Arab summit meeting in October 1974 created a new situation in the area which complicated the question of representation. Since the Rabat Summit, Jordan has been prevented from participating in the peace process. Thus, it was predetermined that the historic peace initiative agreed upon by Egypt and Israel met no positive response from the Palestinians. As the sole legitimate representative of the Palestinians, the PLO alone was granted the right to act, and this organization is a very destructive factor, both literally—by its terrorist acts—and politically. The last and boldest demonstration of its fanatic extremism occurred recently when the PLO turned down Pres. Jimmy Carter's initiative—the PLO would not make any concession relating to Israel's right to exist—although such a concession might result in acceptance by the United States, as well as perhaps recognition and participation in the peace process.

How are these facts reflected in Judea and Samaria? Since the Camp David accords, PLO supporters in control of the West Bank municipalities and other central organizations such as universities, social clubs, and the local press have managed to mobilize the politically minded public behind them in total rejection of the Camp David accords. This local rejection, which was initiated by PLO representatives such as the leading mayors, was characterized by militancy and ideological fanaticism. The few public figures who remained moderate or more pragmatically inclined, and hence willing to support the Camp David accords, were silenced by intimidation, including threats and attempts of physical terror, ostracism, and public humiliation. Some of the West Bank personalities who met Alfred Atherton, U.S. special envoy, were labeled "enemies of the people." This successfully intimidated many other public figures. Thus, when Harold Saunders, U.S. special envoy to the Middle East, asked to meet a large number of West Bank notables, only eight out of approximately fifty invited by the consul general appeared, all of them minor figures.

The liberal Israeli policy of freedom of political activity, especially after Camp David, has apparently backfired. The outcome of this policy was that in several recent political meetings in Judea and Samaria, a very extreme attitude was formulated and endorsed as the only legitimate public position. Slogans, such as a call for a return to Haifa and Jaffa and "a revolution with a rifle in hand," appeared under a map of the Palestinian state which included the area of Israel within its 1948 borders.

In order to comprehend such recent developments, let us imagine for a moment a powerful Mafia organization whose aim is to spread its control over a particular area. It uses violent means to further its aims. But the violent group, the gunmen, are merely an instrument of the big bosses. The law enforcement agency fighting such an organization knows it is not enough to fight the gunmen. The bosses, the heads of the whole organization served by the gunmen, must be fought.

Let us consider the terrorist organizations and the terrorist control of the population in Judea and Samaria. Terrorist organizations have been secretly active in the territories for a number of years. Benefiting from the fact that the authorities consider the activities of certain elements in the population legitimate, they have attempted to attain a position of control over these elements, and they have succeeded in doing so. Judea and Samaria have thus become their domain. Their actual control is manifested through public figures heading various institutions—municipal, financial, social— and having at their disposal very large budgets coming from the PLO, from Arab countries, and also, ironically, from the Israeli government. They also control some local newspapers, which they own. All these components are secured by gunmen who guarantee the full discipline and cooperation of the population. The livelihood and social status of terrorists' families are guaranteed by the terrorist organizations through the so-called legitimate institutions.

On what basis do the terrorist organizations attract or demand the population's support for their activities? The essential basis is the cause, *Kadiya* in Arabic. The cement is the ideas: This is our territory and our fight for control is not subject to discussion; every violent means to achieve the goal is implicitly justified. The essential principles are stated in Article XX of the Palestinian National Covenant, which negates not only the national rights of the Jewish people, but also the historical facts of its past. It states that any claim of historical connection between the Jewish people and Palestine is incompatible with the facts of history. It further states that the group presuming to be the Jewish people is not a people but a religious community and therefore has no right to territorial sovereignty. From early childhood, Palestinians are indoctrinated according to these principles; they are taught that the legitimate way to achieve the Palestinians' goal is through violence. "How can the Palestinian gain his home back?" a popular poster asks. "Only by arms can he do so."

One of the typical elements in the psychological structure of the followers of this *Kadiya* is the reversal of roles. The murderer presents himself as the victim. The Palestinian covenant states that the very existence of the Zionist entity is in itself a continuing act of aggression; therefore, any act taken against it is an act of self-defense. These are precisely the words used by the mayor of Tulkarm, in the northern part of the West Bank, in discussing convicted terrorists. It seems that this way of reasoning appears convincing enough to some naive foreigners. To them it makes no difference who began the circle of violence, nor are alternative ways of political action considered. Another example of this perverted frame of mind is the way the PLO propaganda vehicle, the daily *al-Fajr* paper appearing in Jerusalem, described the death of two terrorists whose car—in which they had planted explosives in order to blow it up in the Central Bus Station in Tel-Aviv—blew up too early, causing their own deaths. The paper, dated June 27, 1979, merely tells its readers that the merchant Mr. X and the engineer Mr. Y were the victims of an explosion in a car in Tel-Aviv. No mention was made that it was their own car or that the so-called victims were on a mission to commit murder. Similarly, the organization makes an outcry that there is a plot to murder its men at the time it is engaged in murdering those, such as Sheikh Hasan Husendar of Gaza, who do not obey the bosses.

It is a fact that at a meeting in Nablus, it was accepted publicly as a norm that the people who step out of the path of the PLO should be liquidated. This position is openly espoused by Farouk Kadoumi, head of the political division of the PLO. In a 1979 interview in the Lebanese journal, *Monday Morning*, Kadoumi said: "It must first be said that the PLO and the Palestinian people in the occupied territories and outside them know very well how to use [violent] methods to prevent certain personalities from being deviated [sic] from the revolutionary path. Our people recognize their responsibility and are capable of taking the necessary disciplinary measures against those who try to leave the right path. The PLO is keenly interested in having everyone stick to the path of the revolution, to the PLO banner, towards the achievements of the people's national rights and the establishment of a Palestinian state. The PLO will take all measures needed to prevent any personality or group, regardless of its identity, from striking out in a different path." The role of the representatives of the PLO bosses—the mayors in the West Bank—is to keep the population on "the right path."

In their support of the PLO, mayors have gone as far as justifying acts of terrorism. For example, the mayor of Nablus, Bassam Shaq'a, justified the murder of German tourists in a bus in Nablus. A very distressing phenomenon is the support some Arab-Christian clergymen give to the PLO. The most notorious PLO supporter is the Catholic bishop Hilarion Capucci, who smuggled large quantities of weapons and explosives. Another clergyman, the Anglican priest Illya Huri, who was a member of an assassination cell and therefore deported from the area by the authorities, was recently elected by his congregation—with the approval of the authorities of the Anglican Church—to a senior position. At the same time, he is holding a high position in the PLO hierarchy. One should also mention in this context the deputy mayor of Ramallah, Rev. Rantisi. When questioned about his views with regard to the assassination of a public figure in Ramallah by a terrorist gang, the Reverend Mr. Rantisi remarked: "If he was killed by the PLO, then it is understandable."

The mayor of Hebron, Fa'ed Kawasmeh, when asked in a television interview about freedom of expression and assassinations, replied: "Freedom of expression depends on one condition, that he who expresses his views is expressing his own view. But he who transmits foreign views is not entitled to freedom of expression." Who will determine which is the transmitted opinion and which is the genuine one? Mr. Kawasmeh and the other PLO leaders.

Therefore, when dealing with the subject of countering population support for the terrorists, we should pose the following questions. Is there any use fighting the gunmen while leaving the bosses who send and support them immune? Can one convince the population to withhold its support for the terrorists as long as the law enforcement agencies abstain from contending with the heads of the organizations which send forth terrorists? Is it possible to fight a terrorist without fighting the political cadre for which it is only an operative? Can the political cadre be fought locally while some of our international allies are conducting a dialogue with it? Can one fight the terrorists while withholding moral condemnation and total discredit of the whole criminal organization and its so-called ideology?

In the light of the analysis I have just presented, it can be said that the topic, "On the Problem of Countering Population Support for the Terrorists in the Administered Territories," though phrased somewhat ambiguously, is rather appropriate. Each of us must confront the problem, ask pertinent questions, and search for solutions in accord with his own moral values. Do we have allies in this struggle? Is it enough to assign the task to some professionals, or should it be viewed as an overall national effort?

Discussion

PARTICIPANT: My understanding of the Israeli policy is that it is a combination of two elements. One is the highest possible degree of liberalism, letting the people live on their own and in prosperity. This is done for humane reasons as well as in order to minimize the motives for joining the terrorists and their activities. The second element is security measures against suspects or people found guilty of terrorist involvement. There are people in the administered territories who are ready to carry out terrorist activities, but their number is not high. Some of the mayors in the West Bank support the PLO and the terrorists' activities, but I do not think they are the bosses. To the best of my knowledge, the terrorists receive their instructions for operation from abroad and not directly from the area.

PARTICIPANT: I would like to raise some questions on the subject. As was said before, there is a Palestinian majority in Jordan, where, I believe, the feelings should be more or less similar to those of the West Bank's population. I do not see any reason why a Palestinian living now in Amman should be less PLO-inclined than a Palestinian enjoying economic prosperity in the West Bank. Yet King Hussein has been successful while we have failed. When I try to analyze what made Hussein successful, though he is under a constant threat, I think one very practical reason is that he is employing more or less the same methods and measures the terrorists are using. It is unfair to call antiterrorist measures "terrorist," but that is really what they are. Therefore, even though liberalism is a fine idea and prosperity is a comfortable state of affairs, it loses out in the face of terrorist harassment and threat. My question then is, has democracy any chance of being truly successful in fighting a terrorist organization, especially when the leadership of this organization is outside the borders of this democracy? Maybe our case would have been much easier if we really could be dealing with the leaders themselves. I do not think that stricter security measures are the answer; that would only cause activity to continue underground. Another question is, do we have the moral license and inclination that would enable us to use terrorist methods the same way that King Hussein does? Again, it is a very difficult feat in a democracy. If the answer to these two questions is negative, I am afraid we can only rest content with the very moderate target of keeping the population for the most part at an optimal degree of satisfaction with its way of life, with very little incentive to join terrorist activity.

PARTICIPANT: It is quite fashionable to assume that democracies cannot always fight terrorism in an effective way, and my inclination is to agree with this view. Yet, at the same time, I am not sure that democracy has really tried everything at its disposal. I think that one of the basic problems in democracies is some lack of conceptual clarity as to what constitutes a counterterrorist policy. Let me give just one example. It has been Israel's policy to provide good economic conditions in the administered territories, on the assumption that once people are basically happy with their standard of living, everything will be quiet and they will not support terror organizations. I am not sure that this is a very intelligent policy from the point of view of countering terrorism. If you take a whole population and very quickly improve its economic conditions, what you do is simply free people to start worrying about their political identity. I am not suggesting that what should have been done was to create artificial hardships or limitations. However, in retrospect, it seems to me that a slow, gradual development would have probably increased the importance of cooperation, and the Arabs would have concentrated on working hard to achieve the status they have today. I think the analogy of terrorism to the Mafia, though appealing, is rather confusing; it puts the terrorist organizations in a light of some sort of criminal organizations, yet the measures that should be taken against them are not typical countercriminal measures.

PARTICIPANT: I think it would be useful to make a distinction between participating in terrorist activities and political support for the PLO or Palestinian-Arab nationalism. These are two very different problems. Active support is much more of a police problem. Israel has had quite a large degree of success in this respect, especially in keeping the Palestinian Arabs in Judea and Samaria away from large-scale participation in terrorist activities. The other problem—political support for the PLO—is really not entirely or even primarily in Israel's hands. There is a definite relationship between the two problems; it becomes easier for the PLO to carry out its terrorist activities in a climate of political support.

PARTICIPANT: It seems to be very difficult to encourage an alternative Palestinian leadership to emerge under these circumstances, unless the potential leaders know their physical security is guaranteed. And I am not sure that this is the case in Judea and Samaria. I suspect that since such guarantees have not been made, an alternative moderate leadership has never emerged. Look at Southwest Africa or Namibia today. National leaders, ethnic leaders, and political moderates are systematically liquidated if they depart from the line of the terrorist organizations. A similar problem exists in Northern Ireland.

PARTICIPANT: Israel is not quite a democracy when it comes to the West Bank and the Gaza Strip. Rather, we run a certain kind of liberal occupation. We apply the original British emergency regulations of 1945, and these permit us to do things that other countries cannot do. The main issue consists of two different objectives. One is to administer these territories with low-level terrorist or resistance activity in such a way that we can go on and live with the problem in the near future. The other objective is to try to reach a political solution and a political agreement with the local population. I think we have no difficulties in dealing with the first kind of problem for three reasons: the first is that the population has no way of winning the war by terrorist activity; the second is that we are not a democracy in the occupied areas, and therefore we can use all sorts of measures which we would not use in Israel itself; the third reason is the use of a reward-and-punishment policy in administering the territories—we are liberal with the local population, but can deny any or all aspects of this liberalism at any time. All these steps have been quite successful in the past. Overall, terrorist success in local terrorist activity against Israel during the last fifteen months has resulted in damage equal to 5 percent of that caused by local automobile accidents. The major problem which we are facing today is the political one. We have now reached the stage where we want to achieve a positive solution which needs positive support by the people, by their local leadership. This, I am afraid, we cannot achieve.

PARTICIPANT: Terrorism is quite a frightening phenomenon for most people, yet statistically, the number of people who have died from accidents during the past years is much higher than the number of those killed due to terrorist incidents. I think we fear terrorism because of its political aims. We are talking about the prevention of terrorism as a means of psychological warfare, from the point of view of public, moral, and political support. Here I think there is one difference between the Israeli situation and other situations in the world, and that is the unclear future of the West Bank. Nobody really knows what the future is going to be, and therefore one cannot apply any psychological rules when dealing with population support of terrorism there.

PARTICIPANT: I think King Hussein was successful in Jordan because he fought the political cadre even before he fought the operational one. We tend to exaggerate the use of violence by Hussein and forget what he did to the political cadre. He actually deprived them of active capacities. I think fighting the political cadre is not a matter of tough declarations, but rather is an action of legalizing the delegitimizing of their activity. Once we accept that the organization is immoral, we should not have any problem in handling those involved. If a Nazi group in Israel asked permission to publish a newspaper, the public would not allow it—even though we are a democracy—because nazism is agreed by all to be an immoral movement. Once we delegitimize the PLO, its purposes and its aims, we should not limit or prevent ourselves from legalizing this conception in actual law. Then we can fight that organization.

With regard to the chances of democracy such as it is in the face of terrorism, by the same token we can ask what the chances of democracy are against the Mafia. Democracy has no chance against either. Forcing terrorist leaders and activities underground can be helpful, because there the movement would be much weaker than it could ever be working within the law.

PARTICIPANT: Forcing people underground would be a great mistake, from a practical point of view. It may even increase the population's support of terrorism as it may then seem more glorified. I think the main problem we face is defining our own political aims with regard to the population's support of terrorism. To the local population in the West Bank and the Gaza Strip, these people are not terrorists; they are freedom fighters. Therefore, any open opposition to the PLO endangers the opposer. As a result, the population of the moderates lives in fear. We come back to this being a political problem.

Also, the Israeli public has a moral problem concerning countermeasures. We cannot handle the Arab population in the administered territories like King Hussein did because the situation in Israel is completely different from what it was in Jordan. The population thinks in different patterns, along different lines. The Israeli problem differs from that of other nations in another respect, and that is that Israelis are fighting Arabs, Palestinians, not Israelis. The Germans, for example, are fighting Germans, which makes the problem easier to solve because there is no question of mass population support.

PARTICIPANT: The main point is the political one, not the technical means of police or security measures to prevent terrorism. The main problem is political, and the objective should be to limit public support given to terrorist activity for two reasons: such public support has political implications; and it allows for recruiting, operations, and active support of terrorism. I think the best possible way to achieve that objective would be to reach a political compromise with the leaders of the population. The only possible solution at present is the idea of autonomy, though I do not know if and how it can be carried out.

3

Guerrilla Warfare and Terrorism

Yehoshafat Harkabi

Our committee's task is to discuss terrorism from a strategic perspective. Our interest in it is not merely due to intellectual curiosity. Rather, we are concerned with terrorism as a praxeological subject, knowledge of which can help us determine the courses of action most suitable to counter and combat it.

How did terrorism develop? What have been and are likely to be its repercussions on world order? Terrorism is an outgrowth of guerrilla warfare, which is perhaps the oldest form of warfare. Prehistoric man fought in some kind of guerrilla fashion, trying to strike fear and terror in his neighbors. This type of fighting and warfare later became more organized as armies came into being, and what we now call "conventional warfare" emerged. The latter was characterized by open clashes between two armies over the control of territory. The spatial boundaries of such clashes grew progressively wider as battles began to be fought on one or more fronts. While fighting, each party constituted a target which his rival tried to hit.

Guerrilla warfare today eliminates the open clash over a front that typifies conventional warfare, for in guerrilla warfare there are no fronts. Violence is waged intermittently and at low intensity. The territorial aspect of warfare is maintained, however, though at times even the territorial aspect has been blurred. Furthermore, terrorism defies the distinction between peace and war.

Terrorism generally involves the use of minimal violence to achieve major results. In the past it often resorted to tyrannicide. In the twentieth century, it has become a device for launching revolution. Karl Marx considered revolution a historical earthquake of sorts, determined by inevitable historical developments. According to Marx, the base for a revolution is the proletariat. Lenin, on the other hand, demanded a more activist stance in order to prevent the forces of history from being diverted. He asserted that the task of the party is to direct those forces. According to Lenin, the party, not the proletariat, is the real engineering agency of revolution. The base of revolution was thus greatly narrowed.

The locus of revolution for both Marx and Lenin was urban. Mao Tse-tung retained Lenin's central role for the party, but widened the revolution's base to include the farmers. Revolution, he maintained, is carried out by the peasantry, not the urban proletariat. The locus of revolution is thus the countryside.

The Chinese model did not suit conditions in Latin America, where establishing a wide base of peasantry for revolution was impossible. Revolutions in Latin America were launched by small groups who wandered about the countryside, attacking government garrisons and thus carrying out, by their feats of bravery, armed propaganda which they hoped would rouse, by force of example, the people to rebellion. This version of revolution suited small countries. However, these ideas were not successful in Latin America after the Cuban revolution which served as the model. (Nicaragua is a mixed example.) Revolutionary thinking then veered from the countryside to towns, to what had been termed *urban guerrilla*, a euphemism for terrorism. The change is significant. Mao and Lin Piau spoke about circumventing the towns, while Fidel Castro spoke of the towns as the graveyards for revolutionaries. Now towns became the big hope for the revolutionaries. This change of direction resulted from the failure of the revolutionaries to make progress in the countryside.

The movement back to urban centers as the locus of revolution contradicts Friedrich Engels's evaluation that insurrection in towns by means of barricades would become impossible, as demonstrated by the failure of the 1848 uprising. Revolutionaries today, however, consider the towns as their hope by a different means: terrorism. In the countryside, recent technological developments—most importantly, the helicopter—appear to have benefited the counterguerrillas more than the terrorists. In the cities, on the other hand, technology appears to favor neither side.

What distinguishes modern terrorism is the indiscriminate manner in which it uses violence. For the contemporary terrorist, there are no innocent victims. This is in marked contrast to earlier terrorist groups, such as the Russian Social Revolutionaries (SR) of the last century. The SR terrorists were sensitive to the problem of hitting innocent people and usually directed their violence toward members of the regime they sought to subvert.

Although terrorists try to develop ideologies with which to justify their acts, the theoretical basis underlying modern terrorism is rather meager. The specific nature of each local conflict tends to be much more important than the general theoretical framework. The analysis of specific cases is thus far more interesting than the attempt to elaborate an abstract theory.

The German military historian Hans Delbrück identified two basic strategies of warfare: decision strategy and attrition strategy. While decision strategy seeks to achieve a given objective by one decisive event, attrition strategy seeks to achieve results through a gradual process. Guerrilla warfare and terrorism both fall within the latter category. An important logical difficulty confronts the attrition strategy; namely, how are the small, incremental events to culminate in a decision, unless the process ultimately leads to a decision or a final assault? Mao believed that guerrilla warfare is the process through which an attrition strategy can evolve into a decision one. He described how the cadres of guerrillas slowly develop into a regular army capable of launching a final assault. With this doctrine, Mao added a strategic dimension to guerrilla warfare, which is a series of tactical operations.

The strategic dimension of guerrilla warfare has both practical and theoretical significance; its continuity and territoriality play a central psychological role in inspiring the combatants with the belief that their daily toils may lead to the final success. Thus, the strategic perspective gives directional significance to guerrilla warfare.

Terrorism, however, lacks a strategic dimension; the link between individual terrorist operations and the achievement of the particular political and social change sought is undefined. Although terrorists believe their operations will cause the bourgeois society to collapse, forcing the fall of the regime, no such change has to date resulted from their acts. The achievements of terrorism have not been significant; the coverage by the mass media has been far greater than the real impact of terrorist acts. In my view, the importance of terrorism lies not in its actual achievements, but rather in its potentialities if it escalates. The norms of civilized behavior have evolved over thousands of years. If the tendency of taking justice into one's hands spreads, civilization will suffer a grave setback. I believe that civilization has considerable resilience and that it will develop forces with which to counter terrorism. Nevertheless, the dangers of terrorism loom heavily and should not be taken lightly.

If terrorism is tolerated, it may become a mode of operation by governments as a form of covert warfare or surrogate warfare. As wars become increasingly difficult to launch, states may choose to weaken their opponents either by launching clandestine, terrorist operations or by instigating terrorism by supporting local terrorists in their adversary's territory. That, too, may destroy civilized world order, especially as modern technologies may serve such trends. The dangers of such developments to world order are only slightly less than the dangers of nuclear war.

Discussion

PARTICIPANT: There is a need to differentiate between different types of terrorism: criminal, ideological, and so forth. Careful analysis of the prototypes, some of which may be a combination of others, may help us construct a useful theory.

With regard to the transformation of terrorism into a strategic success, we must consider not only the phases or levels reached but also the possible schemes involved. We can view manifestations of terrorism not as different levels ranging from terrorism to urban guerrilla to insurgency, but as part of a grand strategic scheme. The Palestine Liberation Organization illustrates this very nicely in some respects. From this angle, the effects of terrorism become much more complex to analyze.

PARTICIPANT: If we could push political terrorists over the line of legitimacy and criminalize them, then the effect of certain kinds of terror on the civil order would be lost, and the terrorists would become prey to ordinary forces. Such was the case with pirates. I think the danger of political terrorism is that on the one hand the terrorists carry with them the advantage of a kind of legitimacy, or a claim to legitimacy (which the ordinary criminal does not have), and on the other hand they disrupt the civil order. This makes it much more difficult to deal with them, and, in a sense, makes it that much easier for them to attain their goals. In a way, the balance tips when the order they are attacking disintegrates. Pirates are treated differently. The pirate is prey—anybody can hang a pirate; it is a perfectly legitimate thing to do. Yet the pirate presents a danger to society strictly in the physical sense, which is not so disturbing. In contrast, the political, sociological, and cultural facets of terrorism make the impact of terrorism more serious and dangerous.

PARTICIPANT: The classical view of terrorism is that its objective is to destroy order and strike at the government level. I agree that this is applicable in many cases, but I think the motives of the various groups tend to differ. Certainly, one can identify groups for which this is not the objective, or find cases where this goal has been abandoned due to lack of success. The major objective of terrorist groups, because of their inherent weaknesses, is to gain international attention, be it in numbers or in effectiveness in the field. Take the Croatian Ustasha, for example, or the PLO. I think their major objective has ceased to be internal disruption; it has become international support. And they have been successful at achieving it. It was the international attention and effectiveness that prompted the Soviets to take a greater interest in the PLO. I think that as far as this aspect is concerned, one could speak of terrorist success.

PARTICIPANT: I would like to bring up other points regarding the distinction between guerrilla warfare and terrorism, a distinction which is very important. First, publicity is much more important for terrorists than for guerrillas. Second, guerrilla fighters have what we call "a third interest," meaning that some people are really interested in their victory. Terrorists believe there is a third interest, but the truth is that there is none. Both guerrillas and terrorists need sympathizers, people who are not full members of the group but are interested in its success. Guerrilla groups usually have a number of sympathizers among the population. Terrorists usually do not; but where they do, their number is very small and does not constitute a body of support.

4

Terrorism-Prone Countries and Conditions

Brian M. Jenkins

Terrorism appears to affect the world unevenly. A few nations suffer a very high level of terrorism, while others seem to be virtually immune to terrorist violence. I would like first to describe the geographic distribution of terrorist acts and, second, to describe some of the more popular theories of terrorism proneness, examining the evidence—or lack of evidence—to support them.

As part of its continuing research on terrorism, the Rand Corporation has for several years maintained a chronology of incidents of international terrorism. This chronology now lists close to twelve hundred incidents for the eleven-year period from 1968 through 1978. Approximately 31 percent of these incidents occurred in Western Europe; 26 percent took place in Latin America; and 20 percent took place in the Middle East–North Africa region. Indeed, ten countries account for 58 percent of the total number of incidents. In order, these are the United States, Argentina, France, the United Kingdom, Turkey, Colombia, Lebanon, Israel, the Federal Republic of Germany, and Greece. Now if these figures seem a bit surprising, as they did to me, it is important to emphasize that this particular chronology includes only incidents of international terrorism; that is, incidents in which terrorists cross national frontiers to carry out their attacks or deliberately select victims or targets because of their connections to a foreign state (for example, diplomats or executives of foreign corporations or embassies); or hijack airliners on international flights; or divert domestic flights to another country. This chronology excludes the considerable amount of violence carried out by terrorists operating within their own countries against their own nationals; it would, for example, exclude the Aldo Moro kidnaping in Italy. Also, it is important to remember that all incidents have the same value in this chronology; that is, there is no weighing for severity. Thus, although a high number of incidents of terrorism have occurred in the United States, they are relatively minor compared to, say, some of the terrorist killings in Spain or Italy.

The Central Intelligence Agency maintains a chronology of incidents of international terrorism, which now lists some three thousand incidents that occurred from 1968 through 1978. It shows similarly heavy concentrations of incidents in Western Europe (38 percent), Latin America (27 percent), and the Middle East–North African region (16 percent). Latin America, interestingly, led in both chronologies from 1968 to 1972, while Western Europe took the lead in 1972 and has held it consistently since then.

It is also interesting to look at where these incidents of international terrorism do not occur. Together, Asia, the Pacific Ocean basin, the Soviet Union, Eastern Europe, and sub-Saharan Africa account for only a little over 10 percent of the total number of international incidents.

A chronology of 5,529 incidents (including national terrorism from 1970 to 1978) compiled by Risks International, a private firm in Alexandria, Virginia, also shows a heavy concentration of incidents in Western Europe, Latin America, and the United States. In fact, Italy, Spain, West Germany, France, Greece, and the United Kingdom (including Northern Ireland) together account for 42 percent of the total number of incidents in that chronology. Argentina, Colombia, El Salvador, Mexico, Nicaragua, Uruguay, Guatemala, and Puerto Rico account for 22 percent. The top ten countries in order of the frequency of terrorist incidents are Italy, Spain, the United States, Argentina, Turkey, the Federal Republic of Germany, Colombia, France, Greece, and El Salvador. Thus, some pattern emerges in that the same countries appear in both the international and national chronologies.

In international terrorism, distinction must be made between the location of the terrorist incident and the nationality of the victim or actual target of the terrorist violence. A distinction must also be made between the location of any incident and the target of any terrorist demands, which in many cases may not be identical. The CIA does not publish figures relating to the nationality of actual targets of terrorist attacks, except for that percentage of attacks that are directed against U.S. citizens or property. The latter figure shows that 42 percent of all incidents were directed against U.S. diplomatic or military officials or property, U.S. business executives or facilities, or private U.S. citizens.

If we break the Rand chronology down by nationality of victims or physical targets of terrorist attacks, it reveals a number of interesting changes from the first list, which dealt only with the locations. Israel, not surprisingly, moves way up as a target nation. Also Yugoslavia, the Soviet Union, and Cuba, which are seldom the scenes of terrorist violence, move up as targets of such violence. Other than that, there are relatively few changes; the top ten countries are the United States, the United Kingdom, Israel, the Federal Republic of Germany, France, Yugoslavia, the Soviet Union, Cuba, Turkey, and Spain. Now, looking at the same kind of breakdown—that is, by nationality of victim or country—and examining the Risks International chronology, which includes domestic as well as international terrorism, we see very little disparity between the locations of targets and the national identities of victims. Here the top ten nations are the United States, Italy, Spain, the Federal Republic of Germany, Colombia, Turkey, the United Kingdom, Argentina, Israel, and El Salvador.

With a few exceptions, then, the same nations dominate all these lists, whether locations or targets of terrorist violence are measured: in North America—the United States; in Europe—Italy, France, Spain, West Germany, Greece, and the United Kingdom; in the Middle East—Turkey and Israel, with Israel the prime target of terrorist attacks. Were this chronology adjusted to include only those incidents in which there were casualties, I suspect that the United States and France would fall considerably in the list, since in both countries there is much bombing but few casualties.

There is no easy way to identify the affiliation of terrorists. For example, the terrorists who took over the Egyptian embassy in Ankara identified themselves as members of the Eagles of the Palestinian Revolution. Some sources claim that this organization is actually an alias of the well-known al-Saiqa group, which is a part of the Palestine Liberation Organization. Still others, however, would claim that the responsible party is the Syrian government, which in effect controls al-Saiqa.

Not only is it difficult to identify the organizational and national affiliation of terrorist groups, we must also be extremely cautious with the data which are obtained. Our major problem is that there is a significant possibility of several kinds of bias in reporting. As mentioned previously, most chronologies of terrorism are derived from the news media. In countries where the press is controlled, reporting of terrorist incidents may be suppressed. Countries in which the news media are primitive or the press is not readily available to those compiling chronologies are probably underrepresented. In contrast, countries in which the news media are well developed and readily available may appear, according to the statistics, as centers of raging terrorist violence. There are ways to adjust for overrepresentation—for example, by dealing only with incidents in which there are casualties—but the problem of underrepresentation remains intractable.

There is a further problem in that urban violence is more likely to be reported than rural violence. To be sure, there may be less terrorism of international consequence in rural areas. For one thing, there are fewer targets; national palaces, embassies, and corporate headquarters are located in cities, not remote villages. But a substantial amount of domestic terrorism may occur in rural areas missed or ignored by the local press, so that countries with serious rural violence problems may be underrepresented in chronologies of terrorism.

Much of the terrorist violence that has occurred in Europe has been carried out by Arab groups and is aimed at Israeli targets. The preference shown by Arab terrorists for operating in Western Europe may be explained by several factors: proximity to the Middle East; the relatively free travel among Western European countries; the absence until the last few years of stringent antiterrorist security measures; the fact that many educated Palestinians are attending universities in Western Europe; the presence of large Palestinian student populations; and the terrorists' perceptions of these countries as allies or supporters of Israel. Note that these are external factors, unrelated to the social, economic, or political conditions of the European countries.

We must also remember that terrorism is largely a matter of perception, so that a few spectacular incidents may give the impression of a serious terrorism problem. Less attention may be paid to more numerous but less spectacular incidents. And there are biases in our own perception. We seem to pay little attention to higher levels of violence in Third World countries, while a single act of violence in, say, a Western European capital is likely to produce major headlines around the world.

Finally, we should keep in mind that the combined strength of all the terrorist groups in the world amounts to perhaps several thousand combatants. If we limit ourselves to those who have received international attention for their acts of terrorism, we are perhaps talking about hundreds. Must we really seek broad social or political explanations behind the acts of so few? Keeping in mind the smallness of the terrorist community, we shall proceed to a listing of hypotheses as to why some countries seem to have higher levels of terrorism than others.

Hypotheses on the distribution of terrorism include political, historical, economic, social, and demographic explanations. In the political category is the hypothesis that terrorism is the violent expression of legitimate grievances in societies where dissidents have no alternative means of bringing pressure on a repressive government. Leftists tend to favor this hypothesis, since the countries most affected by terrorism consider themselves (with varying degrees of accuracy) as political democracies and are regarded as aligned with the West—that is, anti-Communist. The evidence offered to support this hypothesis is tautological: Terrorism occurs here for these reasons, the proof being that terrorism occurs here.

A second hypothesis is that terrorist violence is a by-product of a free society. That is, it occurs primarily in countries that have politically open societies, occurring far less frequently in countries such as the Soviet Union, where the government strictly controls its citizens. Terrorism can be successfully repressed by totalitarian methods or by regimes that become totalitarian in response to the threat of terrorism, such as Uruguay. The evidence for this hypothesis, like the preceding one, is somewhat tautological, but at least it adds the dynamic element that a democratic regime turning authoritarian is able to suppress terrorism. It does not, however, explain the absence of terrorism in some democratic nations.

A third hypothesis is that terrorism is the product of a free press. This is closely related to, but nevertheless distinct from, the second hypothesis. The first element of the hypothesis is that incidents of terrorism are reported where the news media operate without restriction. Being in the news, they are picked up in the statistics. A government-controlled press is likely to be prohibited from reporting such incidents; hence we read little about incidents of terrorism inside the Soviet Union. Major incidents may still be reported by the international press, but not enough to offset significantly the lack of news in countries where the press is somewhat restricted. The second element of this hypothesis is the view that in countries where the press is strictly controlled, potential perpetrators of terrorist action know that their actions will receive little or no publicity; thus, they refrain from carrying them out. Terrorists operating in countries where the press is free can be assured that their actions will receive widespread coverage, and thus they are inspired to carry out such actions. Therefore, the existence of a free press not only allows for more statistical reporting, but in a sense leads to more terrorism.

A fourth hypothesis is that the disparate level of terrorism in Western democracies reflects Soviet, Cuban, or other Communist support for terrorists in these countries. While it is true that many terrorists—even those whose grievances reflect ethnic conflicts—espouse left-wing ideologies, the evidence regarding the degree of direct support for terrorism provided by the Soviet Union and other Communist countries is ambiguous or unreliable.

A fifth hypothesis is that the origins of terrorism are historical. Terrorism is simply a manifestation of unresolved ethnic or ideological conflicts. Thus, it occurs in countries where ethnic or ideological struggles have been most apparent. Terrorist acts in Spain, Northern Ireland, and the Philippines and those directed against Israel certainly reflect ethnic division and in some cases decades or even centuries of struggle. Much of modern terrorism in France also can be traced to separatist tendencies in Brittany and Corsica. Likewise, terrorism in Italy, Spain, Argentina, Turkey, West Germany, Greece (all of which are high on our list) and Japan (which is not) reflect continuing deep ideological struggles going back to at least World War II and often to the beginning of the century. The ethnic and political homogeneity of Scandinavian countries, then, would explain their relative immunity from terrorism.

A sixth hypothesis is that terrorism has been most virulent in the former Axis powers: Germany, Italy, and Japan. According to this hypothesis, the governments of these three countries lost their moral authority, first by becoming Fascists and second by losing the war. According to this hypothesis, with few exceptions the Fascists—particularly industrialists and low-level bureaucrats—escaped retribution and successfully threw themselves into an amoral pursuit of wealth in the postwar years. Dissent was placated in these societies by the thriving economies, which benefited not only industrialists but workers as well. Rejecting the crass materialism and questioning the Fascist past of their elders, the younger generation rejected the rigid social and political structure in which a single political party, generally conservative, merely sought to conserve its power and increase wealth. This hypothesis breaks down under statistical examination, which shows that Japan does not have high levels of terrorism and that France is less immune to terrorism than proponents of this theory suggest.

A seventh hypothesis is that terrorism is most powerful in those countries where anarchism was most virulent earlier in the century and thus represents a continuing historical tradition. Certainly this hypothesis appears appropriate for Italy, Spain, Argentina, Japan, and possibly West Germany. It does not, however, explain the relatively low incidence of terrorism in the Soviet Union or the Balkan countries.

An eighth hypothesis is that local and environmental factors are not the causes of Western European terrorism, which is, rather, a product primarily of Palestinian terrorists. Local extremists have made contact with Palestinian organizations, received training and continued support from them, and have been used by them. This Palestinian connection has thus turned a few domestic terrorists into far more powerful and active movements than they otherwise would have been, so that while all countries experience certain levels of terrorism, the Palestinian connection raised the local level of terrorism in some. This hypothesis might explain the incidence of terrorism in West Germany and Japan, and possibly Turkey and Iran, where Palestinians do play a pivotal role in international terrorism. But it is incapable of explaining terrorism in Spain, Northern Ireland, and Italy, where terrorism seems to be more of a local phenomenon.

A ninth political theory is that left-wing terrorism has resulted primarily from the increasingly conservative orientation of the Communist party. That is, when the traditional revolutionary party became part of the legitimate political system, began to seek respectability, and in fact became part of the opposition to the government in power, rather than to the system in power, it lost its control over the more radical, militant elements, leading to outbursts of terrorism. According to this theory, the origins of terrorism in West Germany can be traced to the beginning of the Grand Alliance in the 1960s, and those in Italy to the increasingly conservative position taken by the Italian Communist party. The theory could also be applied in the case of Brazil, where the Communist party became more conservative and there was a proliferation of fragmented left-wing groups.

There are two economic hypotheses, and they are mutually contradictory. The first is that terrorism is the product of affluence or of high economic growth—two factors that generally appear together. That is, those countries that have experienced high levels of terrorism (such as the United States, West Germany, the United Kingdom, France, Italy, and Japan) also have comparatively high per capita incomes. They have also experienced rapid economic growth (as in West Germany, Italy, Japan since World War II, and more recently, Iran). The theory cannot explain why other wealthy countries in Western Europe—Switzerland, the Scandinavian countries— which also have high GNPs, have not experienced high levels of terrorism.

The second economic hypothesis is that terrorism is the product of economic stagnation. This hypothesis might explain the high level of terrorism in Northern Ireland and Uruguay, where economic stagnation has led to widespread unemployment and lack of opportunities for university graduates, thus providing a pool of economically deprived people from which terrorists could be recruited.

Finally, there are several social and demographic explanations. One is that terrorism reflects the decline in morality and erosion of faith in institutions such as family, church, and state, which began in the early 1960s. Another theory is that terrorism is the product of the prolonged adolescence that is a contemporary feature of society, particularly in the more affluent countries. Terrorism is seen as the product of official policies that place an exaggerated emphasis on university education, thus overcrowding universities and condemning graduates to unemployment. Affluence does indeed permit the prolongation of adolescence. That is something sociologists have noted, and certainly there were explosions of university populations in some countries as governments sought to make university education available to more people.

A last hypothesis is that terrorism is a product of urbanization. This is a favorite with criminologists, who also trace increasingly high levels of crime to the anonymity of city life and the breakdown of traditional institutions in city life. It is true that the countries most affected by terrorism are highly urbanized, but as we have already noted, there is a tremendous reporting bias because terrorism that takes place in urban areas gets reported while that in rural areas does not.

These are fourteen theories that have been advanced to explain the uneven distribution of terrorism. Not one sufficiently accounts for the whole spectrum of the phenomenon, and certainly all of them are open for debate.

Discussion

PARTICIPANT: I would like to note that, for a number of reasons, there are different statistics concerning the same subject. You mentioned the CIA, Rand, and Risks International statistics. I think we have to recognize that data bases, and therefore the statistics on a particular subject, differ greatly because of the varying definitions of terrorism and because the jurisdictions of the data bases differ. For example, FBI statistics deal with domestic issues; the U.S. Department of Defense, on the other hand, has no files concerning domestic terrorist activities, except for very specific cases, such as protection of nuclear weapons.

In addition to the problem of definitions and that of the area covered by a particular data collecting group, there is the problem of overestimation. Some of the incidents attributed to terrorists may actually have been undertaken by criminals or psychopaths. On the other hand, there is the problem of underestimation, for some of the data bases do not incorporate all terrorist incidents. For example, Risks International deals only with *significant* international and domestic cases; it excludes what it deems insignificant cases. Underestimation is also the result of governments not reporting incidents for psychological reasons. The Italians, for example, are obviously not going to give you all the statistics in regard to Italy. We also find that some bases exclude specific incidents. To illustrate: purists would exclude Indo-Chinese or Israeli incidents, deeming these to be guerrilla warfare rather than terrorism.

My point is, that we have to be very cautious because of the multiplicity of definitions and because of the various classifications of terrorist acts. It is very difficult to analyze terrorism when there is no universally accepted definition of terrorism.

PARTICIPANT: I am a little puzzled about the way the statistics are classified. What, for example, is the distinction between rural terrorism and guerrilla warfare? I suppose that if you tallied up the events without distinction, you would find Vietnam at the top of the list for the mid-sixties.

PARTICIPANT: I find one major flaw in the account presented, because a condition of terrorism is mainly a state of mind, not only a matter of statistical figures. According to the statistics presented, the United States ranks very highly, even highest in some cases. But the impression conveyed by some of our American participants is that in the United States there is no condition of terrorism. I think that perceptions are more important than the statistical count.

As far as your compilation of events is concerned, it is useful in itself, but it does not answer the question from an operative point of view: What are the conditions of terrorism? If we do not know what they are, if they are everything as listed here, we still do not have any direction or answer as to possible ways of handling the problem.

JENKINS: I have spent an enormous amount of time with the statistics in these chronologies, and I hope there will not be any misunderstanding concerning them. I am not suggesting these numbers are the final word. I am deeply aware of the tremendous limitations in this kind of empirical effort and have tried to point out some of them. There are biases in reporting, stemming from problems concerning jurisdictions or from perceptions of what constitutes terrorism. I tend to go along with the view that it is probably more a matter of perceptions than a matter of statistical counts. In fact, what always puzzles me is that there are years in which all the indicators, every kind of detail you could count, go up; yet people think that terrorism is going down. On the other hand, there are years when statistics go down; yet everybody thinks terrorism is going up. I have never been able to figure out why the perceptions did not match up with the statistics. It turns out—and this is my own hypothesis—that our perceptions of the problem are governed by a relatively few spectacular incidents of a particular type. Interestingly, hostage incidents attract far more attention and determine perceptions far more than murder, even mass murder. When an airliner with seventy-five people on board crashes, it is news for a week at most. Yet a South Mollucan siege of a train that drags on for weeks and months or the Moro kidnaping drives perception to biases. I am not proposing that statistics be the basis for measuring levels of terrorism, but statistics can help us determine where to examine terrorism, where terrorism seems to be because of factors we can measure.

With regard to the question of classification and calculation, is terrorism in rural areas calculated as guerrilla warfare? This problem has come up a number of times. I can offer only the criteria I have used in my own research of the phenomenon. I certainly make a distinction between guerrilla warfare and terrorism. I think it is entirely possible to be a guerrilla fighter without necessarily being a terrorist. The specific criteria that I would impose for classifying an act as terrorism are:

1. It must include violence or the threat of violence.
2. It must be considered a crime under municipal law. There is no crime called terrorism. Terrorists commit classic crimes: arson, kidnaping, murder, and so forth. Therefore, we are talking about criminal acts.
3. For the most part, the act would also be a violation of the laws that govern warfare. Most terrorists now claim to be combatants, that is, soldiers belligerent in combat. But if we consider the actions and check the rules of war to which just about all of the nations in the world have subscribed, we note that the actions—such as the deliberate application of violence against civilian noncombatants, the seizure of hostages, or the maltreatment of prisoners—are all direct violations of the conventions that govern conventional warfare. Therefore, even if terrorists were to be raised to the status of combatants, they would still be committing a crime.
4. The action has some political objective beyond an individual goal. I am not saying that I share or even comprehend all of the ideologies that are the basis of terrorist violence, but some political goal must be present. A mugger in Central Park or a guy who holds up a bank is not a terrorist, even if he were to meet the other criteria, because he is not doing it for any goal beyond his individual goal. The lunatic who wants to blow up the world because God tells him it is a wicked place is not included in our definition of a terrorist. Yet we would include the act as a terrorist incident.
5. That the person regarded as a terrorist be part of a group or at least working for an ideal. I would insist on this criterion in order to exclude from the statistics the individual lunatic operating on his own.
6. Finally, and perhaps most importantly, that the action is carried out to produce effects beyond those on the actual victim or target of the event. In other words, the overall effect must include some intended psychological impact beyond the shooting of a specific victim. This is recognized, I think, in terrorist doctrine; "Kill one to teach a hundred" is a terrorist dictum.

To sum up, an act of terror has an element of violence; it is a crime under municipal law; it is most frequently also a violation of the rules of warfare; it has political objectives; it expresses the ideal of a group; and it has the operative means to terrorize.

According to this definition, one can be a guerrilla fighter without being a terrorist. One can also be a member of any army and be a terrorist, even though one would technically be a privileged combatant. For example— and I say this with some fervor as a combat veteran of Vietnam—to me, the actions carried out in the My Lai massacre could conceivably, justifiably be acts of terrorists. They were directed against a civilian population; they were perhaps intended to inspire dread and fear amongst the local population; they were certainly criminal; they were a violation of the rules of warfare; they contained the element of violence; and there was no military justification for those acts. What I like about my definition is that one can apply it in a relatively free manner. I do not have to judge objectives; I do not have to judge causes; and I do not have to say some people are not terrorists because they wear uniforms and others are terrorists because they do not wear uniforms. At any rate, I am not offering this as a universal and final definition, for it certainly has many legal shortcomings.

PARTICIPANT: I think that five of the six points of criteria you have presented are common to both guerrilla warfare and terrorism. Violence is perpetrated in both cases; both essentially commit crimes; certainly in both cases you have political objectives; certainly in both cases a group or idea is involved; and certainly in both cases you have at least the intent of effects beyond the individual victims. So what it boils down to is the question of whether there are violations of the rules governing warfare, a matter with which I am not familiar.

PARTICIPANT: I am troubled by the definition of terrorism as acts of violence carried out for political reasons. How does that apply to the Mafia in Italy? Their acts are certainly criminal; they are carried out for economic reasons, however, not for political ones. Yet I think the acts can be classified as terrorism.

PARTICIPANT: I do not see any reason not to use the dictionary definition for terrorism just to understand the word itself. It means terror applied to some defined community or population in order to get some demands free of charge. In this sense, I do not see that there is really any difference inherently between what the Mafia has done and what a political terrorist does. The same method is used, though the content of their demands is different. At times one cannot differentiate between a terrorist act and a Mafia action because the demand is not very specific. We have to inquire into the reasons and the conditions that make a particular population more likely to become the victims of a terrorist act.

JENKINS: It is useful to discuss the definitional issue, but the lack of precision in a definition ought not to stall the discussion. For example, lawyers and judges cannot come up with a definition of pornography. Yet there is something that is pornography. The fact is that despite our inability to agree on a precise definition of terrorism that will satisfy the international community, the lawyers, and the historians, there is something called terrorism; and we can probably generally agree on the kinds of actions which are terrorist actions. With regard to the criteria for compiling the statistics I have cited, ours is frankly the most conservative one in terms of numbers because of these criteria.

PARTICIPANT: Did you, for example, include in your U.S. list the cases where there were victims but the perpetrators were unknown?

JENKINS: No, we did not. Our position on this is simply that if we do not know for sure, we do not count it as an incident. That tends to make our data base very small compared with some of the others.

PARTICIPANT: I take issue with one of your definitions, which is that terrorism must be tied to a political aim. That would exclude all incidents when people carry out terrorist acts for personal reasons, even though they may not be mad (it depends, of course, on how you define madness). When a person hijacks a plane because he believes that he has been treated badly by his superiors, he is not mad. This is terrorism, yet it is not political.

JENKINS: The only hijackings we would exclude are those done purely for economic reasons—for example, the hijacking by an individual who demands two hundred thousand dollars and a parachute—or those where the hijacker is plainly emotionally disturbed, like the one who hijacked a plane in Chicago and wanted to fly to Wyoming. We try to exclude the clearly lunatic and the purely economic cases.

PARTICIPANT: There is a point I think I ought to mention with regard to your fourteen hypotheses concerning the causes of terrorism. Each of these hypotheses is independent and quite often one conflicts with another. For example, one of your hypotheses refers to ethnic grievances while another offers reasons why there is no terrorism in the Soviet Union. Yet, as we know, the Soviet Union has a lot of ethnic grievances. There is no terrorism there because of their security system. These two hypotheses seem to cross one another. Therefore, it is possible that no single one of the fourteen hypotheses is the correct one, but rather a combination of these describes more clearly what terrorism proneness is.

JENKINS: Again, none of these hypotheses is my hypothesis. I recognize the fact that some of them are mutually contradictory. There may be two or three that may suit one country and a different combination that may suit another country. Therefore, I am somewhat skeptical of our ability to create one grand theory. But we can certainly make an effort.

PARTICIPANT: We do have a record of what terrorism is, as was mentioned, in terms of domestic laws. If you look at it from the U.S. perspective, a police officer would say that terrorism is breaking the law. Again, in terms of statistics, you have to look at the laws of the country where the incident took place or at those of the country affected. Also, today there is a record of international documents dealing with terrorism.

I, personally, tried to compile such documents, from a treaty for the extradition of criminals and for the protection against anarchism dating back to 1902 to the Bonn economic summit declaration of July 1978. We have a record related to specific acts of terrorism; for example, hijacking or acts of unlawful interference with civil aviation which are clear violations of international law. Even the Soviet Union would consider them as such. In addition, economic crimes were mentioned. These constitute a different problem, for they are directed against the business community. But altogether, we have today domestic law, regional law, and international law related to terrorism. If we start with that, I think our job will be much easier in terms of compiling facts concerning what terrorism is.

PARTICIPANT: There are acts of terrorism that are meaningless, because they simply do not affect the public where they take place. That is why terrorism is actually a matter of perception. I think the issue at stake is not numbers, but rather the effect of terrorist acts upon the people in communities where they are perpetrated.

PARTICIPANT: I think that is a very important point, because if we say that terrorism is a matter of perceptions, then we can say there are some populations which are more prone than others to be terrorized.

PARTICIPANT: Actually when you talk about populations, you are also talking about governments and their tolerance or submission. It is not just a question concerning a particular group. The target of the terrorist must be considered, as well as the kind of reaction the government will have and the countermeasures the government will take.

PARTICIPANT: I think terrorism against Israel is different because Israel's population is not terrorized so easily, but you must not overlook the results outside the region, such as in the United Nations and in other countries. I cannot see that the PLO carries out acts of terrorism in order to get results here; rather, it is done with an eye to the outside.

PARTICIPANT: The issue under discussion is not the effect of terrorism on people. There is no disagreement that terrorism is a matter of perception. It is not a matter of body counts, incident counts, or any kind of counts. But the issue is how we deal with the task we have been assigned here in terms of terrorist-prone countries. Why does Italy, for example, have more terrorism than Sweden?

PARTICIPANT: I am not sure of it in statistical terms, but let us assume, for example, that in India there are more terrorist activities than in Italy. Yet nobody here, I am sure, has put India on his list. The problem is that somehow, if there are acts of terrorism in India they are simply lost in the overwhelming society. The society there is so huge that there is little or no sensitivity to human life. Possibly, there is also no publicity, so we are simply not aware of terrorism in India if it exists.

PARTICIPANT: Let us be careful with what we ascribe to the Indians. Perhaps it is not a question of Indian sensitivity to human life, but one of our insensitivity to loss of Indian life. It may be that the Indians are as sensitive to human life as we are, but as long as these incidents take place in India we do not care about them; whereas when they take place in West Germany or Italy, we care more about them. Nevertheless, were we to compile these facts, we would find consensus with regard to seven or eight countries: all would agree they have high levels of terrorism. I would bet that those countries would be reflected in the statistics, in some very rough fashion.

Now, can we get to the issue of *why* those countries are hit by terrorism?

PARTICIPANT: There is a very clear common denominator which allows for terrorism, and that is lax security measures. Weakness of authorities is also a very strong element.

PARTICIPANT: Italy is very high up on the list because it has a very free press; it has relatively weak security authorities that have recently been weakened even more; and it has a tradition of criminal-terrorist activity which serves as an example for political terrorists.

PARTICIPANT: May I at this point expand the issue a bit? I fully agree, and I think it is important to look at specific case studies such as Italy. If you look at the Middle East, you must understand it against the background of the tradition of violence and terror in this area. When people discuss terrorism or guerrilla warfare, as some people call it in this region, they talk about contemporary situations; if you go back to the Middle Ages, however, you will see there is a long tradition of terror. I think we have to stress the particular historical tradition of violence and terror in some societies, which makes them more tolerant to terrorism and renders the latter more acceptable. The Middle East is certainly such a region.

PARTICIPANT: Some theories of terrorism are not testable. I do not know how to measure decline in faith in institutions, for example. Maybe one goes around and measures the number of people actively attending church in Italy today in comparison with the number that attended church there fifteen years ago, but I do not know how to do that. Some things are virtually impossible to measure. There is no single hypothesis that holds up with testable data. There is a problem either with the hypothesis or with the availability of the data.

PARTICIPANT: I would say that terrorism-prone societies are those where there is a combination of several factors, including an unstable political system. You mentioned dissatisfaction with a regime, but not its stability, which can be an important factor when combined with social stress among various groups (ethnic, for instance) or with major economic gaps. I would also add that the reasons for terrorism are mainly local; only sometimes are they enhanced by international factors.

PARTICIPANT: It seems to me that an important factor contributing to terrorist proneness that has not been mentioned is excessive amounts of explosives. We know from our own experience in Israel that when explosives are smuggled in, a lot of terrorist incidents occur. Their number goes up proportionally. The number goes down when fewer explosives are available or when only homemade explosives are available. I have a sneaking suspicion that the reason why there is relatively little or no terrorism in countries like Sweden, Switzerland, and so on, may be due partially to the unavailability of explosives. These are countries that have not been involved in wars recently. Although every Swiss citizen has his rifle at home, he does not use it for terrorism. Also, it is rather difficult to get hold of arms and explosives there. In the Soviet Union, too, one cannot possess arms unless he is in the army or is a member of the police force.

There is another factor which may affect the statistics concerning terrorist proneness, and that is the fact that certain countries have reached agreements with terrorists, have given in to terrorist demands in exchange for the promise that there would be no more terrorism in that particular country. We know that this is the case in Italy; for a long time this was the case in France; and there are other countries where this is true. This policy worked in regard to Arab terrorism. Italy is a very good example of this. The Italian government gave in to Arab terrorism, partially due to the promise received in exchange that there would be no more Arab terrorism there.

PARTICIPANT: Practically speaking, the question is what we can do in the academic community with regard to data bases, and so forth. If we use what little international agreement there is as a basis, I think we can get a lot of data. In a practical sense, what can institutions such as the Center for Strategic Studies (CSS) do about the problem?

PARTICIPANT: We have reached no conclusion concerning the causes of terrorism. In fact, we have come to the inevitable question of definition. Although I do not absolve countries like the Soviet Union or often mindless organizations like the UN General Assembly for their obstructionism in coming to a definition of terrorism, I think we have to reduce somewhat the harshness of our judgments of their inability to do so, when a roomful of people who are like-minded about the problem of terrorism cannot come up with a satisfactory definition of terrorism.

Data are nice for the utility of entertaining notions. If we cannot agree upon a common international data base, then, at the very least, we should make the different kinds of data bases in the possession of one country available to other countries. Even if we cannot agree on a common criterion or a common definition, we should keep in mind that we are not going to satisfy everybody. The only thing we can do is be very up-front about what our criteria are, so that anybody using a particular data base can judge it in the correct perspective.

5

Terrorism and the Eruption of Wars

J. Bowyer Bell

Like romantic love, *terrorism* is easy to recognize but difficult to define. We use the term here to refer to the reasoned, if brutally violent, deeds of rebels engaged in an irregular campaign. We thus exclude from consideration state terror and acts committed by criminal or demented figures. A definition of the *eruption of wars* is also somewhat elusive, since it is sometimes difficult to identify exactly when a state of war exists. Civil order may decay into war. Lebanon, for example, slipped into war bit by bit. And, in fact, several lawsuits now pending question whether or not a war exists in Lebanon at all. In the present context, I shall distinguish between wars between nation states and wars within national boundaries. In analyzing the twentieth century, we can further differentiate among world wars, major power wars, middle power wars, and minor power wars— leaving aside whether any of the last two variants were proxy or surrogate wars. Clearly, there were two world wars involving almost all major powers and many of lesser rank. One of these wars was precipitated by a terrorist act, the assassination of Archduke Francis Ferdinand. On a smaller scale are the wars between two major powers: Japan against China or (perhaps) China against the United States in Korea. Most major state wars have been colonial or involved a lesser power—the United States in Vietnam or Britain in South Africa. Next, there are middle power wars: India versus Pakistan or Israel versus the Arabs—although during the last two Israeli-Arab wars, in 1967 and 1973, the weight of materiel was enormous even by previous major power standards. Finally, there are the small power wars: the Tanzanian-Ugandan affair or the Balkan wars.

There are two major varieties of internal wars, both presently labeled wars of national liberation. The first type is the colonial war, from the struggle of the Cypriot EOKA (Ethniki Organosis Kypriakou Agoniston, or National Organization of Cypriot Fighters) for union with Greece, to the Irish Republican Army's (IRA) efforts to expel the British from the six counties of Ulster. Most of these seem to be over. The second type of internal war is the revolutionary war, where the boundaries of the nation have already been defined but the nature of the society is in dispute. These, too, are various, from the Spanish Civil War to the civil disorder in Northern Ireland. Many of these revolutionary wars are defined by the rebels in colonial or neocolonial terms; the Basques, the IRA, and the Saharans all claim to be fighting a national liberation struggle against imperialism.

The relationship between terrorism and the eruptions of external wars is ambiguous. Generally, the more extensive the war and the more serious its causes, the smaller the chance that terrorist acts were the primary cause of the eruption of hostilities. Of course, in waging war, nations have often claimed to be responding to provocations of irregular violence—for example, Polish "intrusions" into Germany in 1939—for no nation has ever admitted greed as just cause. Rarely do terrorists provide more than a rationale for declaring international wars.

The relationship between terrorists and civil wars is more complicated, since hostilities are in part waged by terrorists—urban or rural guerrillas. These wars are conducted by terror rather than instigated by terrorism. Terrorist activities may also provoke military intervention by a foreign power, as, for example, in the case of Pancho Villa's raid into the United States prior to World War I. The United States dispatched an expeditionary force under Gen. John Pershing that wandered about in northern Mexico to little effect but did not lead to a formal Mexican war. More recently, the United States has been involved in irregular wars in places as diverse as Laos and the Dominican Republic directly, and Angola and Iraqi Kurdistan indirectly. It is also possible that such substate actors—terrorists—may provoke a larger power confrontation. Elsewhere, as in Lebanon, motives and events are not so clear. No one knows when or for what purpose the war in Lebanon began, nor can the responsible parties be identified. No one knows if the Fedayeen truly wanted to provoke a Syrian invasion or an Israeli incursion. Thus, the impact of terrorism in the eruption of the Lebanese chaos is ambiguous.

Despite the uncertainties and the reservations mentioned above, it is of interest to examine the issue further. Can terrorists provoke eruptions of conventional wars? Do they want to do so and will they? What of tomorrow's war and today's terrorist? It might be wise to examine in some detail four contemporary arenas for terrorism: Ireland, Italy, Iran, and Israel.

Ireland. Two groups of violent opponents currently dominate Ireland, the Protestant paramilitaries and the Provisional Irish Republic Army. Located in the six counties of Ulster, the Protestant paramilitaries are essentially vigilante groups who murder random Catholic victims in the North and on occasion plant bombs in the South. The Provisional IRA, an all-Ireland group and the oldest operating revolutionary movement in the world, is dedicated to a thirty-two-county united Ireland or, in other words, the dissolution of the Dublin government and the expulsion of any British presence or proxy in six-county Ulster. A third albeit authorized force of violence is the British army, purportedly a peace-keeping force sent to prevent the various gunmen from killing each other. At present, the major confrontation is between the IRA and the British army. After ten years, this confrontation seems as intractable as ever.

Can IRA terrorism lead to an eruption of war, and if so, between whom? All the British governments, Conservative and Labour, have contended that withdrawal of the army would precipitate a civil war between the Protestants and Catholics. In such an eventuality, would such a confrontation prove to be a real war? And if so, would it be possible to say that the eruption was caused by terrorism? Would the transformation from one kind of internal war to another be an eruption?

The other scenario that could involve war would be a British withdrawal, civil strife, threatened Catholics—this would impel intervention by the Irish army. Although greatly improved in recent years, the Irish army is hardly prepared to launch an invasion into and across hostile Protestant territory, and Dublin politicians are horrified by the prospect. Dublin's policy, like London's, is to hope that IRA violence will go away, that the militants of all sorts will exhaust themselves. Thus, neither Dublin nor London wants confrontation. It is therefore difficult to imagine a terrorist act that would engender war after ten long years of unsavory terrorist acts.

Italy. Italy displays a vast spectrum of revolutionary activity pursued by a variety of terrorist groups. Of the many scores of these groups, few are well organized. While some of them are neo-Fascist or vaguely monarchist, most are on the far Left. Essentially, the goal of the leftist groups—the Red Brigades, the Front Line, et al.—is to make Italy ungovernable by instigating anarchy and chaos in order that a new, revolutionary Italy (structure undefined) may emerge. The goal of the Fascist terror groups is to install a single, powerful Fascist leader. They seek merely to create the civil tension which will induce the Italian public to embrace such a figure. Thus, there could be chaos inspired by the Left or a military dictator brought to power by the Right. But what then? Would there be civil war? Would terrorism spread? No one knows. We can say, however, that if the Red Brigades were to take over Italy—an event which seems unlikely—intervention by NATO or by neighbor states would almost certainly not occur. In the case of a coup from the Right, intervention from abroad would be even less likely. Thus the likelihood of Italy's terrorism problem erupting into an international war seems quite low.

Iran. For at least a year Iran has not really been governed. The "system" might be called institutionalized chaos. The country is presently in the midst of a low-intensity internal war involving various ethnic separatist movements, diverse religious armies, guerrillas of the Left and Right, residue state institutions, and security forces. While the present state of chaos cannot be called a war, it could whet the appetites of a neighbor and provoke intervention. Certainly, the Iraqis have been tampering with the ethnic Arabs around the Abadan refinery and the southwestern oil fields. Encouragement of the Kurds has been more discreet for Iraq itself has long had a Kurdish separatist problem (until recently exacerbated by Iran as a U.S. proxy). Various American analysts have worried about Soviet intervention in Iran. Such intervention might as easily be provoked by Iranian aid and comfort to Islamic rebels in Afghanistan as well as by the chaos in Teheran. However, despite the presence of the Russians in Afghanistan and the American fleet in the Arabian Sea, despite the ancient Iraqi enemy at the gates, despite the chaos, there seems only a small chance of conventional war in Iran. Even should there be a Soviet invasion or a Soviet-American confrontation over Iran, would terrorism—state or revolutionary—have been responsible? I think not.

Terrorism in Iran is a symptom of instability, not a cause. The Center has not held for a variety of historical reasons. In the worst possible case— major power confrontation—various factors other than terrorism would have been responsible.

Israel. The terrorist problem in Israel is more various, more interesting, and more relevant to the eruption of war than in the other cases examined, since here the provocation of war has been the professed goal of various Fedayeen. According to their spokesmen, the Palestinians are fighting a revolutionary anticolonial war with the limited support of their Arab and ideological allies. For them, the Israelis are the last vestige of Western imperialism, imposed from Europe and maintained by outside aid, particularly from the United States. For the Palestinians, the struggle with Israel is a war of national liberation. A great many Israelis would insist that it is a surrogate campaign of terror fought by Palestinian Arabs abetted by Arab states, but ultimately directed by the Soviet Union for geo-strategic purposes. For the Israelis, then, the struggle with the Palestinians represents an undeclared middle power proxy war.

This anti-Fedayeen war could escalate into a direct middle power war as a result of terrorist provocation. Such provocation might be intentional or might be the result of error or simple neglect—the instigation of a deed without due reflection on the nature of potential retaliation. For example, Israel moved north to the Litani River when provided with terrorist provocation. The Israeli intrusion was hardly an eruption of war, but it might have led to a confrontation with Syria and an eruption of a formal middle power war. Certainly, the Fedayeen provocations have in the past and can be expected in the future to lead to Israeli retaliation of one sort or another, a heightening of regional tensions, an erosion of toleration. No matter how justified, such Israeli retaliation will erode détente with Egypt and perhaps provoke an Arab response. One terrorist massacre can and has led to escalation, and escalation in the Middle East can be dangerous, indeed. Perhaps, more than any other place in the world—certainly more so than in Ireland, Italy, or Iran—the likelihood of terrorists provoking state response that might lead to a war exists in the Middle East.

It appears, then, that the terrorists acting alone can rarely precipitate a war, especially a major war. The more complex the conflict, the more protracted the prewar confrontation and rivalry, the greater the level of martial violence—the less likely is terrorism to play a major role. As Professor Dror noted, terrorism provides an atmosphere, a milieu that makes the eruption of war more likely, especially in the Middle East. In this region and elsewhere, although terrorism is unlikely itself to cause a war, it may provide a rationale for long-planned intervention or turn an irregular war into an all-out one. In some cases, as in Ireland today, terrorism appears remote from the clash of states, if not from civil war. In other cases, as in Italy, terrorism might lead to sufficient chaos to spark a military coup and civil war, although this is unlikely. In still other cases, as in Iran, terrorism operating in a power vacuum might entice intervention by the greedy, although this, too, is unlikely. Finally, in some cases, as in the Middle East, terrorism remains a clear and present danger, a destabilizing factor that can easily lead to provocation, retaliation, escalation, and confrontation. Thus, while in most instances terrorism is a minor factor in the eruption of wars, in some cases, like the Middle East today, it can play a decisive role.

Discussion

PARTICIPANT: Terrorism creates issues, that is evident. But does it ignite wars? I think the historical record here in the Middle East proves that it did not do so in the past. In 1956 there were other factors; and though the 1978 Litani operation was made possible by terrorist acts, those acts did not ignite a war between Syria and Israel.

PARTICIPANT: One should take into account the use of terror campaigns as an artificial cause of war. Careful manipulation of terrorist strategies can be used to create international semilegitimization to start a war. On a more diffuse but no less important level, terrorism influences not war eruption, but war moods, which increases the propensity of an outbreak of war. A country subjected to terrorism would be more ready to use violence than a country not subjected to terrorism. In a general sense, the mood of violence, of semibarbarism, increases the likelihood of war.

PARTICIPANT: This was a relevant factor in Israel in 1956 and 1967.

PARTICIPANT: This mood of violence increases domestic political readiness and popular pressure to resort to violence. Terrorism can be viewed as hindering the peace process, which indirectly increases the probabilities of war. My main point is to emphasize the indirect influences, other than the catalytic trigger effect.

PARTICIPANT: There is a general influence of terrorism on negotiations, domestic politics, mood, and readiness to use violence, which are all factors that increase or decrease the probability of war. But using a different approach, I would say that if terrorism would cause wars, there might be a greater incentive to get rid of it. Should supporting terrorism endanger the supporting country, which may get involved in a war, the cost of supporting terrorism might increase to a point where a country would have second thoughts about doing so. The very fact that terrorism is cheap under some circumstances increases the willingness to support it. Therefore, if it were clearly recognized by some international custom or law that support of terrorism constitutes a legitimate definition of aggression, there might be strong incentive to reduce this support.

Looking further into the future, should terrorism use mass-destruction weapons or attack high-value targets such as oil lines, then the probability of using countermeasures would be increased. The increasing costs of terrorism motivate and stimulate counteractions.

PARTICIPANT: There is a very interesting question, which is whether supporting international terrorism against a definite country should give that country a right to use the United Nations Charter's clauses on self-defense. I could well imagine a strong legal claim by the U.S. State Department that one is entitled to use a surgical strike against a terrorist training camp in another country. On the one hand, this is dangerous, because it may increase the risks of war; on the other hand, it may be essential in order to motivate counterterror measures in the supporting countries themselves.

PARTICIPANT: How is it possible to punish a certain country, for example South Yemen, for supporting terrorism?

PARTICIPANT: There are a number of ways. As an extreme example, you could destroy Aden. I do not think there is any country or group which is immune to punishment.

PARTICIPANT: Thus far, we have naturally tended to think principally of the eruption of wars and of the acts of terrorism which precipitate or bring the crisis to a peak. I would like to suggest considering, in addition, the effects of terrorism in loosening up or altering certain elements of the international order, or the redrawing of lines in international politics. Perhaps the one element of modern international politics which should be considered is international frontiers, particularly in the Third World. One of the ways of dissolving a frontier or making it less solid than it would appear to be is by continual acts of terrorism. It seems to me that an example of this is the way in which the Provisional IRA has succeeded in making the United Kingdom–Irish Republic frontier appear a very questionable thing.

PARTICIPANT: I would like to support the comments made about the drawing of political lines. There is no doubt terrorism plays a very important role in the drawing of political lines. In the case of Palestinian terrorism, we must admit there was a Palestinian strategy and one of its objectives was to draw such lines. They succeeded to a great degree. We must have a better understanding of the combination of terror acts and political aims. I think that the case of the Fedayeen in Israel supports the thesis of the redrawing of political lines. I agree also with what was said about Israel's case with Syria. The Syrians are using Fedayeen to promote a deterioration and escalation in tension between them and Israel. It is not necessary for them to use their own force as in the case of war. For them, an all-out war would be a costly affair, so they would rather create a situation wherein Israel has to attack them while they can try to exploit the advantages in the defensive. This is especially true if their aim is to continue building themselves up, as in fact they are trying to do.

PARTICIPANT: It is not clear to me whether you really consider terrorism an autonomous factor in determining state decisions concerning war, or is it more a kind of pretext, rationalization, or cover-up? Is it a continuation of war using other means? If so, interests in outcomes and costs would determine the decision rather than the occurrence itself. Is terrorism autonomous?

PARTICIPANT: I think the subject is more or less inappropriate because the questions and reactions differ according to the audience. The successful antiterrorist operations of the Israel Defense Forces in Gaza were rather painful to Nasser; therefore, his posture changed with regard to that subject matter. It is a qualitative judgment as to how important a terrorist act is in all these particular cases. Yet a specific war that starts on a specific day because of a specific terrorist act is, I think, quite rare. Causes for war are usually varied and vague. I think that you cannot measure the exact effect of terrorist activity on the outbreak of war.

PARTICIPANT: I think it has been shown that in the major varieties of wars that have occurred around the world since 1945, that is, the internal wars, terrorism was in fact an omnipresent factor. If you look at Southeast Asia and Africa and examine the conflicts in those areas, it becomes clear that terrorism is an ongoing element. Insofar as it escalates and raises the stakes for intervention in those conflicts, it is a war-inducing characteristic. It is not just the redrawing of frontiers that is at stake here, but the takeover or change of regime which is, of course, the common objective of the revolutionary movements. To that extent, I think terrorism becomes a more significant weapon. This was manifest in the areas I have just mentioned, and also in Latin America.

With regard to the development of terrorism and rural guerrilla war, the implication of much of the discussion—for instance, in Prof. Walter Laqueur's book on guerrilla warfare—is that the rural emphasis is dying away, that guerrilla warfare of the traditional kind is no longer a major option for revolutionaries. According to Laqueur, as terrorists realize that technology is loaded against them, they will give up terrorism. I do not see the historical evidence for that assumption. I do not think that there are any universally valid principles in this matter. In some areas, rural guerrilla warfare still counts and is capable of winning real strategic gains. In that context, terrorism—both rural and urban—seems to me to have a key role. In its auxiliary role in a revolutionary war, it is still very important.

PARTICIPANT: A prominent case indicating that guerrilla warfare has not died out is Nicaragua. In Nicaragua we have seen a comeback of guerrilla tactics.

PARTICIPANT: I would like to make the distinction between what I would call autonomous terrorists who act on their own and agent groups. Whereas at times the means may be identical, the purposes and the effects are ultimately very different. One of the principal functions of political terrorism is to raise the subject on the international agenda, to make it an issue, as in Nicaragua. The Somoza family had been in power for forty years or so. The Sandinistas made their cause an issue because they created violence, and the violence has been continuing for a considerable period of time. The attitudes to Nicaragua by states, people, and firms have altered as a consequence of the fairly successful actions of the Sandinista groups. This is exactly what the PLO achieved in the Middle East: they made it an issue; they raised it on the international agenda. If you do something which is undeclared, you may be punishing your enemy, but you are not affecting politics.

PARTICIPANT: Is there a trend towards mass-destruction type terrorism as opposed to the so-called selective killing? An example is the Iranian terrorist act, when three hundred people were killed in a movie house.

PARTICIPANT: The general consensus is that terrorists are interested in influencing people, not in killing them. The fact is that the number of people killed by terrorists is very small. The number of anonymous terrorist acts is very small. The bombing at La Guardia Airport that killed eight people was apparently an act nobody wanted to take credit for. There have been a few assassinations in Europe that no one has taken credit for. These incidents are few, though technically the people and the equipment for an anonymous campaign are available.

PARTICIPANT: It is true that terrorists do not seek to kill large numbers of people. But perhaps the most important aspect of their propensity to use nuclear or chemical weapons is not the commission of murder, but the psychological effects. If terrorists can hijack a plane, take hostages, and threaten to kill everybody including themselves, they can also take over a nuclear plant somewhere in the eastern United States and blackmail the government as well. I think we should study ways to prevent this kind of event.

PARTICIPANT: Terrorists have never done this. There has been sabotage on nuclear plants, but not to the extent of causing widespread damage. Also, no one knows why it was done. Revolutionaries tend to view the nuclear option as an imperialist one. Big nasty powers have nuclear means. Terrorists sabotaging nuclear plants (the Basques, for example) have done so to prevent the plant from being built, rather than to use nuclear power in order to cause trouble.

Also, for a revolutionary organization, the priorities, capacities, and possibilities are very limited. It is unnecessary to build a bomb in a basement if all you want to do is blow up a hotel. To steal the material, to manage it when people are chasing you, when the police are searching for you— all this makes the feat more difficult. If you have ever seen bombs made in Belfast and Beirut, you know why they are not making atomic bombs. The technical problems of an active revolutionary organization, the kind of fighting that goes on amongst themselves, the difficulties of just existing in this kind of life are very harsh. We have talked more about revolutionaries at this table over the last few days than they have ever talked about themselves. They do not even have time to make a bomb, or to think ahead.

Besides, revolutionaries are very conservative people. They are creatures of habit, and it is unusual to find a novel revolutionary technique. Hijacking, for example, was first done in the thirties. Since then, it has been done over and over again. Terrorists prefer to do things that are military. As you increase your capacity, you do not continue to use terrorism; you get rid of it as quickly as you can because you want to be an army. Therefore, you would rather shoot soldiers than assassinate political leaders, even if the latter would be more effective.

The great difference in flexibility and in tactics that I have seen has been due to satellite television. Everybody can watch what you are doing in one place; the "crazies" can watch and do the same thing.

As for biological warfare, chemical warfare, nuclear warfare, why worry? I could turn New York into chaos if I had twelve replaceable people with nothing but ice picks. Nobody would ride the subway; nobody would go to the theater; no one would go to work. The chief of staff of the IRA told me the best weapon that the IRA had was a match. So if these things work, there is no need to escalate. Those primarily concerned about the matter are not the terrorists, but academics and some people in the government who see the potential in escalation.

PARTICIPANT: Returning to the eruption of war, I do not believe we can distinguish between internal and international war as sharply as we have been doing. There is obviously the cumulative effect of takeovers in certain regions. I am not arguing the old domino theory. What I am suggesting is that the overall strategic balance is affected by the internal takeover of a regime. To that extent, an internal disturbance clearly causes a widening conflict over scarce resources, strategic bases, and so forth. The more successful a war proves to be for revolutionary groups, the more Western states will feel closed in and isolated. Terrorism is a war-inducing element insofar as it is a constant threat, a present element in revolutionary wars. Terrorism is used at every stage in a protracted war—in both the rural and urban contexts—and has a strategic value insofar as it weakens the regime or as it brings in extra aid and comfort from supporting states. There is always some outside source of arms or aid. Certainly in Central America you would not have to go very far to find a supplier of arms and training for the guerrillas active in that area. Thus, we have to look at the intelligence collection and the international measures taken by, for example, the NATO states, as part not only of our national defensive measures, but of our Western security posture as a whole. This part is not necessarily the most important one, but it is certainly an important vertebra. Therefore you have to devise an international strategy for the NATO states that will deal with this problem.

At the moment we do not have such a strategy, because anything that occurs outside the central front of NATO or the North Atlantic area is considered immediately a nonstart; nobody wants to know about it; it is left to ad hoc measures. I think we have to give some prominence to thinking about how Western society can be served by the appropriate kinds of aid, response, subtle forms of inexpensive intervention, cost effective intervention. That would really help to contain the expansion of revolutionary movements in these problem areas among which I include the Middle East.

6

"The Blow at the Center": The Concept and Its History

Zeev Ivianski

The engagement between terror and established society, developing into a long protracted war, is now a hundred years old. The first revolutionary organization to adopt the terrorist struggle as its tenet and strategy was the Russian People's Will (Narodnaya Volya) party, founded in July 1879. At its first founding conference held in Lipetsk (near Voronezh) on July 19–21, 1879, the decision to carry out "the blow at the center" (referring to the assassination of Czar Alexander II) by means of dynamite marked the split in the Land and Liberty organization and the turn toward terrorism.

The struggle between the insurgents and the regime in Russia assumed, *ab initio*, the character of a duel between an isolated ruling class lacking social backing and a determined revolutionary minority. Seizure of power was seen as the precondition for control of the masses. The duel between the two was fought out in a social vacuum; society was no more than a spectator. The absence of mass participation in the confrontation forced both sides to concentrate on the center as the source of their future power. This accounts for the impersonality of the decision to assassinate the czar. However, this is not to say that there was no element of retribution or revenge and no thought of pinning personal responsibility on Alexander II. Yet, from the outset, both wings of the Land and Liberty movement made it clear that the problem was not the liquidation of the czar as an individual, but rather that of striking a blow at the center as a foundation for revolutionary strategy. A broadsheet issued by the executive committee after the attack on the railway line near Moscow on November 19, 1879, proclaimed:

Thus we appeal to all upright and freedom-loving citizens ... we repeat to the public—Alexander II is the symbol of a debased, bloodthirsty, cowardly, all-corrupting tyranny, he is the major representative of those who sap the people's self-government, the major stay and support of reaction, he deserves the death sentence. Yet he is not our sole concern. Our aim is the people's freedom, the people's good. Our goal is to free the people and transform it into one which has supreme authority over its own fate.[1]

This strategy of terrorist warfare and the force of threats and intimidation leveled against the regime were viewed as more important than merely liquidating the czar. Indeed, as Georgi Plekhanov put it, ridding the country of Alexander II was only likely to clear the way for the rise of an Alexander III, but imprisoning him within his own palace, curtailing his movements and his freedom, laying siege to the whole ruling entourage, laying bare the regime's vulnerability and weakness, bringing down its authority and prestige—in these lay some measure of victory for the terrorist underground and defeat for the regime. The February 5, 1880, explosion in the Winter Palace caused a stir that was more important than the actual attempt on the life of the czar.

One of the manifestations of the modern age, in which totalitarian and individual terror meet, is the dehumanizing of the enemy and the impersonalization of violence. Another feature of the modern age lies in the fact that intimidation has ceased to be the monopoly of governments or rulers. Science has given individuals and small groups the weapons that enable them to sow fear and wage war without troops. Every revolutionary minority, every gang, every lunatic can now terrorize thousands.

The appearance of the slogan "propaganda by the deed" in 1877 represented a turning point in terms of the character of modern assassination, the strategy and tactics of the revolutionary movement. Assassination is no longer aimed at the mere slaying of the ruling tyrant. It has become the living demonstration of a public pronouncement, an act of protest, a concrete realization of justice, a demonstration of active refusal to accept the situation as it is, a revolutionary move.

Two developments of the modern age were decisive in determining the new course of events: the spread and increasing sophistication of mass communications systems; and the increasing importance of public opinion. The development of newspapers, the telegraph system, radio, and television gave an extra dimension to terrorist acts, transforming them from isolated acts into world events. These same new means of communication magnified public opinion, which turned terrorist acts into an effective and influential

1. Literatura Socjalno-revoljucjonnoj Partji "Narodnoj Voli" (Paris: Tipografja Partji Soc. Rev., 1905), pp. 167, 168.

pressure force. The force of the printed word, carried large distances by mass communication means, became greater than ever before—both for good and for evil.

Writing in 1877, Paul Brousse declared: "Propaganda by the deed is a fantastic tool for awakening popular consciousness ... ideas will no longer be confined to paper, to journals, to writing desks, they will become clothed in flesh and sinew, presented before the very eyes of the people, and the people will salute as they pass by."[2] The idea is to be demonstrated, to be given living form on the stage of history. Thus was born the slogan "propaganda by the deed," although Brousse, the man who coined it, was himself to abandon it before the onset of the wave of terror and assassinations that gave it concrete expression. Peter Kropotkin, the theoretician of the idea, never considered himself responsible for the concrete conclusions to which it was carried. Prior to the slogan's adoption as a resolution at the London International Congress of Anarchists in July 1881, Kropotkin advocated "a permanent revolution, to be carried on verbally and in writing, with the dagger and the gun, and with dynamite."

The efficient, planned, and scientific use of dynamite as one of the terrorist-revolutionary arts of warfare was pioneered in Russia, and it was here that it also reached perfection during the thirty years of virtually continuous struggle waged by the Narodnaya Volya and their successors, the Socialist Revolutionaries. Yet the myth and worship of dynamite belonged to the anarchist underdogs, the intelligent and semieducated alike.

The assassination of Czar Alexander II on March 1, 1881, marked a turning point in the history of anarchist terrorism. Anarchist leaders and thinkers viewed the assassination as a harbinger of the future, a concrete realization of propaganda by the deed. On July 14, 1881, the International Congress of Anarchists met in London. It was attended by forty-five delegates representing each of sixty federations and fifty-nine groups of individuals, or more than five thousand persons. The wave of anarchist terrorist attacks tied to the slogan "propaganda by the deed" had had its own effect even without the endorsement of the International, but that endorsement was quick. The London Congress accepted two explicit resolutions that left their mark on the entire sweep of attacks that were carried out in the latter years of the nineteenth century and at the beginning of the twentieth.

Growing tension, the unfulfilled expectations of the masses, disappointed hopes, and a social atmosphere that was conducive to violence provided the background against which the anarchists turned to terrorism in translating their slogan into concrete terms. The same social climate was also responsible for the growth of desperate individual protest.

2. Cit. *L'International Documents et Souvenirs*, par J. Guillaume, T. IV (Paris, 1910), pp. 225–227.

Revolutionary syndicalism served to channel mass bitterness, but it was individual anarchist terror that was the stream into which individual despair flowed. The individual anarchists of this period did not come from the intelligentsia. For the most part, they were a cross section of an oppressed class. Only a few were industrial workers; most were casual laborers, craftsmen, or vagabonds. Their response to the call for propaganda by the deed was quite spontaneous; they were the echo answering the call that rang through the void of their world. They burst out from the very depths of society, but they also echoed a disappointment with mass revolution, a disillusionment with revolution as a tool in the hands of the masses. They had no thought-out strategy; there was about their acts a likeness to suicidal war. Terrorism was intended to wake people up, to put an end to their tranquility, to wipe out their indifference. They saw themselves as emissaries of the masses who would give concrete expression to the masses' desires.

A wave of anarchist assassination attempts broke out simultaneously in Germany, Italy, and Spain in 1878, and spread to France and to the United States in the 1890s. To be a king, concluded Umberto I of Italy after the first attempt on his life (November 7, 1878, by the anarchist Passanante armed with a dagger), is from now on a "professional risk," which kings and prime ministers must take upon themselves.[3] The risk cost him his life: on July 29, 1900, he was assassinated by the Italian anarchist Gaetano Bresci, who had come from the United States expressly for this purpose.

In 1893 an anarchist's bomb exploded in the Liceo Theatre in Barcelona, killing twenty bourgeois and injuring scores of other persons. This was a bad omen for the future. Dozens of attempts on the lives of kings, presidents, and prime ministers followed this event. One of them was particularly shocking: the assassination of Empress Elizabeth of Austria in 1893, who was stabbed to death by the Italian anarchist Luigi Luciani.

Looking at the wave of anarchist attacks that struck out at rulers, monarchs, and heads of state both in Europe and elsewhere, one is apt to get the impression that what was at work here was some immense worldwide underground working with total dedication at the dictate of a well-organized, secret conspiratorial organization. A closer look, however, reveals quite a different picture, for—with the exception of the incidents in Russia—all of the attacks were the work of isolated individuals. They were backed by no organization; no one encouraged them, no organization gave them support or know-how. In each case, the attacker was an unknown, isolated individual who alone and unaided bore the responsibility for his

3. Ernest Alfred Vizetelly, *The Anarchists* (New York: John Lane, 1911), p. 214.

act, for the decision that had led up to it, and for its final implementation. Yet, for all that, there was a conspiracy of chain reaction, an element of revenge, of paying back, of spontaneous, worldwide solidarity. There was, too, a shared personal background in the cases of all the anarchist attackers: they were all men with no way out, men trapped in a world which offered them no refuge. Surely few other periods in history can show a series of characters so daring, so bitter, so bent on destruction and annihilation. Bakunin, Nechayev, Most, Ling, Duval, Descamps, Ravachol, Henry Vaillant, Caserio, and Lucheni—all were bewildering rebels "individually waging their leading conflict with the world."[4]

There is an amazing parallel between the blow at the center as conceived by revolutionary syndicalism (the myth of direct action being one of its expressions) and the myth of the blow at the center as it appeared in individual terror and propaganda by the deed in the anarchist wave. The struggle of labor against capitalism was consciously directed by the syndicalists with the aim of gaining control over the centers of economic might. The fact that a paralysis of transport and of sources of power was well within their capability, and that the technical possibilities presented by the science of chemistry permitted an increase of terrorism, determined the nature of the struggle and its methods. It was often pointed out with what ease the entire industrial structure might be damaged via sabotage of the electric industry and the sources of electric power. Together with this there developed a consciousness of the strength possessed by the revolutionary minority and a shrugging off of all criteria of morality.

The ideological place of origin of this new strategy was France. But nowhere was this new message applied more thoroughly, bitterly, and unscrupulously than in the course of the bitter and brutal class struggle between labor and capital at the end of the nineteenth and beginning of the twentieth century in the United States. The most radical American exponents and practitioners of the new "catastrophic idea" were the "Wobblies," or Industrial Workers of the World (IWW). Strikes became occasions for confrontations; and they were decided by force. Employers hired ruffians, strikebreakers, and private detective organizations. The workers, for their part, reacted by blowing up factories. In the spring of 1899 the Bunker Hill Company was blown up and damage amounting to $250,000 was done. The governor of Idaho, Frank Steunenberg, a former union man elected by a workers' vote, was killed on December 30, 1905, by a bomb placed at his front door because he adopted a very tough line toward labor unions during his term of office. Between 1905 and 1910

---

4. R. Hunter, *Violence and the Labour Movement* (London: Routledge and Sons, and New York: Macmillan, 1916), pp. 90–91.

dynamite became the prime weapon of the iron workers' struggle. If, in the course of this struggle, their wages rose from $2.50 for a ten-hour day to $4.30 for an eight-hour day, this must be offset by the dynamiting of 150 buildings and bridges throughout the United States and Canada. One of the most tragic episodes in the "march of dynamite" was the explosion that took place in the editorial offices of the *Los Angeles Times* on October 1, 1910, when dozens of innocent people were killed. This atmosphere of violent struggle, vicious attacks, bloody strikes, and their equally bloody suppression brought on its decline into crime. Dynamiting became a matter of hiring the right thugs. The recourse to crime, which had been common even before the great industrial upsurge, increased dramatically.

The use of dynamite became crucial not only because of its destructive character but because its invention coincided with the development of the modern communication media with their thirst for shocking scoops and their ability to carry the news of any shocking event to the most remote corners of the globe, turning it into a great propaganda event.

As mentioned earlier, the revolutionary movement in Russia, almost in its entirety, turned to terrorism largely under the magic spell and promise of dynamite. From 1879, all the attempted assassinations of the Narodnaya Volya party were carried out with gelignite. Dynamite was not merely of technical significance, but served also as a dramatic symbol, distinguishing acts committed with it from acts of ordinary murder.

The blow at the center thus became the gospel of a new, permanent, scientific revolution. But the real aim of the blow at the center in this new exposition of the modern revolutionary terrorist warfare was not so much the intimidation of future pretenders for the crown, nor the elimination of ruling tyrants. Its real aim was to hit the center in order to arouse the masses, for such a blow could serve as a mighty propaganda means. Thus, their aim was less to kill the living czar as to destroy the myth of the czar. To undermine the czar's authority, to make him a prisoner in his palace, to reveal his human weakness—these were the real aims of the eleven attempts on the czar's life. Another aim was the desire to replace the myth of the czar by a new myth of the almighty Revolutionary Executive Committee.

If the history of terrorism in its various manifestations is a hundred years old, so, too, is the history of counterterror.

In the course of the protracted engagement between terrorism and counterterror, a few outstanding facts must be stressed. What we might call counterterror policy has never been a premeditated, clear-cut course of action, but rather the outcome of trial and error. At the same time, there has also been an exchange of ideas, tactics, and methods on both sides; revolution and counterrevolution; terror and counterterror.

There is much truth in the observation that the Russian revolutionary movement was, in the course of its struggle with the regime, contaminated by that regime's characteristics. In some fatal manner the revolutionary state of the future was shaped by the czarist model. Dialectic development, the twists of history, the ghosts of former generations, and their inheritance all stamped the road to change and revolution with the imprint of the past. Clearly, there was no magic at work here, but rather the violence of the regime's structure, the worship of force, and the hierarchical and centralist character of the bureaucratic machine that prepared the ground for the myth of force, the myth of the state as a means towards revolution, and of violence as the motor force for historic and social change. The Nechayev structure of the revolutionary general staff, of the Executive Committee with its agents and networks, was not only the result of invention or ideological warping; it was carved out of a warped reality. The craze for dynamite for the blow at the center and the seizure of power sprang from the manner in which the image of the enemy was projected onto the image of the revolution. It may be this that explains why so many of them—men such as Kablitz, Tikhomirov, and Romanenko—eventually took refuge in the monarchist camp.

One of the most noteworthy characteristics of the confrontation between the regime and revolutionary terror was the manner in which, on both sides, weaknesses were turned into strengths and strengths into weaknesses. Centralism, the very foundation of the absolutist bureaucratic regime, worked in two directions. It turned the "state that hung in the air" into a relatively easy target for terror attacks, hence that state's extreme sensitivity and vulnerability to terror. The very source of its strength became the weak point of the whole structure, the true soft underbelly. But the revolutionary movement adopted its own forms of centralism, setting up a general staff (the Executive Committee) and under it a network of organizations subordinated to it by the severest discipline in what the constitution termed a *vassal* status. In this instance, too, centralism was a source of strength. It gave the underground purpose and the ability to stand firm; it turned the movement's former powerlessness and its numerical weakness into strength. The advantage it had over the regime's central organization lay in its being a secret organization. If to these advantages one adds those of self-imposed discipline, devotion, and readiness to sacrifice, then what we are presented with seems, on the face of it, to be an all-powerful central body. True, the regime's central body also rested on a secret arm of its own and fenced itself in with an army of detectives, informers, and secret police, but the true center still remained exposed, for the regime itself could not go underground.

In effect, both sides aimed their attack at the center of the opposite side. But the centralist principle that was, in one sense, the strength of the underground was, in another sense, also its weakness. In the first place, it was sufficient to inflict one severe blow at the center for the entire strength of the underground to collapse. This was one of the reasons why all terrorist revolutionary movements set up since the beginning of the twentieth century chose to keep their central bodies far from the reach of the regime (i.e., abroad) despite the concomitant difficulties. In the second place, those same human qualities and superiority of morale that the terrorist center enjoyed also made it more vulnerable, for the regime's central bodies were in most cases less sensitive to the loss of the key personnel. The blow at the center in the case of the latter was, it is true, painful, shocking, and confusing; but it was not fatal. As compared with this, the blow at the terrorist center was likely to prove fatal to the entire movement. The experience, authority, and prestige of the members who formed the terrorist center was not transferable, as the fate of the Narodnaya Volya showed once the Executive Committee was liquidated. Furthermore, failure of the human element, lack of caution, feelings of solidarity, and the desire for revenge were all at times responsible for endangering the entire structure of the movement. Alexander Mikhailov, the "pedantic watchman" of the party, the man who formulated its discipline and its secret character, was caught and arrested in an attempt—which broke every elementary security precaution—to commemorate two of his comrades who had just been executed. Sofya Perovskaya was caught needlessly wandering the streets at midnight, totally self-forgetful and lacking in control, shocked by Zhelyabov's capture. Worst of all was the human weakness in the face of solitary confinement, the threat of execution, the tricks and skill of the interrogators, the trials which at times broke even the best—Goldenberg, Mikhailov, Stefanovich, and Rysakov—and led to the uncovering of all of the underground's secrets. Thus, the source of strength became the very source of weakness when the regime was able to penetrate the heart of the movement.

One of the crucial battles in this protracted war is the intelligence battle. Carlos Marighella, the leader of Brazilian urban guerrillas (killed in a clash with the police in November 1969), contended in his *Minimanual of the Urban Guerrilla* that "to compensate for his general weakness and shortage of arms compared to the enemy, the urban guerrilla used surprise ... to prevent his own extinction, the urban guerrilla has to shoot first."[5] In order to do so, he must have a superior intelligence system.

---

5. Carlos Marighella, *Minimanual of the Urban Guerrilla* (Havana: Tricontinental, 1970), cit. A. Parry, *Terrorism: From Robespierre to Arafat* (New York: Vanguard, 1976), pp. 258–259.

Relating to this intelligence battle, Raymond Momboisse states that "intelligence is the key to counter-insurgency operations. Without it the police are as a blind man trying to defend himself against a pack of wolves. With proper intelligence, the rebels can be harassed, hounded, and destroyed. Intelligence is as vital to police as it is to the military in the battlefield."[6]

Intelligence superiority is also vital to the terrorist underground. Thus, one of the main battlefields between terror and counterterror is the battle over and for intelligence. The crushing of the intelligence center of the adversary turns out then to be, on both sides, one of the main targets of the blow at the center strategy.

In the war between terror and counterterror, one of the central issues will always be the struggle over popular backing. One may describe it in tactical terms as a fight for bases of support. In order to achieve this aim, blows are dealt not only to crush the enemy, but sometimes only to discredit him, to hit and crush his prestige, to destroy his morale. Thus, the terrorist group may impose on the state or government a state of siege. Eleven attempts on the life of Alexander II turned him into a prisoner of his own palace; four attempts on the life of Harold Macmichael, the British high commissioner for Palestine, did the same. In all cases of this kind, terrorists caused a state of siege, drained the resources of the government, harassed its nerves, and thus made the price of governing very high. When it turned out to be too high, as in Algeria, Cyprus, or Palestine under the British mandate, the rulers withdrew and the terrorists won.

The terrorist killer has many tactical advantages. It is not easy to find an effective counter to the ruthless killer, states Momboisse. "It will only be a matter of time before a patient killer will find a safe opportunity to kill." Counterterror turns then to reprisal, a dangerous double-edged weapon. It may provoke more brutal terror and bring down in turn more ferocious reprisals. It causes a vicious circle but it may be unavoidable, since one of the basic rules of this brutal struggle is that he who strikes efficiently and first will always have an ascendancy. Speed becomes of essence in the struggle. Both sides are anxious to gain prestige by the force of their actions; by their propaganda; by the extent to which they manage to win over society, world opinion, and sympathy.

In the struggle for that support, an effective blow at the center may be vital and sometimes even decisive. It may help to keep the initiative and to improve morale. One of the main objectives of counterterror is

---

6. Raymond M. Momboisse, *Riots, Revolts and Insurrections* (Springfield, Illinois: Thomas, 1967), pp. 83ff., 121, 463ff., 472–476.

to separate the terrorist forces from local support and from supporting states; a crushing blow at the center may be very helpful to achieve it only temporarily.

King Hussein eliminated the terrorist menace in Jordan in his September 1970 blow (Black September). Time will tell if his crackdown permanently rid Jordan of terrorism. However, in terms of the relative historical process, it seems to have been efficient and decisive. He achieved it by fighting the guerrillas on their own terms—using arbitrary tribunals, carrying out public executions. These are the privileges of authoritarian regimes, which are ruthless and free from the inhibitions of democratic governments. But their victories, too, may prove to be illusory because they rest, usually, on one vulnerable individual.

A successful blow at the center by counterterror may be efficient as a means to stop or prevent the initiative of the terrorist group; to keep and support its own initiative; to gain more public and international support; to crush the morale of the enemy; to disorient and destroy the enemy's plans and to nip in the bud his attempted or planned blows; to ruin his intelligence system; and to intimidate the underground and its potential civilian supporters. Yet, the most effective blow at the center seems to be not the physical elimination of the center, but rather the more complicated and morally dubious provocation in the center—the infiltration of the regime's agents to the very heart of the terrorist movement.

If it succeeds, the blow at the center may halt the spread of terrorist danger, even if it cannot eradicate it. Since counterterror and terror alike are both often involved in a long protracted war of attrition, halting the wave must also be considered an achievement.

Even if the blow at the center seems to be more efficient than blows at the periphery, one should keep in mind that its impact will be stronger if it coincides with an unremittingly and simultaneously conducted war of attrition against the terrorist periphery; if the physical elimination of the center cannot be conclusive, one should nevertheless not underestimate its results. Its impact will depend on many circumstances. There are leaders with charisma who cannot be replaced. In some other cases it may take time; it may cause internal strife, and time may be crucial.

History teaches that there were blows at the revolutionary centers which proved to be fatal. Such was the ruin of the Executive Committee of the People's Will party. At one time the Jewish Lehi underground in mandated Palestine was paralyzed after its center had been destroyed by the British. In both cases, however, terrorism eventually sprang up again and more vigorously. Still, in the face of the very limited scope of open alternatives, the blow at the center remains the aim of both sides in the secret, unconventional, brutal war.

7

Political Terrorism—
The German Perspective

Hans-Josef Horchem

Terrorist activities in Germany during the last decade have been numerous and serious enough to warrant special study. In order to shed some light on the German problem, I would like first to present some relevant statistics; secondly, to describe the three main German terrorist organizations; and finally, to discuss the steps the German government has taken to counter terrorist activity.

Between January 1970 and April 1979, thirty-one people—including nine policemen, four justice officials, and three diplomats—were killed by terrorists in Germany. One hundred eight Germans narrowly escaped being killed. Ninety-seven people were injured in bombings and shootings for which terrorists were responsible. One hundred sixty-three people were taken as hostages. In terms of property damage, terrorists were responsible for ten serious cases of arson; twenty-five bombings; and thirty bank robberies, in which total losses equaled DM 5.4 million.

The majority of these acts were committed by three main terrorist organizations currently operating in Germany: the Red Army Faction (RAF), also known as the Baader-Meinhof gang; the 2d of June Movement; and the Revolutionary Cells.

The RAF is the oldest, the most political, and the most dangerous of the three; its history is thus worth examining in some detail. In 1972, six important members of the group—Baader, Meinhof, Meins, Raspe, Ensslin, and Gerhard Müller—were arrested as a result of information received from the German public. Their arrests followed six serious bomb attacks in Frankfurt, Munich, Augsburg, Hamburg, Karlsruhe, and Heidelberg in May of 1972. One year later, in the summer of 1973, the group began to rebuild, establishing strongholds in Hamburg, Frankfurt, and Amsterdam. This group, whose main goal was the release of the imprisoned RAF members, was destroyed on February 4, 1974, by concerted action on the part of Hamburg, Frankfurt, and Amsterdam security forces. Nine RAF members were arrested and condemned to lengthy prison terms.

A year later, a third group was formed. Its tactic was to murder senior West German officials and diplomats. In April 1975, the group seized the German embassy in Stockholm, killing both the military and the commercial attachés. The purpose of this attack was to force the German government to release jailed RAF prisoners. The government did not yield, however, and the terrorists were overpowered by security forces and put into prison.

By 1976 it became clear that a fourth RAF group had been created. On November 30, 1976, two lawyers, Siegfried Haag and Roland Mayer, were arrested during an Autobahn check. Papers found on the two showed that new actions by the RAF were being planned. Bank notes found on the men were identified as having been stolen during bank robberies in Cologne and Hamburg. Nevertheless, despite the arrest of its leader, Haag, the RAF became strong enough to carry out serious violent actions in 1977. These included the murder of Attorney General Siegfried Buback and his guards; the murder of banker Jurgen Ponto; and the kidnaping and murder of Hanns-Martin Schleyer after his guards had been killed.

The RAF was able to continue functioning even after the arrest of its most important members because of its reliable circle of supporters, who maintained links between the arrested terrorists and the operational ones. It is worth noting in this regard the RAF's considerable success in attracting the support of persons hitherto uninvolved in illegal activities. Several lawyers, for example, played important roles in linking the jailed terrorists with their free colleagues. The lawyers also succeeded in recruiting new members, mostly other young lawyers. These lawyers now constitute one of the three central groups within the organization. In addition, there are approximately twenty-five operating terrorists, of whom more than half are women. There are also supporting groups that organize campaigns to mobilize RAF sympathizers inside Germany and abroad. Concentrated in Hamburg, Baden-Württemberg, Hessen, and Berlin, these supporters number approximately 150 and form the pool from which operating terrorists are generally drawn.

The Berlin-based 2d of June Movement has never had the consistency of the RAF, nor has it formulated clear political aims. In practical tactics, however, the movement has often been ahead of the RAF. This was shown in the kidnaping of the Christian Democratic politician Peter Lorenz in

Berlin on March 27, 1975. Unaware of Lorenz's location, the federal government gave in to the terrorists' demands to release five prisoners, who were flown to South Yemen.

Following the Lorenz incident, the movement was essentially destroyed. Then, four female members of the group escaped from a Berlin prison in 1976; in 1978 another terrorist, Till Meyer, was freed from the same prison. But these individuals have not committed any further terrorist attacks in the name of their group. Moreover, on June 22, 1978, Till Meyer and three other terrorists were arrested in Bulgaria and returned to the Federal Republic.

Since November 1973, the Revolutionary Cells have committed more than twenty incendiary attacks and bombings. Several people were killed in two Frankfurt bombings in June and December 1976. Unlike the RAF, the cells do not appear to operate entirely underground; however, the majority of their members are not known to security authorities.

To aid the authorities in deterring terrorism, the German parliament recently passed several new laws strengthening the security forces' abilities. Since 1971, the hijacking of or attack on an airplane carries a penalty of not less than five years imprisonment. Manslaughter in this context carries imprisonment of not less than ten years. Another law makes it no longer possible for one attorney to defend several accused terrorists. The right of defense has also been partly altered so that, under current law, a defense attorney suspected of involvement in the defendant's crime may be excluded from the trial. In 1974, the right to carry on a trial in the absence of the accused (during a hunger strike, for example) was extended. In 1976, a law was passed imposing greater penalties for membership in a terrorist organization. The law concerning the arrest of terrorists was strengthened and control over written communication between the defending lawyer and his client was made possible. In 1977, a law was passed preventing contacts between arrested terrorists and their defending lawyers if such contacts are deemed to enhance the prisoners' chances of escape. As of 1978, all apartments in an apartment block may be searched, and the police may establish control points during large-scale searches. The use of dividing panels during a discussion between the accused and his attorney was also authorized in order to prevent the exchange of objects.

The search for German terror organizations is extremely difficult. Their members, particularly those of the RAF, are intelligent, work conspiratorially, have the support of ideological sympathizers, can operate openly in an open society, and are determined to resist official action by the use of lethal weapons.

The search for terrorists is further complicated by conflicting social considerations. While the discovery and arrest of terrorists is clearly desirable, the extent of the search is limited by fears of totalitarianism. Moreover, an overreaction by the German authorities would undoubtedly play into the hands of the terrorists. Thus, authorities generally perform selective, rather than general, searches based on information obtained from intelligence sources. The use of intelligence gathering is limited by several factors, however. First, agents infiltrating terrorist organizations face considerable personal danger, including death, if exposed. Secondly, in execution of their infiltration activities, such agents may themselves break the law or act as *agents provocateurs*. Thirdly, none of the three main organizations maintains headquarters, offices, or logistical apparatus per se. Thus, unable to wiretap or penetrate their offices, the security authorities are forced to search for the terrorist within the anonymous world of the city at large. Such efforts are extremely difficult and have not always been successful. The large computer of the Federal Office for Criminal Investigation succeeded several times in detecting safe houses of terrorists, but in all cases the houses were empty when searched.

In the overwhelming majority of cases, success in discovering terrorists has been the result of information received from the public. During the logistic build-up of the RAF between 1970 and 1972, such information was not forthcoming. Only when the state showed itself determined to counteract terrorism through large-scale searches did the public come forward with information. Between 1975 and 1977 the number of wanted lists on show in the Federal Republic diminished considerably; at the same time, the willingness of the public to assist the security authorities also dropped. The criminal police were able to post only one-fourth the previous number of notices in small shops. What this fluctuating level of willingness to cooperate shows is that a democratic state can be shaken when the population begins to believe that it is more dangerous to do something for the state than against it.

Aided by information obtained from the public, the security forces—using surveillance, wiretapping, and other technical devices—may face a rather good chance for a successful penetration of a terrorist organization. The best way for an operation to begin is by evaluating the publications of the terrorist organizations and support groups. A few members of support groups generally maintain contacts with a few terrorists living underground. The supporting organizations also serve as the basis for attempts to recruit new terrorists. The security forces should therefore concentrate their efforts upon these groups by means of surveillance, wiretapping, and bugging of safe houses and the flats of supporters—if justified, of course, by the seriousness of the terrorist threat. In addition to the search apparatus, there are three measures which are important in combating terrorism:

1. Adoption of special security measures for vulnerable persons and institutions.
2. Constant use of intelligence resources to monitor terrorist organizations and their supporters.
3. Consistent demonstration of decisiveness on the part of the government, especially during and after a terrorist attack.

Policy towards terrorists has been shown to be a decisive factor influencing the incidence of attacks; successful terrorist action is usually followed by fresh violent crimes. The 1975 occupation of the German embassy in Stockholm and the murder of the two German diplomats resulted, *inter alia*, from the government's capitulation to terrorist demands during the kidnaping of Peter Lorenz. The resolute attitude by the government during the attack on the Stockholm embassy contributed to the fact that there were no further serious attacks for the next year and a half.

A firm attitude by the government is made more difficult by the publicity given to terrorist actions in the mass media, which to a certain extent are often part of the terrorist action itself. During the Stockholm embassy attack, Swedish television had a camera focused on the embassy for several hours. After the kidnaping of Hanns-Martin Schleyer in 1977, the first ultimatum of the terrorists contained two demands of the media: at 10 a.m. an RAF prisoner was to affirm on television the departure of the RAF prisoners who were to have been set free; a government announcement was to have been broadcast on the evening news at 8 p.m. In the third message, the kidnapers demanded that a videotape of Schleyer reading a letter be broadcast. Copies of videotapes and Polaroid photos with ultimatums and announcements were constantly sent to the domestic and foreign press. However, at the government's request, the German press conducted itself with remarkable restraint during the Schleyer case. The terrorists thereby lost the publicity which they had calculated would be forthcoming.

The German government's firm, steadfast position vis-à-vis the terrorists' demands was put to another test in the course of the Schleyer affair when a group of Palestinians hijacked a Lufthansa airliner in an attempt to increase the pressure on the government further. Rather than yielding to the terrorists' demands as they expected, the German government sent an assault force of the GSG-9 unit which overpowered the hijackers in Mogadishu, Somalia. The hijacked passengers were freed, but Schleyer was murdered by his kidnapers, who realized that the German government was not going to yield to their demands. Undoubtedly, the event had a marked demoralizing effect on the terrorists. Four of the jailed RAF members whose release was demanded by Schleyer's kidnapers committed suicide in Stuttgart-Stammheim prison after they received the news of the successful rescue in Mogadishu.

It should be recognized, however, that improved personnel and technical resources of the security authorities will not prevent terrorists from committing crimes. While the new laws help state institutions to combat terrorism, they are only one of several means which can contribute to the solution of the problem. The guiding principle for the realization of new legal solutions must be the recognition of the magnitude and complexity of the problem. All generalized responses should be considered skeptically, as they easily become routine and thus ineffective. Terrorists have always been ingenious enough to deal with generalized laws and can adapt to them easily.

While each terrorist attack requires a unique response determined by the particulars of the situation, one principle must guide the response to all terrorist actions: the responsible organs of state must not capitulate to terrorist demands. Such a response only encourages repeated attacks. The state must consistently demonstrate that it will not give in to blackmail and that violence will not be tolerated. Otherwise, a problem which is essentially a problem of security could well become a question of the future existence of free societies and states.

8

The Real-World Problems of the Terrorist Organization and the Problem of Propaganda

Paul Wilkinson

Terrorism, in my view, is a special form of unconventional warfare, a method of coercive intimidation, generally, though not invariably, for some political objective (there are religious movements in the terrorism business). Terrorists use the threat of murder, injury, and destruction either to coerce the target group or government into submitting to their demands or to create some kind of climate of collapse, fear, or uncertainty, which they intend to exploit in order to publicize their cause or inspire insurrection. Almost invariably, terrorism is used in combination with other forms of unconventional war, and here I underline my agreement with General Harkabi in seeing terrorism as one thread in a much more complex strategic design. Terrorism is essentially a psychological weapon aimed not only at its immediate victims, but also at a wider audience.

Taking up the point made by Professor Dror about disaggregating the concept of terrorism, I would like to propose a brief typology which will help us differentiate the main active terrorist movements. I shall examine these groups in relation to propaganda and organization.

The first distinction is between state terror and terrorism by factions or revolutionary movements. I think it is quite useful that in the literature, *terror* now seems to be established as the term used in relation to regimes. *Terrorism* generally seems to be applied to revolutionary groups. This does not imply any moral superiority on the part of states. The terror of states—in terms of fatalities, in terms of damage to individual life and liberty—has had a far more devastating effect on the history of humanity than the terrorist acts committed by individual revolutionary movements.

Another important distinction I shall make is that between domestic and international terrorism. It is very difficult to find an instance of terrorism which is confined entirely within the frontiers of one state. However, many terrorist campaigns do have a prime location in the state in which they are attempting to achieve their objectives. It is helpful to distinguish between these types of organizations and the internationally operated movements, which have special organizational, tactical, and strategic problems (which do not arise in a group active within one country or even within one region).

Of the terrorist organizations most active in the contemporary world, the most conspicuous are the nationalist or ethnic minority movements which are active, of course, not only in the Third World developing states, but also in well-established states in Europe. Second in prominence are the revolutionary ideological sects, among which I include the Japanese Red Army, the Red Army in Germany, and the Red Brigades in Italy. These groups are much smaller than the nationalist groups, with far smaller constituencies. They are nevertheless very damaging to the democracies in which they are active, because of the fanaticism with which they pursue their terror campaigns. The nihilistic or anarchistic spirit which they adopt seriously damages the legal system and disrupts the democratic life of the societies in which they are active. I believe this is particularly true in Italy, where the impact of terrorism on political life has been powerful. A third category of terrorist organizations comprises exile groups, such as the South Moluccans, the Armenians, and the Croats. These are groups that operate abroad—in some cases because of police or military action in their country of origin; in other cases because they have been inspired into support for a terrorist group while living in a host community which they see as unsympathetic to them or in some ways unjust. The South Moluccan community was completely divided in Holland. There are South Moluccans who still regard any violence as totally illegitimate and argue against terrorism. But some of the younger members of the community treat those involved in terrorist incidents as heroes, glamorizing them and promising to act similarly when the time is right. Fourthly, there is the transnational group, the one that has achieved, I think, rather exaggerated attention in the media. One example of this is the Wadi Haddad faction of the Popular Front for the Liberation of Palestine (PFLP), which organized its operations transnationally. It recruited people from various terrorist movements and used them simultaneously in transnational operations. As General Harkabi noted, there is a trend towards greater international collaboration and the development of state sponsorship on the part of the rogue states. A number of regimes strongly favor terrorism, actively finance it, arm terrorist groups, and use them to wage proxy wars.

These four types of organizations are not entirely discrete; a terrorist group may fall into more than one classification. I would say the most powerful mixture of all is the nationalist liberation movement which adopts a neo-Marxist ideology, as most of the terrorist groups now have. This puts them straight on the waveband of the international terrorist communications network.

The question, "Is terrorism futile?" was raised. I think the track record and significance of terrorism show that, by itself, terrorism has been singularly unsuccessful in winning strategic objectives such as the destruction of a whole regime and presumably its replacement by a regime congenial to the terrorists. One can conclude that it is the weapon of the weak. Indeed, this is brought out quite dramatically by examination of the growth of terrorism since the mid 1960s. Note the exponential growth of international terrorist incidents in the wake of the defeat of the Arabs in the Six-Day War. This underlines, perhaps more dramatically than any breakdown of individual incidents or chronology of incidents, the extent to which that dramatic moment of defeat catalyzed the use of terror on a really massive scale by the Palestinian groups. These groups have been responsible for a very high proportion of international terrorist incidents since 1967. Until 1974, the proportion was about 15 percent. Between 1975 and 1978 it declined to about 7 percent, and it is now climbing to above 10 percent. I think we can expect it to continue to rise in the wake of the Camp David agreement. This seems to me to show very clearly the validity of the weakness argument, because if the Palestinians had the opportunity of achieving the military capability necessary to confront Israel, then I think terrorism would have been reduced to a merely subordinate role. In fact, there are very few cases in which terrorism by itself has actually defeated a liberal democracy. One of the cases that is often mentioned is Uruguay. Montevideo's urban guerrilla war in 1971–72 undoubtedly weakened the government of Uruguay. But note that it did not bring about the government the neo-Marxists wanted. In the longer term, in fact, the revolution was not a success, ushering in as it did a right-wing military government.

If one examines autocratic regimes, the efficacy of terrorism alone is no more impressive: I cannot think of a single autocracy in the modern period that was destroyed by terrorism alone. Weakened, yes, certainly damaged; yet not destroyed. Only in the case of colonial regimes, during the 1940s and 1950s, do we find examples of terrorist activities achieving strategic objectives and causing the withdrawal of the colonial powers. This happened to the French in Algeria; and to the British in various places, of which Cyprus is a prime example. Such colonial struggles inspire considerable hope in the hearts of the modern terrorist. If you ask Irish

Republican Army people what they hope to do, they take Cyprus as a model, and many of them claim to have been influenced by Cypriot terrorists in jail. They look to Algeria, and they talk about Britain being guilty in the same way as France when it was castigated as the oppressor power in Algeria. So the colonial paradigm is still a very powerful one.

Terrorism is also seen as an attractive weapon because of the tactical advantages that it can reap. The short-term gains of publicity, cash ransoms, and release of terrorist prisoners still seem to make it worthwhile. The importance of sensational publicity, aided in democratic countries by free media, is particularly noteworthy. Terrorism feeds on publicity.

In combination with other methods of revolution and subversion, terrorism can seriously damage a society or government or other groups. Even when a group's ultimate objectives cannot be achieved through terrorism, terrorism may still appear attractive in that it can weaken the regime, divert its security forces from other tasks, and attract sympathizers. There are also many other tactical advantages that may be reaped. In the *Minimanual of the Urban Guerrilla*,[1] the militarizing of the political situation in democratic states is discussed. Many terrorist movements, particularly those in Germany and Italy, have latched on to this doctrine. They try to force the government into an overreaction which would throw the population into the arms of the people's revolutionary movement. This crude but effective means of polarization can be used for other purposes. Ethnic minority movements often use it to polarize a community against any moderate preaching or bridge building between communities or ethnic reconciliation. Terrorism is also frequently used by revolutionary movements to control their own members. All these tactical uses help to justify acts of terrorism in the eyes of the terrorist directorates and their backers and supporters. Terrorism is thus more than simply a nuisance. It is a constant challenge no responsible democratic state can ignore with impunity.

The search for root causes of terrorism is a matter of great debate in the literature, and I would not like to commit myself firmly to any particular theory. But one can identify certain conducive conditions which explain this massive growth in terrorism statistics. First, there is the general strategic situation, which favors unconventional war as a whole. The balance of terror and the fact that all major states wish to avoid an escalation of violence that could lead to a possible nuclear conflict are important factors. Most states today are even afraid of becoming involved in protracted and vastly expensive conventional conflicts which might escalate. Unconven-

---

1. Carlos Marighella, "Handbook of Urban Guerrilla Warfare," in *For the Liberation of Brazil* (Harmondsworth: Penguin Books, 1971), pp. 61–97.

tional war thus becomes relatively more attractive. In terms of cost-effectiveness, it is the best means of achieving political-diplomatic objectives by coercion.

The balance of terror is also an important factor in the creation of a climate of thought about use of violence. The balance of terror provides a paradigm of a mode of deterrence, and it is possible that revolutionary movements see terror and the holding of hostages as appropriate weapons to use in microconflicts.

There is also the fact that since the end of the colonial independence struggles, national borders have become firmly established. It is now very difficult for any minority movement to achieve a renegotiation of frontiers in its favor through some general diplomatic conference. Hence the desperation, the argument from weakness I mentioned earlier.

Another factor, about which Ted Gurr has written a great deal, is relative deprivation psychology—the feelings of injustice felt by particular groups.[2] Research has shown that feelings of political injustice—deprivation of political rights or exclusion from power or influence within a community—are especially likely to lead to violent rebellion.

The weakness of the international community in general, and individual states in particular, in responding to terrorism has also contributed to the rise in terrorism. This was particularly true up until 1972. Since then, certain Western European states have begun to take a firmer line; and the tough line that Israel adopted has been followed by other states, inspired by the Entebbe rescue.

The shift of revolutionary theory away from the rural guerrilla concept toward the idea of urban struggle is an important feature of contemporary terrorism. The hunger for publicity tends to drive the revolutionary to the cities. As one Front de Libération Nationale (FLN) leader put it, "It was more effective propaganda to shoot a couple of French businessmen in the middle of Algiers than to shoot a hundred or so soldiers in a lonely gully." Other factors precipitating the move to cities are technological opportunity and the vulnerability of industrial societies and cities to the terrorist technology. One should also stress the contagion effect, about which Amy Redlick has written. She deals with the information flow effects of terrorism over a long span of time and shows how this can cause a kind of bandwagon reaction.[3] There is also the growth of proterrorist

---

2. See Ted R. Gurr, "Psychological Factors in Civil Violence," *World Politics*, January 20, 1968; and for a much fuller exposition, Ted R. Gurr, *Why Men Rebel* (Princeton: Princeton University Press, 1970).

3. Amy Sands Redlick, "The Transnational Flow of Information as a Cause of Terrorism," in Yonah Alexander, David Carlton, and Paul Wilkinson, *Terrorism: Theory and Practice* (Boulder, Colorado: Westview, 1979), pp. 73–95.

ideologies and subcultures in Western cities, right in the hearts of the countries that had the highest numbers of terrorist attacks in the last decade. Rogue states have also been active in funding and giving sanctuary to terrorists. But the support apparatus for terrorism needs far more than this. It is often not appreciated just how much effort goes into the propaganda for subversion and violence in the Western world. Throughout the non-Communist world, the Soviet Politburo deploys a vast apparatus for promoting subversion and violence in the interests of Soviet power and the expansion of Moscow-style communism. An elaborate, highly centralized machinery for supporting terrorist groups exists that can operate at various levels. When the Soviets wish to intervene at arm's length, they can use the indirect agency of the local Communist party. Or they can "adopt" or initiate a national liberation movement quite distinct from the local Communist party, disowning responsibility if the mission fails. They can also, of course, use the Communist bloc parties and intelligence services as surrogates for the Communist party and KGB. The East European states currently play a very active role in terrorist support—in training, in funding, and in providing propaganda. These states operate in southern Africa and increasingly in West Africa. I was amazed on a recent visit to find how many East Germans and Poles have entered West Africa. The efforts of the satellite states are apparently reaping returns. One should add to these the secret weapon of Cuba, which merges so well with the background in African countries. Cuban support has made a vital contribution to world subversive and terrorist movements.

Even if such training facilities, money, and weapons were not available through this machinery, the nationalist ethnic minority movement would still be very much in business. The resources available to fund many of their wealthier political wings would be reduced considerably. And many of the revolutionary ideological sects, which—except for the Red Brigades with its estimated 150,000–200,000 sympathizers—have no mass constituencies, would be unable to carry out their operations for lack of these essential elements of support. Nevertheless, the clear *raison d'être* and fanaticism of many of these groups would sustain them. Other movements, however, would not have gotten off the ground had they been left to their own devices. Without either seizing control of a political movement or winning mass support, they would have withered away. The Russians are probably having second thoughts about pouring money into groups of this kind. Might they not lead to revolutionary ideological sects operating within the Soviet Union? I think events in Germany have certainly made them reconsider the matter.

Now let us consider the terrorist personality, organization, recruitment, and propaganda. David Hubbard attempted a hijacker profile in the United

States, but his investigation covered only criminal hijackers.[4] Even after the latest German study, we still have no really convincing profile of the political terrorist. One would suspect that this is partly due to the problem of disaggregation that Professor Dror mentioned. What we need are many more good case studies of movements. These are hard to obtain, of course, because while a movement is still active it does not welcome academic probing of its organization. When we can study an organization carefully at firsthand, we will be able to obtain much badly needed data.

There are certain things we do know from the figures on apprehended terrorists and from information obtained from defectors and others. The typical terrorist is in his or her early twenties (some movements have a 40 percent female membership). He generally possesses above-average education. The exception to the latter generalization seems to be the nationalist ethnic minority movements—where there is often a working-class base, as in the Provisional IRA and the Basques—who seem to have wider strata of social origin among their activists. Most members of the more active international terrorist groups are both highly educated and affluent. Most of them were recruited in extremist political circles or wings of organizations operating in universities, colleges, institutes, and so on. Very often, such recruits are not tested until they have been through political screening for some while, and they may be employed on very low-level missions until they have received more training and experience, perhaps including a stay at a terrorist training camp.

The cell structure tends to be almost universal among contemporary terrorist groups. Those groups which had a more paramilitary style of organization discarded it largely in favor of the secure cellular structure that was pioneered by Russian terrorists in the nineteenth century. Broadly speaking, "firing groups" or cells comprise four or five people, one of whom is the "key man," the link with the rest of the organization. Great emphasis is placed on the maintenance of security. The division of labor within the cell tends to become more specialized as the group becomes more professional. In addition to the bomb manufacturer and the quartermaster, who obtain the materials and necessary logistical support for the group, there are communications and transport specialists, as well as intelligence specialists whose job is to organize the collection of data on targets. I think we underestimate the terrorist groups if we think of them all as amateur nineteenth-century anarchists with bombs sticking out of their pockets and smoke coming out of their ears. There are still some true amateurs, but there are now many highly professional groups operating. Some Palestinian terrorist movements, with vast sums of money

---

4. David Hubbard, *The Skyjacker: His Flights of Fantasy* (New York: Macmillan, 1971).

behind them, have managed to purchase a great deal of expertise, which they pass on to other groups. Thus, they provide information on circuitry for bomb making, on weaponry, and on sabotage techniques to groups which have little or no common ideological ground with them. These ad hoc bilateral links between terrorist movements have been growing steadily.

In addition, the Palestinian movements are being used as a Soviet proxy and as a conduit for support to other groups that might sow disruption and cause damage to the West. Since the Havana and Badawi meetings of the late 1960s and early 1970s, terrorist movements throughout the NATO area have benefited from participation in international meetings. They exchange tactics, supply weaponry, and provide each other with useful intelligence data. It should be emphasized that distance is no longer any barrier to such alliances.

But what about the other aspect of terrorist organization, the political side? Every one of the serious terrorist movements we have discussed has a political wing. I think it is a big mistake for academic students of terrorism to concentrate on the military violence aspect and forget that these organizations are engaged in a frantic propaganda campaign. Much terrorist propaganda is very crude and difficult to read with concentration. But if we want to know what we are up against in order to try to counter it effectively, we need to read and try to understand the literature.

Sponsor states play an important role in the context of terrorist propaganda. They fund publications as well as conferences and provide some of the political expertise. There is much evidence that the front organization of journalists organized by the Soviet Union has provided a great deal of "in-house training" for propagandists working for terrorist organizations in Eastern Europe and elsewhere; sophisticated knowledge is being passed on to these organizations. You may say that this is a flattering comment on Soviet propaganda. I know that some Soviet propaganda is a dismal failure, but there have been some recent successes.

In his study of the *coup d'état*, Curzio Malaparte writes, "What is the bravery of soldiers worth if the masters are not aware that the art of self-defence consists in knowing your weak points?"[5] I really believe that the moral and political weaknesses of our democratic societies are the Achilles' heel the terrorist can exploit. It is neither our lack of technology nor our lack of funds. We have greater firepower than the terrorists in all Western states that are threatened by these kind of movements. What we may lack is the moral and psychological strength and sensibility to measure up to the requirements of this kind of war.

Very few of the judicial systems in the Western world have appropriate

---

5. Curzio Malaparte, *Tecnica del Colpo di Stato* (Florence: Vallecchi, 1973).

means for dealing with the man who actually plans, sets up, funds, and organizes the terrorist operation. We are much more likely to apprehend the man at the end of the chain who actually carries out the mission. One is reminded of a simile used by Maxim Gorki, that an act of violence is "sometimes like a stone thrown by an unknown hand. Is the stone therefore guilty?" In a way, this raises a dilemma with regard to the judicial response to terrorism. In law and in our legal philosophy, the man responsible for the action is, of course, punishable for that offense. Yet the man who is most guilty gets away scot-free. Therefore, I will just ask whether we need to look at terrorism legislation that has been passed in certain countries in order to determine if there is some way to include the organizers behind the scenes, the one who commits the crime of conspiring to carry out an act of terrorism and the one who promotes acts of terrorism.

Terrorism is, of course, a preeminent mode of psychological and propaganda warfare. And ultimately the terrorist and the government fight a war of wills. The political propaganda war to win positive support from the population against the terrorists and to demoralize the terrorist groups must be won if terrorist movements are to be extinguished, and if new terrorist groups are not to be formed.

The ideal setup is a good intelligence network. Such a system requires a high degree of international intelligence cooperation. This is very important because the terrorists themselves operate internationally. It requires sensitive and responsive governments capable of coordinating domestic antiterrorist measures, including systems of joint control to coordinate police, army, and intelligence responses. It also calls for international coordination at the level of countermeasures. And, finally, it demands effective voluntary cooperation from the mass media. Careless or irresponsible media coverage can completely undermine the effectiveness of antiterrorist measures. The media must recognize values more important than being first with a story. Occasionally there is evidence of malevolence and cryptoterrorist propaganda in the media.

There is also the need to identify and destroy the terrorist propaganda bases which are active within our communities. The Soviet apparatus would still remain, and so would the East European proxies. But there are groups busily engaged in propaganda and recruitment in most Western capitals. They are very important to the terrorist movement because you cannot hope to lead an ethnic separatist or class revolutionary movement without including some of the constituents you claim to represent in the leadership committees and in the cells, at least. You cannot run a movement which claims to be liberating Italy or conquering Japanese imperialism for the Japanese revolutionaries if you do not even have some platform in the country you claim to be liberating. Thus, it is very important that the propaganda and recruitment setups of terrorist organizations within democratic societies should be put out of business.

Where do we look for these? Publishing organizations and journals are often a kind of cover for this kind of activity. There are also certain danger spots within the university systems. I am not suggesting for a moment that we close down certain universities. What I am suggesting is that we should identify, and most of us can do so very easily, those university departments and those individuals within departments who carry out tasks for terrorist organizations as propagandists, agents, and recruiters. They are the key initial point of entry for most active terrorists, the point at which most impressionable young people with some sort of political malleability and utopian enthusiasm may be mobilized by extremely ruthless people determined to keep up the numbers of their terrorist organization. Remember they are losing some all the time. Some are put in jail; others defect or just run away. They need to have this constant flow of recruits.

If you could stop the flow of recruits into the terrorist organizations, you could prevent much of the violence and damage done to society later on, and you would save many young people. One might save many young people from the fate of becoming pawns of a terrorist organization, from being exploited by them. And indeed, they are exploited. Many do not really want to stay in the movement. Many of them try to get out. But they cannot because once the terrorists have a recruit, they use terror to keep him. The threat against his family or against his own life is enough to keep the average man or woman in the organization. It is therefore important for us to try to locate the centers of recruitment and cut off the flow of recruits before the damage is done. In democracies, the government and intelligence agencies should make a top priority of examining the development of university bases of recruitment by the terrorist organizations operating in their region. And they should work closely with the academic authorities to get their cooperation to avoid engaging as university staff those people likely to act as terrorist agents and propagandists. Part of the war against terrorism has to be fought out in the seminar and lecture rooms of the universities of the Western world; there is literally a struggle for the souls of the young. The Italian police discovered this reality, though rather late in the day perhaps.

The media in a free society have a key role in this propaganda. They must establish popular credibility. They must tell the truth. They must expose the propaganda of atrocities, defamations, and myths of the terrorists. They must call a murder a murder, not an "act of revolutionary execution." They must avoid interviewing terrorists on television and radio and glamorizing or sensationalizing their activities. Even an experienced broadcasting service like the BBC has been guilty of unwittingly aiding terrorism. There must be a conscious effort to ensure balance in reporting and comment. No democratic institution should be above media criticism. But the media should avoid pillorying officials and agencies of law and order. Policemen, lawyers, and soldiers are also citizens. They do a tough job for society in terrorist situations. At the very least, they should be given the chance of replying to allegations against them in the media.

Political will and propaganda alone cannot win the war against terrorism. The military, security, and political fronts all need to be conquered. But there are two key conclusions I think we can draw. You cannot win the war against terrorism by military methods alone, except perhaps in a totalitarian state in which none of us would want to live. And you cannot win solely by better propaganda. Charles Roetter, in *Psychological Warfare*, wrote, "Propaganda is no substitute for victory. It cannot unmake defeats. It can help prepare the way for the former and speed its coming; and it can mitigate the impact of the latter. It cannot act in isolation. To be effective, it must be closely related to events."[6] This rather wise comment applies to the terrorist situation. The gravest danger of all, in situations of severe and protracted challenge by terrorists, is that the moral integrity, the will, and the loyalty of a democracy may erode under the impact of cynicism and the blind pursuit of self-interest by powerful groups, such as the oil companies or the media. Any liberal state demoralized and strained by inflation and recession could be pushed into destruction without a shot being fired. If one injects the element of terrorism and the probable disorganization that could be provoked by simultaneous terrorist attacks in many parts of a democratic state, it does not take great imagination to envisage a scenario of political collapse.

It is essential for us to view terrorism in the context of a worsening climate of conflict. It may be only one element, but in certain key crises it may be the decisive catalyst for the destruction of democracy. A democratic system that is undefeated at the ballot box can still be destroyed by its failure to defend itself against determined attack by the enemy within the gate. Terrorism may well be the Trojan Horse.

Discussion

PARTICIPANT: It is important to point out that in the face of a serious problem, governments cannot absolve themselves simply by turning it over to the military and intelligence, saying it is their problem. The problem must be treated in an integrated fashion. For example, the fact that there are certain nuclei of revolutionary movements that come from a certain

6. Charles Roetter, *Psychological Warfare* (London: Faber, 1974).

social strata can present an educational problem. But governments in liberal countries have a tendency to regard it as something in the domain of intelligence or of the military. The integrated approach is very rarely taken; but only this approach can enhance our chances of success.

Furthermore, it is important to get at the problem as early as possible. I would say that in Israel we recognized the problem early, but we did not fully understand it early enough. Moreover, we could not have changed the situation very much politically. Yet, I think that if we had taken a longer-range point of view, we could have prepared ourselves much better. To give only one example, the matter of infiltration along the borders—which we finally solved successfully—could have been dealt with in a much easier and cheaper way at an earlier stage.

PARTICIPANT: I would like to make a contrary argument. There is the danger of overreacting to the problem of terrorism, and I see some trends in this direction in what you have been saying. For instance, terrorism may contribute to what is called the "new barbarism." Nevertheless, I would say that unless or until terrorism escalates with mass destruction devices or psychologically shocking devices of different forms, I would not trouble too much about it. It is not worth more of an effort. I would hesitate to put terrorism in most European countries as a top priority problem. Therefore, I have my doubts regarding a conclusion that the present level of terrorism justifies a much larger effort in combating it.

PARTICIPANT: I think in a way this does mark a very basic difference between us. In the first place, I would claim that there are countries where the war against terrorism is by no means a low priority problem. The Basque region of Spain and Northern Ireland would give it a very high priority. I think Italy seems to have an extraordinary tolerance for high levels of violence; it is part of their cultural tradition. I am not suggesting, however, that they would be satisfied to have terrorism placed outside the first ten items of priority. I think most Italians in the center of the political spectrum would want to place it among the first six problems. But I would certainly say that in the case of Israel, given the dangers of escalation of conflict that always exist in this area in a deteriorating situation, I would regard terrorism as an ongoing problem of a high level of seriousness.

PARTICIPANT: Let us examine European countries. With regard to some of them, I would present the following argument: If the present trend of underemployment of university graduates continues, there will be more terrorism because there will be greater political dissatisfaction. Now, is this a problem of terrorism or a problem of the labor market?

WILKINSON: Well, actually it is both. I am not suggesting that we close down democracy. We just need to defend our free institutions better.

PARTICIPANT: On this everyone would agree. It is a question of the marginal decisions. I would agree to checking university teachers if there is a certain level of danger. Some levels of danger justify it. At present, for instance, I would control the teaching of toxicology. But I ask myself, in what countries is the risk so high that paying this marginal price is worth the marginal benefit?

PARTICIPANT: It is a question of proportion. Let us assume that you have to advise a certain prime minister whether to activate a surveillance system in the university. One has to consider the costs and benefits. We have to give responsible advice. I have the feeling that in many countries the cost of imposing more surveillance at the universities at the present level of violence is higher than the benefits involved. Of course, costs are not only monetary.

PARTICIPANT: Perhaps we can turn the question around a bit. Are we talking about an incident or about a consequence of the modern urban civilization? Are we talking about an instrument of policy manipulated by certain states or certain revolutionary organizations, which is not incidental but rather a direct and deliberate threat to certain societies? If this is the case, then it is something which has to be met as one meets any threat. Ultimately, the question is, who is being threatened and what is the extent of the threat? And there are certain threats which cannot be dealt with. It may be a domestic problem, with certain ramifications, which may or may not be dealt with by the authorities. The political problem of the Middle East, however, is quite different. It is not educational and has nothing to do with the labor problem. It is a totally different kind of problem. We are talking about two quite distinct kinds of activity, and one has to consider who is being threatened in each case, and whether the threat can be met.

WILKINSON: I think I would agree that you have to look at the whole spectrum and not just offer a simple solution for all groups and all contexts. I tried to argue that in each case where you have a serious active terrorist organization which is actually organizing operations, even on a low intensity level, you have to look for the propaganda bases of that organization. I think the country must look for its recruiting bases in order to reduce that threat. In the case of the threat to Israel, I would say you do have the problem of people within the universities who are proterrorist. This is certainly known to my Israeli friends at this conference. There have been cases of people within the university structure helping the Palestinian terrorists attain the aid, training, and support that they need, using the educational process as the point of contact. I think, therefore, that it is not a labor problem here, but a problem similar to that in the European context.

PARTICIPANT: One of the reasons that Western democracies have had difficulties coping with the problem of terrorism is that political terrorism is not an integral part of their countries. Their institutions are not qualified to deal with it. When you fight terrorism in Western societies, you have to be careful not to use methods which will change institutions, thereby threatening the stability of the society. In other words, you have to minimize pressure levels as much as possible. You have to strengthen other aspects and not attack those institutions that symbolize liberal democracy in the West.

PARTICIPANT: I think the state of political affairs is such that the attitude of most people to this problem is largely influenced by the regime in question, the cause in question, and so forth. It is also worth mentioning that terrorism does not necessarily entail hitting the "innocent" people. If a prime minister is assassinated, for example, would you call him an innocent person?

PARTICIPANT: Yet in the process of assassinating a prime minister, those carrying it out are going to risk killing other people, taking the law into their own hands, and putting themselves up as executioners. If that sort of thing were to be done, would one really think it a step forward in the interests of democracy? I very much doubt it. I think it is just possible that the case General Harkabi mentioned concerning tyrannicide would have covered the assassination of Stalin or Hitler. Indeed, the people who plotted Hitler's death justified it in these terms, in terms of the classical doctrine. I do not think we could extend that kind of protection or justification to cover acts of individuals within the democratic system. Terror was invented, one might say, to use threats of death and destruction on society as a whole. It has been written that terrorism is the weapon of the modern age against bureaucracy, whereas tyrannicide was the weapon in the age of kingdoms. I think if one takes a strong line against terrorism as such, then it really does not become a purely national problem. It becomes a problem with international legal dimensions and repercussions.

PARTICIPANT: I was distressed by one thing in your presentation. You showed us the diagram of the Soviet system for subversive action, for what might be called intelligence gathering and covert action. That disturbs me. In fact, that is their network for recruitment, penetration, propaganda, and espionage. It does not necessarily mean that they use this for supporting terrorism in general or for supporting any particular terrorist group. I think that one has to make a distinction. They have had this setup for many years, well before the phenomenon of international terrorism existed. They have used it for their own purposes, what we would call revolutionary purposes, or covert actions—subversion, espionage, and so forth. What surprised me is the fact that the distinction you made was almost entirely opposed to the one that I am convinced exists. The Soviets do not seem to be terribly interested in the so-called revolutionary-anarchist movements, whether in Italy or in Germany, and there has been a great deal of difficulty in proving a link between them. There has been Soviet support for national liberation movements and the PLO. Nevertheless, there are questions as to the support they give to the terroristic methods used by these groups. The questions concern the kind of support they give and the amount involved. I would like to hear some evidence about the USSR–Baader-Meinhof connection.

WILKINSON: I am glad you raised that point, because I think your doubts are likely to be resolved during the course of the conference, for quite a number of us have chapter and verse that will substantiate that connection very clearly. Even many national liberation movements that seem to be quite unlikely to be championed by Marxism-Leninism nevertheless receive financial and propaganda aid, as well as facilities, weapons, and supplies from Eastern European countries.

PARTICIPANT: I have great doubts about this holding true for the anarchist movements.

WILKINSON: On the side of the anarchist movements, too, there is quite a lot of documentation concerning the help that Eastern European countries gave the Baader-Meinhof group.

PARTICIPANT: I would like to see some of this. I am sure there are situations where the Soviet Union is very glad about terrorism, but I do not have any evidence about this.

PARTICIPANT: In many conversations with Eastern Europeans of various nationalities—Russians, Poles—they expressed their outright indignation at the idea that the Soviet bloc supports terrorism. For ideological and tactical reasons they are opposed to it. The idea that they are funding these organizations infuriates them.

WILKINSON: Still, it is not so farfetched to think they might be channeling funds to the terrorist organizations, which then use these funds to finance operations off their own backs. I think this is what is happening. A lot of money which is handed over in very large sums to Palestinian groups cannot be controlled. How much of that is in fact passed on to groups which are ideologically a long way off from the Soviet Union?

Then, of course, it is not quite as indirect or remote as you might imagine, because transnational gangs have used people who were trained in Soviet camps and have encouraged their operatives to get that training. This is apparently quite easy to get because of the Palestinian connection. It is more likely a kind of network which is being financed at one end by Soviet allegiance to certain movements that have the national liberation aura, which then pass on the benefits of that benevolence to revolutionary–national liberation groups or to revolutionary-ideological groups. The Soviets must know this is going on. There is some evidence that before 1973 or 1974 they were fully aware of assistance given by the East German authorities to the Baader-Meinhof group. The assistance included sanctuary in East Berlin, aid while members of the group were on the run, money for *Konkret* [Ulrike Meinhof was a member of the staff of this journal and practiced political journalism]. The money so provided was useful to the movement in a crucial stage of its development.

I am not saying, however, that they are financing the current activities of the new generation of terrorists in West Germany.

PARTICIPANT: Is there information concerning the training of the Red Brigades in Czechoslovakia?

PARTICIPANT: Very early, before they got into the killing business, some dissident Communists, formerly associated with the Italian Communist party, went to Prague.

WILKINSON: There is no conclusive proof of that. But there is a pretty well documented link between East Germans and the Russians and the Baader-Meinhof group in its earlier phase. I am not saying that is continuing now, but I want to give you the source material on the basis of which that was concluded.

PARTICIPANT: The first generation of the Baader-Meinhof gang went to Palestinian terrorist camps to be trained.

PARTICIPANT: I think the KGB operates at certain levels without checking home with the Politburo and that it carries out much covert action without having it necessarily approved at the top level. But I think what is impressive here is the fact that the Soviets are exploiting a number of factors, but are involved only indirectly. That is not quite the same thing as active or direct support. I agree in particular with the point that much of the Soviet link is worked through the Palestinians—not even through Fatah, but through Habash. For a long time, the Soviets had very little contact with Habash. Now the relations have improved.

WILKINSON: There is some evidence that the Soviets are nervous about terrorism being brought into their country. After the metro bombing in Moscow, they issued a statement that corrupt bourgeois elements had brought in this form of violence.

PARTICIPANT: Research has found that the Soviets began changing their position on international hijacking once they had been subjected to it.

PARTICIPANT: Although the links between the Soviet Union and terrorist movements operating in Western Europe are well disguised, they are still visible. Not all the links go directly through the Palestinian channel. In the case of the Provisional IRA, a lot of the political propaganda support was given without even a request having been made. This is done because the Soviets consider the IRA's struggle useful to them. If you say this is exploitation, then exploitation is important. The fact that they are exploiting terrorism to the limits shows that propaganda and other subversive activities are a force to be reckoned with, insofar that if we do not answer that propaganda, we are naive, ignorant, or being misled. The point I am trying to raise is that the propaganda dimension that accompanies the terroristic efforts, and is often not taken seriously, needs to be met face on. We must fight it because there are people who are foolish enough to believe it.

9

The Impact of Mass Media on Terrorists, Supporters, and the Public at Large

Hillel Nossek

Theories and research from the field of mass communications provide many insights into several aspects of terrorism. Of the many issues related to terrorism and the media, I shall deal with two: the ways in which the terrorists exploit the media and the effect of mass media coverage of terrorist incidents on the public.

In planning and executing terrorist acts, terrorists, particularly the PLO, consider the impact of mass media coverage. Several factors, known in the communications literature as "media selection criteria," are considered.[1] These include:

1. Timing. Terrorists stage massive attacks on dates of historical significance in order to attract media coverage. Acts are also staged as immediate responses to unfavorable political developments. The latter is consistent with the news selection criterion of reporting events which are part of a set of expected occurrences but are still unpredictable.
2. Place. The physical target is usually chosen on the basis of the available news media resources in the area.
3. The number of people affected. The more people affected by an event, the higher is the probability that it will become news and the greater is the chance that it will receive extensive coverage. This is consistent with the news selection criterion of personification. Furthermore, the higher the number of casualties, the more negative is the perception of the event; and the more negative an event appears, the higher is its probability of being reported.

---

1. On media selection of events as news, see: J. Galtung and M.H. Ruge, "Structure of Foreign News," *Media Sociology*, ed. J. Tunstall (London: Constable, 1970), pp. 259–298.

4. Target and goal. When targets which are conducive to the taking of hostages, such as international airliners, are chosen, one of the goals is presumably to open negotiations and thereby involve government officials. Government officials are elite persons and qualify as news-makers. Furthermore, the involvement of representatives of elite (i.e., Western) governments in the negotiations and the threat to the lives of citizens of elite nations increase both the probability and the amount of coverage.

Each terrorist act need not incorporate all of the features of the news selection criteria. Forceful representation of only one or a few of the necessary characteristics is sufficient for the attack to receive extensive coverage.

I believe that the terrorists' communications theory is based on the assumption that the only way to convey different messages simultaneously to the various target audiences is via a dramatic attack characterized by media-oriented features. My analysis[2] of the Maalot (1974) and Savoy Hotel (1975) cases supports this hypothesis. In both instances, political developments which the PLO viewed as unfavorable were expected. In the case of Maalot, the disengagement agreement with Syria was nearly concluded; in the case of the Savoy Hotel, Henry Kissinger was on his way to the Middle East to start negotiations on the second disengagement agreement with Egypt. Furthermore, the attack on Maalot was scheduled to take place on May 15, the day chosen by the PLO to commemorate the invasion of all neighboring Arab armies into Israel in 1948. All features—time, place, the number of people affected, target, and goals—were taken into account in planning the missions. PLO spokesmen used the international news media to convey their messages to their respective target audiences as follows:

1. To members of the PLO: "We're alive and fighting to achieve our ends."
2. To Palestinians in Israel: "We're fighting for you. It's time you join us."
3. To the United States: "You can't solve the problems of the Middle East without us."
4. To Israel: "Your existence is not secure without solving the Palestinian problem."
5. To Arab countries: "Our way of dealing with Israel is the only way."
6. To international public opinion: "We are still oppressed."

I believe the same pattern can be deciphered in other well-known incidents. Moreover, success in capturing worldwide attention has encour-

2. H. Nossek, "Terrorism and the Mass-Media: An Analysis of Two Cases in the Israeli Media" (Hebrew) (unpublished study).

aged repetition. This means that when Palestinian terrorists feel the need to send messages to all of their audiences simultaneously, they will try to launch a massive, dramatic attack.

What impact does such publicity have? According to Paul Lazarsfeld and Robert Merton[3] in their well-known article on the functions of the mass media in modern society, publicity in and of itself confers status. I cannot imagine Yasir Arafat appearing in the UN or meeting with Bruno Kreisky had he not achieved that status, which was, to a great degree, a media creation.

According to Lazarsfeld and Merton, the mass media also have an effect which they term the *narcotizing dysfunction*. The public, exposed to large and repeated doses of media versions of political and social issues, becomes apathetic while believing that it is participating. This may, at least partly, explain why citizens of democratic nations remain complacent in responding to the horrors of terrorism and the dangers to democracy which terrorism poses.

Now I would like to try to assess the impact of the media on the public in a state which is a direct target of terrorist acts. Tsiona Peled,[4] in her research based on public opinion polls, tried to determine how Israelis' feelings of security—both locally and nationally—are affected by terrorist acts as reported in the media. She found that the terrorist incidents raised the level of fear but did not change the feeling of assurance in the future existence and security of the state of Israel. These findings are, to the best of my knowledge, the only empirical information available on the effects of exposure to media coverage of terrorism. Therefore, my analysis of the impact of mass media coverage of terrorism on the public will be based on research dealing with the general concept of media effects. I shall ignore, in the present lecture, the vast body of research on the effect on children of exposure to media portrayals of violence, since the focus there is on aggression as a response to these contents.

All general theories on the effect of mass media on the audience—Direct Impact, Two-step Flow of Communication, Agenda Setting, and Uses and Gratification—concur in finding that attitudes and opinions are not changed by exposure to mass media content. On the contrary, both psychological and sociological research have found that the effect of the mass media is to strengthen existing attitudes and opinions.

---

3. P. Lazarsfeld and R.K. Merton, "Mass Communication, Popular Taste, and Organized Social Action," *The Processes and Effects of Mass Communication*, eds. W. Schramm and D. Roberts (2nd edition) (Urbana: University of Illinois Press, 1971), pp. 554–578.

4. T. Peled, "Stability and Change of the Attitude: Structure of the Israeli Public from the Six-Day War to December 1970" (unpublished doctoral dissertation) (Hebrew) (Jerusalem: The Hebrew University, 1976).

Wilbur Schramm, in his article on the Kennedy assassination,[5] found three major functions of the mass media. According to Schramm, the media provided information, which served to prevent panic; they allowed the public to take part in national grief and to let out deep emotions; and they reassured the public of the continuing existence of the state and government.

Hadley Cantril's research on the public's reaction to Orson Welles's famous radio broadcast on the invasion from Mars[6] found that only those persons with certain predispositions misperceived the broadcast as a true news bulletin and panicked.

In my own study, I tried to uncover the latent symbols and messages perceived by media viewers exposed to coverage of terrorist events. I found that in Israel, the Holocaust serves as a point of comparison and distinction, and the message perceived is that despite some similarities between terrorist attacks and the Holocaust, the Holocaust will not be repeated in Israel. I believe that this perception has an effect on the public and partly shapes Israeli leaders' reactions to terrorist attacks. Their reaction to exposure to media coverage of terrorist incidents is then more emotional than practical. This kind of effect theory needs much more research, both in Israel and in other countries where the symbols and latent messages will, of course, be different.

To summarize, the effect of the media on terrorists is twofold. In the short run, media coverage of terrorist incidents encourages repetition. In the long run, conferral of status on terrorist leaders and on the issues they represent reinforces the attitudes of terrorist supporters. In a country in which terrorist acts are frequent, publicity may increase fears over personal safety, but positive attitudes may also prevent panic and uncertainty and, in the case of casualties, such coverage may enable the public to share emotions with the victims' relatives.

As for why the mass media give such enormous coverage to terrorist acts, I suggest that the structure, professional norms, and technical and aesthetic constraints of the media demand a predictable product; events like terrorist attacks perfectly conform to the desired formula.

With this in mind, I would like to close with some general remarks which can serve as guidelines for a discussion of practical measures to minimize possible exploitation of media coverage of terrorism.

First, a blackout of coverage might cause future acts to be more violent, since a main goal of terrorist violence is to attract media attention. A blackout might also cause rumors and panic, especially in a small state like Israel.

---

5. W. Schramm, "Communication in Crisis," *The Processes and Effects of Mass Communication*, pp. 525–553.

6. H. Cantril, *The Invasion from Mars* (Princeton: Princeton University Press, 1940).

Next, a call for self-restraint or self-imposed censorship by the media themselves is impractical given the vast number of media organizations and journalists, the differences in their political beliefs and, most importantly, the competition among and within the various news media.

Also, the opening of a channel for messages sent by the enemies of free societies should be controlled by limiting the type of information transmitted. Guidelines regarding the type of information which could harm police and military personnel involved in terrorist attacks, should be published and distributed to editors to help them make judgments on what to exclude from their broadcasts or pages.

Finally, as for minimizing the effects of status conferral, only a well-planned and well-executed public opinion campaign might achieve some success. This campaign should be based on messages aimed at strengthening existing negative attitudes toward and opinions against the phenomenon of terrorism.

In conclusion, I think the best way to avoid the impact of the mass media is to prevent the occurrences of terrorist attacks. By concentrating on how to fight the terrorists, we can have much more success than by fighting a losing battle against the media.

Discussion

PARTICIPANT: The guiding principle all of us should keep in mind is that most journalists would sell their countries for a headline. The corruption of the media in this respect has much to do with this very simple opportunistic factor. A sensational news story is very hard to resist. This explains not only the undue prominence of some stories involving terrorism, but why information of a kind that is helpful to terrorists regularly finds its way into the feature pages of the newspapers. I would like to devote some time to some of the structures of disinformation in the media which I think are helping terrorist interests and the interests of those who support terrorists.

When you look at the growing legitimization of the PLO, the image of the PLO as a valid constructor of statehood, a political movement rather than a terrorist gang, you come up again and again with the fact of the influence of one or two organizations in Western countries that have been singularly successful in feeding stories favorable to the PLO and other radical causes to the Western press. I am thinking, in particular, of a Washington-based institute which is by far the most influential radical think tank in Washington today. It has, of course, tremendous entrees into the administration, into Congress, and into the media. The role of this institute in isolating and destabilizing the shah's regime in Iran was very important. Most of the significant anti-shah newspaper articles that appeared during the two years before his exile are a tribute to the network around that group. Part of that network in the United States is the Breira organization, which was founded by left wing American Jews who favor a dialogue with the PLO and in some cases go far beyond gentile Americans in their support for the PLO.

I have followed this particular subject in some detail, and I mention it because if you want to talk about the media, about psychological warfare, or about the presented image of terrorist groups, generalizing will not do; we must deal with specific issues. Let us examine the particular centers of influence and see what we can do about them. Indeed, I think something can be done. The operations of the institute are very devious indeed, and its financing is worthy of official investigation in the United States. That is one setup which is doing a lot to create a climate that legitimizes terrorist activity and affects all Western countries. As I say, it has direct interests in legitimizing the PLO, but it has similar interests in discrediting Western institutions, Western corporations, and Western intelligence, turning them into acceptable targets for terrorism. Another institute, in Amsterdam, maintains a very large data bank on Western corporations, specializing in the kinds of material that will discredit them, including information concerning the private lives of the directors. It is functioning as an intelligence service for the radical Left, which feeds into the terrorist network.

Another aspect to consider that is of growing importance in the media—particularly in Europe—is old-fashioned bribery of journalists and those influential in the media. I know of two British journalists who travel regularly to the Washington area to meet with a Libyan who lives in Florida and is a paymaster of the Libyan secret service. I have seen documentary evidence that these two journalists receive checks or cash for a large sum in a bank in Virginia. And that is only the tip of the iceberg. I do not think there is anything of the sort as yet in the United States, but in the case of Europe we are dealing with direct financial attempts to influence journalists and whole news organizations. That is something which can be handled very easily by exposure. More determined efforts have to be made by all Western governments, including the Israeli government, to make available information of a kind that will discredit and disrupt the terrorist networks and their support groups. This involves all aspects of psychological warfare.

PARTICIPANT: Western perceptions of the entire Middle East problem are constantly changing. If the price of oil were to be doubled tomorrow, you might find changes in opinion. We are therefore working against a dynamic factor in trying to influence opinion in Europe, which is already strongly guided and controlled by the need for oil. We need to examine the uses that are made of some Palestinian groups by other interests, such as radical Arab governments or the Soviet Union.

PARTICIPANT: The importance of the media lies in that the media are a way of giving a terrorist act political significance. The question is whether there is any way to prevent this. It was said, and rightfully so I think, that most reporters would do anything to publish a story. We must keep in mind, however, that by doing so they are serving what they perceive as the best interests of the public. For this reason, I think little can be done to prevent publication of stories by trying to persuade a journalist that he is serving a wrong cause. Still, any publication of terrorist activity puts the terrorists on the political map, which is why they need the supplement of publication, of the media, in order to advance their political case. As I have said, we can do nothing to prevent publication of such events, but we should always strive to show the other side of things, to stress the negative and dangerous in the manifestations of terrorism and terror organizations.

PARTICIPANT: There is a big debate taking place in Britain at the moment because the BBC filmed an interview with one of the IRA or Irish National Liberation Army (INLA) assassins, thus airing his viewpoints. At the same time, British media give very little coverage to individual terrorist acts perpetrated by the IRA. This growing tendency to publicize the aims and justifications of the terrorist group is very worrisome. It is the legitimization of the terrorist group rather than the publicity for isolated episodes that is most worrisome. There is a growing tendency to believe that wherever terrorism exists, there must be a good reason for it.

PARTICIPANT: Another aspect of the subject that is often ignored is that many terrorist groups, especially the fringe ones in Europe, are probably far less influenced by what is said in the mainstream press than by what is said in the relatively small circulation publications which are read by their own political constituents. There is now a proliferation of new Left publications in Europe, many of which are including weekly incitements to violence or terrorism. This is important because the kind of articles they publish about governments, police, and intelligence services are designed to dehumanize those institutions and render them attractive targets to terrorist attacks. The dehumanization of the enemy is a precondition to the emotional readiness to kill in cold blood. We have yet to learn how to deal with this problem.

PARTICIPANT: I believe that journalists are approachable and can be converted and inspired to better coverage since terrorism is something about which we all basically agree. It is not a partisan issue; it is not a political party issue; it is not a conservative versus liberal issue. Most people in the West agree that we must end terrorism. Most people see it as a common threat. This is an enormous asset.

You will not find any editor who will be unsympathetic to an approach on the subject of terrorism and its coverage that calls for a campaign to end terrorism everywhere. Let us remember that the media, in some respects, run the United States and some other Western countries. They have brought down presidents and therefore feel strong and self-confident. There is thus no way that the media in the United States will tolerate direct influence from any government institution. Influence must be subtle. It must appeal to the appetite which the Western press has developed for investigative reporting, for big exclusives, for big exposés. This can be done very effectively by providing information needed for these stories through sought-after channels such as government and intelligence services.

10

Desensitizing the Public to Terrorist Attacks: Methods and Dilemmas

Nehemia Friedland

What is meant by a *desensitized public*? To my knowledge, advocates of desensitization have failed to describe precisely what is meant by the concept. I take the term to refer to a situation where the daily lives, emotional well-being, and sociopolitical attitudes of the citizens of a target nation are little affected by terrorism, much as they are little affected by fatal traffic accidents or vague threats of natural disasters. This analogy is problematic, however. In desensitizing a public in the face of, say, natural disasters, our effectiveness is measurable on a single dimension, the extent to which the public's sensitivity is indeed lowered. However, in desensitizing a public to terrorist threats there is a second critical dimension: the extent to which the implementation of desensitizing measures might be construed as victories by the terrorists. It is the need to chart a pragmatic course between these two conflicting dimensions which makes the desensitizers' task a very difficult one.

Assuming, for a moment, that a public could be desensitized to terrorist threats, can we take it for granted that this should be done? I find it difficult to give an unqualified answer to this question, and I would suggest for consideration the following dilemmas. First, a desensitized public represents a serious obstacle for a terrorist organization, which may thereby be forced into escalating its efforts. On the other hand, a highly sensitized public provides positive reinforcement to acts of terrorism. Which is preferable: a sensitized or a desensitized public?

A second dilemma involves the fact that sensitivity is positively correlated with alertness. As experience accumulated in Israel shows, public alertness is an important counterterrorist measure. It is thus imperative that the distinction between sensitivity and alertness not be blurred, and that the close interdependence between the two not be ignored.

I would like to turn now to some comments concerning means by which a public can be desensitized to the effects of terrorism. As a social psychologist, I must admit that with regard to desensitization, the content of the psychological bag of tricks is rather meager. At any rate, the brand of desensitization we are considering seeks to counter fear and anxiety, which are exacerbated by the potential severity, the randomness, and the unpredictability of terrorist attacks. The process of desensitization must be founded on two bases: information and coping skills. I will start with the latter.

It is a widely accepted and well-documented psychological observation that threatened and stressed individuals react and behave more confidently if they are certain of their mastery over the situation, if they believe that they know how to behave when faced with the threat, and if they are confident that their responses will be effective. One may conclude then that the public has to be provided with, indeed trained in, a repertoire of responses which might be useful in the face of terrorist attacks or threats. Yet there exists a counterview: namely, that such training might achieve the opposite result of enhancing the salience of terrorist threats and thereby breed fear and anxiety.

In terms of information, I identify the following types of information which could be useful in desensitizing the public:

1. Background information about terror organizations can conceivably demystify, deglorify, and depict terrorism in valid, mundane dimensions. On the other hand, such information might also contain frightening elements. It is, of course, inadvisable to present information which is intentionally biased to highlight the reassuring facts only. In addition, the dissemination of such information might provide terrorists with the publicity which is so dear to them.
2. Information about counterterrorist tactics, means, and devices can reassure the public. However, for obvious reasons, one may doubt the authorities' willingness or ability to disclose such information.
3. Information and forecasts about the future nature, frequency, and intensity of terrorist attacks may reduce the role of unduly pessimistic expectations in contributing to fear. Without such information, the public may envision attacks far more terrifying than those actually anticipated.

As the issue of the mass media has already been discussed extensively, I shall offer only two comments. First, mass media reporting of terror incidents must be factual, accurate, reliable, yet devoid of the so-called human interest element. When a reporter interviews a released hostage about her emotional reactions, he might instigate in his audience a process of identification, thereby bringing the event closer to each person's home and heart. There is nothing like such identification to sensitize individuals. Secondly, the media must be very careful about terminology. If desensitization is to be aided by the media, it should avoid terms such as *freedom fighters, revolutionaries, guerrillas,* and *commandos,* making use, rather, of terms used in reporting common crimes. Let me hasten to emphasize that I am not expressing here an ideology or a value judgment. I am merely suggesting that by criminalizing terrorism, we place it in a context to which the public is better accustomed and thus move towards the goal of desensitization. At the same time, by suggesting that the mass media adopt a different terminology, we may indeed be suggesting the adoption of an inaccurate terminology, which could damage the media's credibility.

Discussion

PARTICIPANT: When considering preventive measures, you have to take into account public opinion, but you cannot make your decisions according to it.

PARTICIPANT: When you start the campaign to educate the Israeli public on how to react in hostage situations, you have to ask yourself whether this is really the best way to prepare the public for future incidents.

PARTICIPANT: The question which arises is, to what extent can one take preventive measures in order for them to be optimally effective? One can surround a school with a battalion of guards, or one can put just one guard there. A balance must be obtained between operative efficiency and the right level of sensitization of the public.

PARTICIPANT: Public sensitivity is needed in order to combat terrorism effectively.

PARTICIPANT: In general, and particularly in Israel, a logical policy has to be adopted and followed. It should preserve the needed balance of desired concern and not reach the level of induced anxiety.

PARTICIPANT: I think that saying we have to do something is a kind of blanket solution. Several different aspects of the issue can be considered. One of them concerns the struggle against terrorism. Is it to our advantage to cultivate a highly sensitive, excited public? I think it is definitely one way of reinforcing terrorist acts. The complementary view is to say we need a desensitized public that will assure one that the terrorists are not succeeding. On a different level, the question is, to what extremes does one go in order to prepare the public for different terrorist events? There is enough information nowadays on what could be defined as adequate or proper hostage behavior. Are we or are we not going to train people in such behavior? Here, I think, the question of our taking the initiative is a legitimate one.

PARTICIPANT: How can you train three million people on the assumption that one of them may become a hostage? It seems impractical.

PARTICIPANT: I am not arguing the logic of it, but just presenting this as an example of the main issue at hand. The problem is not to assess the public's degree of sensitivity. Training programs should be balanced, adapted to the situation as needed.

PARTICIPANT: The question is what one does in order to save lives, what information must be passed on to achieve this goal. The media have a free hand here to a great extent; we can only try to influence them in the desired direction.

PARTICIPANT: Israel, of course, presents a special situation in which the public is highly educated and aware of problems concerning terrorism. But we should not underrate the degree to which the public in any other country can be educated. For example, people in London were panicky for a while when IRA bombings first became commonplace and preventive measures were being taken; after a time, however, it became part of the accepted normality of life. Of course, public behavior does depend a lot on national temperament.

PARTICIPANT: People become desensitized as they become used to things. Israelis do not panic when they see a man with a gun, because it is a normal scene. In Rhodesia (Zimbabwe) or Northern Ireland it is the same. The security problem is of the highest priority, and the public must become accustomed to it.

PARTICIPANT: I am not sure the idea of getting used to a situation is sufficient in order to reduce sensitivity to it. I think getting used to a threatening situation should be combined with counter or security activity. The public cannot simply become accustomed to failures or to daily losses. There is a need for action in which the civilian population participates as well. However, there should be a balance between operational activity that limits any terrorist activity and the picture presented to the public concerning the situation.

PARTICIPANT: In countries such as England, Germany, or Israel, where there is a state television, the latter can be used to counterbalance the threat of terrorism to a certain degree and serve as a helpful educational tool for the public.

PARTICIPANT: There is another aspect of sensitivity that should not be disregarded. I do not think there is a clear-cut distinction that in one case makes the problem of sensitivity nonexistent, and in another makes the problem so complex that it cannot be dealt with. Although we Israelis appear to be perfectly desensitized, there are definitely some issues concerning which we are overly sensitive at times. For example, there was the case where some seventy terrorists were released in return for one single Israeli hostage. As far as I could tell, there was no overly sensitized public; yet the political decision was made as if such a pressure existed. Such sensitivity cannot be handled by adequate security measures.

PARTICIPANT: The basic question is, do we retain our sensitivity towards other human beings? In Israel there is no question about this. Personally, I think we should hold on to that sensitivity.

PARTICIPANT: One of the reasons we are becoming desensitized to particular kinds of events is that we are beginning to have very clear expectations about these events; that is, we expect them to happen in market places, on buses, and so forth. Unintentionally, the stability of tactics used by the terrorists has desensitized the public to certain kinds of events. People can get used to anything, provided it has a pattern. The moment a slight change is introduced, sensitivity rises again.

PARTICIPANT: I am not sure the idea of getting used to a situation is sufficient in order to reduce sensitivity to it. I think getting used to a threatening situation should be combined with counter activity or security activity. The public cannot simply become used to failures or to everyday losses. There is a need for action wherein the civilian population participates as well.

PARTICIPANT: In many European countries, and certainly in places like Latin America, we witness the demoralization of the entire dominant group of community leaders because they have become targets of terrorist violence. This specific problem can only be dealt with by means of security measures, not through verbal desensitization alone.

PARTICIPANT: I think the knowledge and feeling that security measures are being practiced serve more to desensitize the public than the mere knowledge of patterns of events.

PARTICIPANT: One other helpful factor is that we manage to teach the population specific behavior patterns that enable the public to deal more calmly with the situation.

11

Terrorism and the Soviet Union

Yonah Alexander

Terrorism, the threatened and actual resort to ideological and political violence by nonstate groups for the purpose of achieving limited or extensive goals, has become a permanent feature of contemporary life, with grave implications for free societies. Recognizing the menace posed by terrorism to the rule of law, the safety of the individual, the stability of the state system, economic development, and the survival of democracy, Western nations have adopted various approaches to terrorism. Non-Communist countries spend billions of dollars annually on improving security and increasing protection for citizens and for civilian facilities. Special defensive measures have been developed for ensuring the safety of diplomats and government officials. More than a dozen nations have set up commando units designed to fight terrorists and rescue hostages from their grasp. Multinational corporations provide their executives with instructions on protecting themselves and their families, and spend huge sums safeguarding their investments.

But despite all efforts at control, the level of terrorist violence remains high. There are many reasons for this, but there is one dominant factor: the toleration, encouragement, and even support of terrorism by the Soviet Union. The purpose of this paper is to examine briefly Moscow's behavior within the framework of its revolutionary doctrine of peaceful coexistence and the implications of that behavior for the West.

It is becoming increasingly clear that ideological and political violence is, to paraphrase Carl von Clausewitz, a continuation of war by other means for the purpose of compelling an adversary to submit to specific or general demands.[1] Indeed, terrorism is escalating into a form of surrogate warfare,

---

1. Carl von Clausewitz, *On War*, vol. 1 (London and Boston: Routledge & Kegan Paul, 1968), pp. 2, 23.

whereby small groups are able, with direct and indirect state support, to conduct political warfare at the national level. Such groups may ultimately even succeed in altering the international balance of power.

It is not surprising, therefore, that the strategic thinking of Communist states, as exemplified by the Soviet Union's policies and actions, calls for the manipulation of terrorism as a suitable substitute for traditional warfare, which has become too expensive and too hazardous to be waged on the battlefield. By overtly and covertly resorting to nonmilitary techniques, and by exploiting low-intensity operations around the world, the Soviet Union is able to continue its revolutionary process against the democratic pluralism of the Free World, as well as against a wider target area.

Three points must be noted in analyzing this phenomenon. First, the scope and nature of Soviet involvement in terrorist activity—ranging from the political legitimization of violence to the supply of funds, training, arms and other operational support—has fluctuated over the years in accordance with Moscow's changing appreciation of its interests. Secondly, promotion of specific terrorist operations has often been no more than the largely unintended by-product of Soviet behavior at particular stages of its history. And finally, because of Russia's position as an undisputed superpower controlling or influencing to a greater or lesser extent the foreign policy conduct of other Socialist countries which subscribe to its ideological line, it is not always easy to determine whether a particular terrorist action or series of actions sponsored by one of these countries is, so to speak, home grown, or whether it is Moscow-inspired. Bulgaria, Cuba, Czechoslovakia, East Germany, North Korea, and Vietnam spring to mind in this context. The support provided by these countries to various Communist and non-Communist terrorist movements in both developed and developing countries is generally attributed to the decision makers in the Kremlin.

Socialist states, then, serve both as intermediaries between the Soviet Union and terrorists, and as essential actors in assisting the promotion of ideological and political violence throughout the world.[2]

In sum, terrorism, whether directly or indirectly backed by the Soviet Union or independently initiated, is an indispensable tactical tool in the Communist struggle for power and influence within and among nations. In relying on this supplementary instrument, Moscow aims at achieving strategic ends when the use of armed force is deemed either inappropriate or ineffective. The broad goals the Soviet Union hopes to gain from terrorism include the following:

---

2. For some details on assistance given to terrorists by various governments in recent years, see, for instance, *Congressional Record*, vol. 123 (May 9, 1977), S7253.

1. Influencing developments in neighboring countries. For example, Moscow planted subversive Communist seeds in Iran for decades, contributed by proxy to the fall of the pro-Western shah, and is currently helping local Marxist-Leninist factions in Iran to prepare the requisite conditions for the overthrow of the revolutionary Islamic government.[3]
2. Drawing non-Communist states into the Soviet alliance system or at least into the Soviet sphere of influence. For example, Moscow's activities in Portugal—ranging from subsidizing the local Communist party to infiltrating the administrative machinery of the country—culminated in chaos and almost enabled the revolutionaries to seize power.[4]
3. Helping to create new states in which it will have considerable influence as a result of its support of those countries' claims for self-determination. The Soviet assistance rendered to the Palestine Liberation Organization aims at achieving this end.[5]
4. Weakening the political, economic, and military infrastructure of anti-Soviet alliances such as NATO. A case in point is the Soviet support of the Irish Republican Army (IRA). Moscow hopes that if violence in Ulster continues, Britain, a member of NATO, will be weakened as a potential adversary.[6]
5. Initiating strategic proxy operations in distant geographic locations where direct conventional military activities requiring long-distance logistics are impractical. For instance, the Kremlin's manipulation of the South West African People's Organization (SWAPO) aims at setting up a Marxist regime with a pro-Soviet orientation and thus gaining strategic and economic advantages in this region.[7]

Russia's justification of the use of terrorism as a legitimate political tool has its ideological roots in the works of the founders of orthodox Marxism-Leninism and other prominent Communist authors. To a greater or lesser extent they all advocated the employment of confrontation tactics, including terrorism, for achieving Communist aims. In *Das Kapital*, Karl

---

3. *The New York Times*, June 16, 1979. See also James A. Bill, *The Politics of Iran* (Columbus, Ohio: Charles E. Merrill, 1972); and Marvin Zonis, *The Political Elites of Iran* (Princeton: Princeton University Press, 1971).

4. On recent developments, see "Europe," Risks International Report, February 1979, pp. 85–87. See also Michael Harsgor, *Portugal in Revolution* (Beverly Hills, California: Sage Publications, 1976).

5. *The New York Times*, June 11, 1979. See also Galia Golan, "The Soviet Union and the PLO" (London: IISS, Adelphi Papers, 1976).

6. See, for instance, J. Bowyer Bell, *The Secret Army: The IRA 1916-1974* (Cambridge, Mass.: MIT Press, 1974).

7. See, for example, Muriel Horrell, *Terrorism in Southern Africa* (Johannesburg: South Africa Institute of Race Relations, 1968); and Michael Morris, *Terrorism* (Cape Town: Howard Timmins, 1971).

Marx asserted: "Force (*Gewalt*) is the midwife of an old society which is pregnant with a new one."[8] Writing in 1848, Marx expressed a strong belief in the necessity for political violence: "Only one means exists to shorten the bloody death pangs of the old society and the birth pains of the new society, to simplify and concentrate them—revolutionary terrorism." A year later, he predicted that "when it is our turn, we shall not hide our terrorism."[9]

This belief in the necessity for violence persisted not only in the later writings of Marx, but also, with some modification, in the works of Lenin. He, too, held that the revolutionary struggle might appropriately include terrorism. Lenin and the Bolsheviks saw, for instance, the usefulness of terrorism as a tactic of disorganization of the czarist enemy and as a means of acquiring experience and military training. Writing in 1906, Lenin responded to critics of this approach by asserting that "no Marxist should consider partisan warfare (including political assassination) . . . as abnormal and demoralizing."[10] Indeed, terrorism was regarded by Lenin and his successors as a part of the proletarian revolution, but to be employed only under the direction of the party and only where conditions existed for its success.

Thus, from the first Marxist-Leninist revolution against czarism—when more than a thousand terrorist acts were perpetrated in Transcaucasia—to the present day, Moscow-oriented communism has encouraged and assisted terrorist groups which follow a strict party line and are highly centralized.

Insurgent movements—including the New Left, and even Trotskyists (working for the furtherance of international communism but generally hostile to the Soviet Union)—have also received some support from the Russians. Moreover, for considerations of political expediency rather than ideological solidarity, a great variety of sectarian, nationalist, separatist, and anarchist extremist groups have frequently been supported by the Soviet Union. Many of these movements have adopted Marxist ideologies as a "flag of convenience," rationalizing Marxism as a model for revolution against the state. Affiliation with the Soviet Union grants a sort of international respectability, affords a sense of affinity with other revolutionary movements, and guarantees some assurance of direct and indirect

---

8. Karl Marx, *Das Kapital* (Berlin: Dietz Verlag, 1962), reprint, p. 779.

9. Arnold Kunzli, *Karl Marx, Eine Psychographie* (Vienna, Frankfurt, Zurich: Europa Verlag, 1966), pp. 703, 712, and 715.

10. V.I. Lenin, "Partisan Warfare," in *Modern Guerrilla Warfare: Fighting Communist Guerrilla Movements 1941-1961*, ed. Franklin M. Osanka (New York: Free Press 1962), p. 68. See also V.I. Lenin, "Left-Wing Communism—An Infantile Disorder," in *Selected Works* (Moscow: Progress Publishers, 1975), vol. III, p. 301.

support by like-minded groups and socialist states. With the adoption of a Marxist philosophy, however, some of these terrorist movements have fallen victim to internal ideological debate, division, and conflict.

Notwithstanding such ideological differences, the Soviet Union does not hesitate to provide assistance to a multitude of groups, holding that social discord and political turmoil in "enemy" territory is likely to advance Moscow's cause. It would, however, be a gross exaggeration to assert that most terrorist operations are Soviet sponsored. As Lord Chalfont correctly observed: "I do not believe that the forces of international terrorism are centrally inspired or centrally controlled, but I do suggest that when it suits their purposes, the forces of international communism will support terror groups throughout the world."[11]

It is also true that practical considerations have dictated that Soviet policy towards terrorism must necessarily be adapted to changing circumstances. Moscow has long recognized that it, too, is vulnerable to various forms of terrorism. In fact, as early as the 1920s, Russia was the object of terrorist attacks by White Guard émigrés who used neighboring countries as operational bases. Exercising its right of self-defense, the Soviet Union sent troops into Mongolia and China to liquidate these bands.[12] During the interwar period, Moscow supported various international efforts to eliminate certain kinds of terrorism, particularly armed attacks.[13]

More recently, as a superpower with political, diplomatic, economic, and military interests all over the world, the Soviet Union has become increasingly vulnerable to various forms of terrorism, including the hijacking of Soviet aircraft, the assassination of Soviet officials and diplomats, and the bombing of Soviet embassies and trade missions.

For these reasons, Moscow has adopted a more cautious and restrained stand. Indeed, the activities of various terrorist groups, including some which espouse Marxist revolution, have even been branded as "adventurist." At times, the Soviet Union has also acted in concert with capitalist states in condemning subnational violence. It supported, for example, the United

---

11. Lord Chalfont, "Freedom in Danger: The External and Internal Threat," *Atlantic Community Quarterly* (Fall, 1976), pp. 234–325.

12. See, for example, Ian Brownlie, *International Law and the Use of Force by States* (Oxford, 1963), pp. 241–242.

13. See, for example, Treaty of Peace between Lithuania and the Soviet Union, signed on July 12, 1920, *British and Foreign State Papers*, CXIII, p. 1121; the protocol of the Riga Conference, March 30, 1922, to which Estonia, Latvia, Poland and Soviet Russia were parties, in J. Degras, *Soviet Documents on Foreign Policy* vol. I (London, 1951), p. 296; and Ian Brownlie, "International Law and the Activities of Armed Bands," *International and Comparative Law Quarterly*, VII (1958), pp. 720–721 for other agreements to which the Soviet Union has been a party in the years 1920–1932. For other Soviet attitudes on the question of terrorism, see J. Stone, *Aggression and World Order* (London, 1958).

Nations Declaration on Principles of International Law concerning Friendly Relations and Cooperation among States in Accordance with the Charter of the United Nations, adopted by the General Assembly as Resolution 2625 (XXV) on October 24, 1970. This document asserts, *inter alia*, that terrorist and other subversive activities organized and supported by one state against another are a form of unlawful use of force.

As a country with dissidents who sometimes perceive aerial hijacking as the only means of escaping to the West, the Soviet Union became a party to the 1970 Hague Convention for the Suppression of Unlawful Seizure of Aircraft and to the 1971 Montreal Convention for the Suppression of Unlawful Acts against the Safety of Civil Aviation. In addition, it has concluded bilateral agreements with Iran and Finland, which provide for the return of hijackers to the state which registered the aircraft.

Thus, the Soviet Union has clearly attempted to achieve a balance between opposition to terrorist activities to which it itself is vulnerable and support for operations that attempt to tear down the fabric of Western society and weaken other non-Socialist governments. For example, subtle psychopolitical encouragement of nonstate violence was provided by the Kremlin when it frustrated efforts to obtain United Nations backing for a comprehensive international convention for the prevention of terrorism. While affirming its opposition to "acts of terrorism ... such as the murder and kidnaping of foreign citizens and aerial hijacking,"[14] the Soviet Union refused to join the Western powers in applying to the term *international terrorism* a broad interpretation which would include acts committed by national liberation movements.[15]

Notwithstanding the discrepancy between the antiterrorist public stance of the Soviet Union and its actions, Moscow's support of ideological and political violence expanded in the post-Khrushchev era. Two major factors contributed to the Kremlin's determination to play a more active role. First, the turbulent 1970s saw some surprising developments in different quarters of the globe: the failure of the rural guerrilla movements in Latin America and the resort to urban guerrilla warfare and terrorism; the defeat of the Arabs in the June 1967 war and the subsequent rise of Palestinian terrorism; the Vietnam War and the widespread demonstrations against it; and the French students' revolt of 1968. Secondly, many subnational movements adopted a "comradeship" in their struggle against "imperialism," "capitalism," "international Zionism," and for the "liberation" of

---

14. United Nations General Assembly, 27th Session, UN DOC A/C 6/SR 1389, December 13, 1972, pp. 4–5.

15. United Nations General Assembly, UN DOC A/AC 160/I/ Add. 1, June 12, 1973; Ad Hoc Committee on International Terrorism, July 16–August 10, 1973, p. 26.

dependent peoples. As Ulrike Meinhof writes in her "Manifesto": "We must learn from the revolutionary movements of the world—the Vietcong, the Popular Front for the Liberation of Palestine, the Tupamaros, the Black Panthers."

Capitalizing on these welcome developments on the world scene, Moscow became intimately involved with a substantial number of terrorist groups, however misguided their operations might be designated. Of course, as a respected member of the "family of nations," the Kremlin could not openly support these movements, lest it jeopardize "peaceful" relations with various countries. The policy of détente, which has brought the Soviet Union considerable benefits, also dictated clandestine support.

Although the evidence is often circumstantial, it is clear that there exists a carefully developed terrorist infrastructure which serves Moscow's foreign policy objectives. The International Department of the Central Committee of the Communist Party of the Soviet Union (CPSU), the Soviet Security Police (KGB), and Soviet Military Intelligence (GRU) have played a major role in this process.

The CPSU, headed by Boris Ponomarev, has been the most important Soviet agency for the support of terrorism. For example, it established the Lenin Institute in Moscow (it is also known as the Institute of Social Studies, the Institute of Social Sciences, and the International School of Marxism-Leninism), directed by F.D. Ryshenko, with G.P. Chernikov and V.G. Pribytov as his deputies responsible for the supervision of the curriculum and liaison with the Central Committee of the party. Selected members of Western and Third World Communist parties following the Soviet line have been trained there in propaganda and psychological warfare as well as in armed and unarmed combat and guerrilla warfare.

The CPSU also built Moscow's Patrice Lumumba Friendship University, to serve as a base for the indoctrination and training of potential "freedom fighters" from the Third World who are not Communist party members. More specialized training in terrorism is provided at locations in Baku, Odessa, Simferopol, and Tashkent.[16]

The CPSU has also been involved in setting up terrorist groups for its own purposes. There is evidence, for example, that it had a hand in the establishment of the Solidarité and Aide et Amitié terrorist support network. Directed by Henri Curiel, a Communist Egyptian Jew who died in 1978, this organization has connections with some seventeen illegal groups, including the Popular Revolutionary Vanguard (VPR) in Brazil,

---

16. *Annual of Power and Conflict 1973-1974* (London: Institute for the Study of Conflict, 1974), pp. 230–258.

the Movement of the Revolutionary Left (MIR) in Uruguay and Chile, the Quebec Liberation Front (FLQ), and the African National Congress (ANC) in South Africa.[17]

Moreover, at its Moscow headquarters, the KGB established a special section for recruiting and training terrorists. According to several sources, Carlos—the "International Jackal"—is a product of the KGB. Originally recruited in Venezuela, Carlos studied under Col. Victor Simonov at Camp Mantanzas outside Havana, and was later sent to the Soviet Union for further training at the Patrice Lumumba Friendship University and other specialist institutions run by the KGB. It was Carlos who established liaison with Dr. Wadi Haddad, chief of operations for the Popular Front for the Liberation of Palestine (PFLP); with the German Red Army Faction (RAF); the Japanese Red Army (JRA); the Turkish Peoples' Liberation Army (TPLA); and the Italian Red Brigades.

Like the CPSU, both the KGB and the GRU have tried to establish various terrorist movements and to gain control of existing ones. V.N. Sakharov, a defecting KGB officer, has revealed that the KGB sought to form terrorist cells in Saudi Arabia and the smaller Arab states in the Persian Gulf and in Turkey. The Soviets also sought to penetrate and control the Palestinian movement in the early 1970s. Attempts have been made by KGB members to establish links with the IRA through the British and Irish Communist parties and the Marxist wing of the IRA itself. Moreover, since the KGB is believed to control the Cuban Intelligence Service (Direcion General de Intelligencia, or DGI), it is probably able to influence the activities of a number of Latin American and African Castroite terrorist groups.

The work of the KGB has been greatly facilitated by Soviet client states in Africa and Asia, including Algeria, Angola, Iraq, Libya, Mozambique, South Yemen, Tanzania, and Uganda. These countries have become centers for promoting terrorism in the Middle East and beyond the region, and thus serve the aims of Moscow.

Terrorist groups, aided directly and indirectly by the Soviet Union, are becoming increasingly potent and are even affecting the balance of power between the West and the Communist bloc. Since the lip service paid to détente and peaceful coexistence has not been accompanied by any manifest weakening of the Soviet ambition to achieve regional and global hegemony, the West must develop a realistic strategy to deal effectively with the Soviets' exploitation of terrorism as a tactical tool to disturb the status quo.

---

17. *Le Point*, June 21, 1976. See also John Barron, *KGB: The Secret Work of Soviet Secret Agents* (New York: Bantam Books, 1974), pp. 76–77.

Discussion

PARTICIPANT: My experience is that people do not readily accept the general line of Dr. Alexander's presentation: that the Soviet Union is the mastermind of international terror, that there is an international terrorist infrastructure aimed, conceived, and supported by the Soviet Union in order to weaken the democratic institutions. In order to convince people of this we must present facts concerning, for example, the Soviet backing in training terrorists and their leaders in the Soviet Union itself. I know very few hard facts to testify to this beyond a few episodes. Can we prove the overall planning and coordination in any way beyond the conjecture of a meeting at a given date and an act of terrorism taking place a day or a week later?

As to weapons, it is true that the standard weapon is Soviet-made, but that is still not enough proof to an observer who does not subscribe to a certain theory.

Bear in mind that the ideology behind what Dr. Alexander mentioned ties in with détente. Those in the Western world who support détente today demand very strong proof before they will accept the theory of Moscow's role in international terrorism, since support of this theory contradicts their support of détente. Without this proof we can perhaps convince ourselves, like the people who already subscribe to this theory, but we will not convince the West to take effective action. Thus, I would like to see some concrete facts presented here.

PARTICIPANT: I have some doubts with regard to the direct responsibility and planning of the Soviet Union with respect to international terrorism. On the contrary, I think there is a lot of evidence that terrorist organizations in various countries are in fact counterproductive for local communism and are apparently not at all influenced, run, or directed by the Soviet Union or the Communist establishment. It is true that the Soviet Union does help international terrorism indirectly by supplying arms and means to various organizations, but it seems that, for political reasons, the Soviets close their eyes to the uses these weapons will be put. I think there is very little evidence to connect the Soviet Union directly with international terrorism as we see it today.

PARTICIPANT: The Soviet Union may have contributed to the spread of terrorism indirectly by weakening the security services of democratic countries. We find this in countries like Italy and to a lesser extent in Germany. In other countries, too, there has been a very concentrated attack by local left-wing elements against the security services, which to a certain extent has led to the weakening and near destruction of local security systems, thereby enabling local terrorism to spread. Whether this was done for the purpose of spreading terrorism or not is a separate question. Presumably, the real reason was to weaken the security system in its operations against local Communist activities; but indirectly, it led to the promotion of terrorism.

PARTICIPANT: Let me try to summarize what seems to me is emerging as an issue of debate thus far. A case has been made that terrorism often serves Moscow's interest; and I do not think there is a major disagreement on this issue. I also think that there may be some Soviet exploitation of terrorism in a political sense, that is, by calling attention to its existence in certain countries. The Soviet Union may exploit terrorism to its advantage in a political sense; and thus far, I have not heard any major challenge to that. It has been pointed out that the Soviet Union does indeed provide encouragement and moral support, in some cases ideological support, to some movements that have used terrorist tactics. Also, it has been noted that the Soviet Union may directly or indirectly be providing various kinds of support for certain groups which meet its criteria as movements of national liberation. A point was raised that there are cases in which local terrorist groups may be operating contrary to Moscow's interests or the interests of the local Communist party; and perhaps a distinction should be made between those groups in line with Moscow and those groups operating contrary to Moscow. It has also been mentioned that the Soviet Union may provide indirect support for certain terrorist groups through pro-Soviet countries, such as Syria.

The questions which arise as major issues, however, are: What is the evidence for Moscow's direct support of terrorist movements and terrorist activities? What kind of support are we talking about, beyond encouragement? Do terrorists undergo training in the USSR? Are they all getting their orders from Moscow, are they all on Moscow's payroll? Another area that gives rise to questions is whether this support, be it moral or physical, leads to any sort of control or coordination. Are the Soviets really running terrorism? Does terrorism, with or without Moscow's aid, pose a danger to democracy? Does it have the inherent power of altering the world balance of power as it exists?

PARTICIPANT: I think it is a bit grandiose to view terrorism as influencing the world balance of power. It is very hard for me to see how the balance of power between West and East is going to be affected by terrorism as we now know it, unless you are predicting it will escalate to levels unknown at the moment.

PARTICIPANT: It has been said that terrorism endangers the survival of democracy. In my opinion, this exaggerates the situation. Currently, terrorism is no more than simply a nuisance to democracies. I must reiterate the fact that many more people are killed by accidents and other forms of violence than by terrorism. Why is it, then, that we do not deal with those problems first?

PARTICIPANT: We have to look at the evidence; otherwise, we are just theorizing on a very sensitive and very complicated subject. I would like to consider some of the points raised and respond briefly to specific questions.

With regard to the threat to the continuity of democracy—to me, terrorism is tyranny. By its very nature it is a challenge to democracy, for it represents rule by the minority. As to the extent of terrorism, we should not talk in terms of how many people are killed or wounded, but about the wider psychological impact. This is a very significant factor, which we sometimes tend to minimize. If there is an increase in terrorist activity and the government is unable to cope with it, the public is obviously going to lose faith in the government.

When we discuss terrorism, at present we talk about conventional means—some of which are quite dramatic, such as the use of SA-7 missiles to shoot down a civilian aircraft. But there is no end to the imagination of terrorists. Obviously, there is no end to the imagination of security forces. In a democratic society, however, overreaction by the government threatens the freedoms which such a society seeks to preserve. Exactly this kind of criticism has been voiced against the reaction of the German government, a democratic government. Even in the United States there are those who object to being searched at airports, as if this were a violation of one of their basic freedoms.

As to the role of the Soviet Union—it seems to me that there is enough evidence, however ambiguous it may be, to suggest the Soviets are directly or indirectly involved in terrorism. The fact that the Soviet Union abstains from voting against terrorism at the United Nations and tries to obstruct UN action concerning acts against terrorism, such as the attempt of the United States to pass a UN comprehensive treaty dealing with terrorism, is in itself evidence. Even lack of action is, to me, indirect support of terrorism. Obviously, there are enough facts to indicate that the Soviet Union is playing a role, however circumstantial the evidence is.

With regard to statistics—I think the general trend is well known. Take, for example, terrorist activities in Western Europe. Between 1970 and 1978, worldwide, there were 5,529 cases of terrorist incidents of all types. In Western Europe alone during this period, there were 2,607 incidents, 1,840 of which occurred between 1976 and 1978. Moreover, because of the role of the media, terrorists today are able to achieve far greater impact than their revolutionary counterparts in the nineteenth century. At any rate, I think we have enough data to indicate that there has been an increase in terrorism, at least in some areas, and this trend is expected to continue.

As far as the balance of power is concerned, I do not think we can reach a final conclusion and say that the terrorists will surely alter it dramatically. I suggest only that terrorism is an instrument, a tool of politics used to advance certain aims. The Soviet Union, like China for a period, has used it against particular targets. I am not saying that in terms of the balance of power there is a dramatic shift today or that we are talking about an immediate change. It is a slow process. Yet, from the studies made it seems that if some of these small groups were to have access to sophisticated weaponry (though this would be a very difficult task), their impact would increase considerably. Not that at this particular stage in history we should be too concerned about it; at the same time, I do not think we should ignore it.

PARTICIPANT: I would like to look at specific cases now. For example, what has the Soviet Union done for the Red Army Faction in West Germany? What specifically has Moscow done for the IRA or for the Basques? What specifically has it done for the Red Brigades, what indeed has it done for the Palestinian terrorists? In the United States, despite a great effort to find a direct connection between the Soviet Union and various terrorist and subversive groups during the Vietnam War period, the intelligence community was, at least publicly, unable to find persuasive evidence of a direct link between Moscow or other Communist countries and these movements. Money, weapons, training—what is the evidence for such support? If there is a direct example of provision by the Soviet Union of money, weapons, training, direction, or control, let us examine it carefully and list some of the examples (within, of course, the boundaries imposed by the use of public sources).

PARTICIPANT: In the course of the last twelve years, Israel has detained several thousand suspected and convicted terrorists. If, for example, one of them proved to have been trained in the Soviet Union or by a Soviet instructor in the Middle East, that would not, I think, constitute Soviet involvement. But if fifty of these terrorists were proven to have links with the Soviet Union, then I think that would have constituted evidence admissible by circles outside this group. If we are unable to convince ourselves in this forum, which is obviously more prone to believe and support this thesis of the Soviet role, then very few outside of this circle will accept this theory. As a result, public sympathy toward terrorism will not be diminished. If anything concrete can come out of such seminars, it is a means by which to convince decision makers in democratic societies to take some actions which might indeed infringe on certain liberties of the public. We can only do this by presenting solid evidence of Soviet involvement.

PARTICIPANT: How many of the Palestinian terrorists captured in Israel could be traced back as having had direct training in the Soviet Union?

PARTICIPANT: I think it can be safely said, and I shall show some evidence later, that thousands of Palestinians were trained in the Soviet bloc countries. There is no doubt about it. There is also no doubt that most of the weapons used by these terrorists are Soviet weapons.

PARTICIPANT: I find I have to be the devil's advocate, because we are becoming too used to looking at the Soviet Union as a factor playing a dominant role in terrorism, which leads us to overlook other factors. What about the United States? When the United States refrained from supporting a democratic regime in Rhodesia [Zimbabwe], was that not an implicit support of terrorism? When the United States refrains from supporting [Nicaragua's Anastasio] Somoza, is that not an act of support for a terrorist movement? When the United States maintains contacts with the PLO, is that not support for them? Why do we always scrutinize the Soviet Union in this context and refrain from examining the role the United States is playing?

PARTICIPANT: I think it would be very difficult to agree on what would constitute adequate evidence. It is easier for us to agree on what counts for inadequate evidence. Three things can be said here. First, it would be a mistake to equate outcomes with causes and to say that, just because terrorism serves Soviet interests, it is an indication that the Soviets are responsible. With respect to indirect support, I think the fact that a state supported by the Soviet Union supports terrorism is not even an indirect indication of Soviet support for terrorism. The government of Israel, for example, is doing many things contrary to United States policies. By similar logic, in supporting Israel the United States supports everything Israel does. That, of course, is untrue. Therefore, such a conclusion concerning the Soviet Union is also false. The third point concerns the problem of escalation. Whenever we say there is little evidence for Soviet involvement in terrorism that can affect the balance of power, we always add that this is the situation at present, but that there is a process of escalation in technology that can affect the balance of power drastically in the Soviets' favor. I disagree with this statement very strongly. I think that if there is an escalation in the means used by terrorists, the result, essentially, would be a Soviet withdrawal from supporting terrorists, because the Soviet Union hates circumstances where the situation gets out of control. I think that if a number of groups were to possess all kinds of weapons and tools that would strongly increase their capabilities, that would constitute a very strong constraint on Soviet support. The Soviets, I believe, would back off from supporting terrorists if circumstances were such that they would have very little control over the events, or if the events would have the potential of creating very serious outcomes.

PARTICIPANT: As to the problem of definitions, the questions are: What do we define as a terrorist group, and what do we define as a group supported by the Soviets? What is international terrorism and terrorism in general? What is the use of terror as a tool? Such definitions may help us delineate the role of the Soviet Union here. I think that, generally speaking, we have to divide terrorist groups into at least three main categories: groups that define themselves as national liberation movements and are viewed as such by the Soviets; groups that may be called separatist groups, meaning groups that try to obtain more rights in their own countries, such as the Basques or the Kurds; and groups with very vague aims, whom we may call anarchists. If we agree about this general classification of groups and try to see where we can fit in the support of the Soviet Union, we can easily conclude that when it concerns liberation movements, there is no question about Soviet support and aid in all manners mentioned—money, training, weapons, and so on. On the other hand, I think there is no clear indication or evidence of Soviet support given to any separatist group in the world. I think the Soviets do not want to be involved in any such activity, although, in the end, the actions of the groups serve Soviet goals. Unrest in the Western democracies no doubt serves the goals of the Soviet Union.

PARTICIPANT: I think we have a fourth type of group: the revolutionary group. This is the group that wants to change the regime in its own country; yet it is not anarchist. Its members are terrorists because they use means of terror. This fourth kind of political terrorism does not really represent a threat to democracy, but only to regimes that exist within the boundaries of the free world. We have a feeling that should this kind of regime be overrun, the balance of power will shift and this will be to the advantage of the Soviet Union. I am not sure that this feeling is justified in the long run, because the outcome depends on the kind of new regime that emerges in place of the old one. Even if the balance of power changes, you cannot classify the change as a direct threat to democracy. It is an indirect threat because it makes the West more feeble, because you lose some of your allies; but it is not a threat to the democratic system. In general, however—and I think that this is a very strong point—our personal freedom is becoming more and more limited because of terrorism.

PARTICIPANT: I generally accept the classification of terrorist organizations as they were categorized here. Nevertheless, I am not convinced that aid given by the Soviet Union to what they consider liberation movements is necessarily aid given to terrorism. It is true—and here I refer to the evidence mentioned before—that there were hundreds, if not thousands, of Palestinians who were trained in the Soviet Union, including training in the use of arms and explosives. But to what extent was this done with the intention of preparing them to carry out terrorist acts? This training, which included political indoctrination, was given for the purpose of preparing these movements for what was considered as more military than terrorist action. Therefore, I am not quite certain that this proves any direct Soviet support for terrorist operations.

PARTICIPANT: We have to emphasize the counterconsiderations on the part of the Soviets, that is, the constraints imposed on the Soviets that limit or preclude their support for terrorist organizations. This raises important questions. Do the Soviets distinguish among the different types of organizations in determining the kinds of support they give? My guess is that they do not give these groups all they want. If we take the Palestinian guerrilla organizations, for example—and we have about eight of them— I think the Soviets do differentiate between the more Marxist and the less Marxist; the extremists and the nonextremists. As mentioned before, they might differentiate between organizations they consider liberation movements and others. They give weapons on a very selective basis. Do the Soviets differentiate amongst kinds of terrorist activities? Do they differentiate among hijacking, massive assassinations, small-scale activities? They may not support massive assassinations at times because support may bring about unwanted retaliation.

PARTICIPANT: We have not dealt sufficiently with the question of whether terrorism is or is not a threat to democracy. There cannot be any doubt whatsoever that the use of terrorism undermines the conception of democratic civilization as we know it. Terrorism is the use of blackmail instead of the rule of law, and in that sense it certainly undermines democracy.

PARTICIPANT: The statement that terrorism undermines democracy is an understatement, because terrorism actually feeds on democracy; it uses the characteristics of democracy as its weapons. It has already been demonstrated that the actual damage inflicted by terrorism is very small, even relative to traffic accidents. The impact of terrorism is through the inherent structure of democracy—by the effect it has on democratic life, on the regime and political structures, and in terms of the state of mind of people. Thus, it feeds on democracy like a cancer.

We have also seen that democracy has no strong countermeasures to terrorism. Therefore, the threat is a very serious one, because if democracy has no strong countermeasures, it may lose the battle—it may limit people's freedom or even shift from being a democracy to being some other system. This is an inherent danger and a problem of democracy. We do not see the success of terrorism in countries which are not democratic because when terror groups there become dangerous, they are wiped out, as they were in Jordan, for example. There, an all-out war was fought to wipe out terrorism. The danger lies within the democratic nations.

PARTICIPANT: What effects has terrorism had so far? Iran was mentioned in terms of the effects on the balance of power. But is Iran a case of the success of terrorism? There is no question that as far as principles are concerned, terrorism opposes democracy and therefore is a threat to democracy. But I would not say that one can conclude that by definition terrorism is antidemocratic, because terrorism was also the foundation of democracies in previous eras.

PARTICIPANT: As a historian, I would challenge severely the idea that today's democracies were built by the use of terrorist tactics. I would hesitate to credit the success of the American Revolution to the use of anything that by today's standards falls into the category of terrorism. In order to show that this is not some kind of an American chauvinistic remark, I would say that a good Marxist historian, looking back upon the Soviet revolution, would also give no great credit to the Black Banner or other movements of late nineteenth century Russia in bringing about the success of the Soviet revolution. I challenge the claim that what Palestinians or other ideologically oriented groups do today is not different from what was done in Boston two hundred years ago.

PARTICIPANT: Talking about the extent to which terrorism is to be considered a threat to democracy, I think we can examine Germany and Italy—two democratic countries that are always in the headlines as far as terrorism in Europe is concerned. Is the daily routine of the average citizen in these countries affected by terrorism? I am under the impression that Lufthansa flights are cancelled at times and that there are fewer passengers on Alitalia. But generally, I do not see any change in those countries. The daily life goes on as usual.

PARTICIPANT: There was an earlier remark concerning the distinction between the degree to which the average citizen is directly affected by terrorism and the perceptions of that individual. It is true that in the recent history of Germany, only twenty-eight people were killed due to terrorist acts. Even in Italy, where some two thousand terrorist incidents occurred in one year, the average citizen has not been seriously threatened. The lifespan of the average Italian has not been greatly reduced by terrorist activity. Nonetheless, the perceptions of the average Italian, German, or American (for whom the terrorist threat has been even smaller) may be quite different. I refer back to the public opinion poll that indicates that 90 percent of the American public believe that terrorism is a serious worldwide problem and, by a ratio of 55:30, they support the creation of a special international force that would operate anywhere in the world to apprehend and summarily execute terrorists. This is public opinion in a democracy. I recently went to Italy and saw the preliminary results of a poll taken by the Italian Communist party (PCI), investigating the public's attitude towards terrorism and appropriate countermeasures. The preliminary results of this poll show that the average Italian, even the average Italian party member, is deeply offended by terrorism and feels directly threatened. If these results accurately capture the sentiments throughout Italy (the poll was taken in Turin), then people in Italy are willing to support all sorts of extremely repressive measures in order to deal with the terrorist threat. Therefore, I think it is important to separate actual threat from perceptions.

PARTICIPANT: I am glad that we have reached some general consensus on the role of Soviet support. The original paper presented here was challenged on the basis that the evidence to support it is ambiguous. There were a number of remarks about different types of support, with agreement that the Soviets may provide more indirect support and encouragement, perhaps less direct support. Questions were raised regarding distinctions between movements and the kinds of organizations that get Soviet support. It was generally accepted that movements of national liberation probably receive more support than those that are anarchistic or nihilistic. A comment was made regarding the state of our knowledge as to how the Soviets distinguish between the qualities of support they will give to the various groups—what they will give, what they will withhold, under what conditions—and what constraints, in terms of various kinds of tactics, are exercised. It is certainly not simply a matter of providing unlimited support for certain kinds of movements as opposed to no support for others. It is much more complicated and sophisticated than that.

I think it was generally accepted that the persistence of terrorism has had a harmful effect: it has diminished the degree of personal freedom. The fact that now people have to subject themselves to searches when boarding airplanes or the fact that there are more controls are due examples. Whether or not this constitutes a threat to democracy is not a point which was universally accepted at this meeting.

Governments which are strongly democratic have reacted to the threat of terrorism with very cautious limitations on personal freedom in specific areas. Governments which were weak democracies or already had totalitarian tendencies, or where democracy was not well established—such as Turkey or Uruguay—reacted characteristically with authoritarian measures. With regard to the threat posed to the world balance of power or to democracy in a broader concept of that word, we have seen again some losses to the so-called free world by some of the states on the edge of it, whether one talks about Iran, or potentially Nicaragua. Finally, whether or not their loss or the change of political complexion will, in the long run, affect the world balance of power is a question that perhaps we can reserve for future historians.

PARTICIPANT: Returning to the question of convincing the public of the necessity of countermeasures, my own experience in the United States is that there is support for the political goals behind the PLO's terrorist acts. The answers I got to my pleas for countermeasures included suggestions which usually meant appeasing the terrorists, giving in to them on certain issues. If we are to come out of this conference with anything useful, it should include ways of changing public reaction and generating media as well as public support for strict countermeasures.

12

Forms of State Support to Terrorism and the Possibility of Combating Terrorism by Retaliating against Supporting States

M. Asa

In our discussions thus far, we have noted that terrorism has usually been employed as an instrument to achieve particular goals. Not only individuals, but states, too, have given aid to terrorists, directly or indirectly. We can now discuss the forms of support granted to terrorism by states and the possibilities of handling this problem of support. The first point shall deal with potential support.

Since terrorism is a tool whose aim generally is to achieve long-range political targets, the political support of terrorism is no less important than its material support. We often emphasize quantitative aspects—the number of missiles, the amount of ammunition, and the capability of terrorists to produce nuclear weapons. These parameters are necessary in order to conduct terroristic warfare. But terror groups have other considerations as well:

1. Theorists do not specify in detail what is necessa in order to accomplish a revolution. A terrorist group has to decide what should be done and attempt to carry it out.
2. Political terrorism is aimed at long-range targets. Terrorism has a rather low strategic value, but it has a catalytic potential, such as precipitating a war. For that purpose, the practical backing and the political support of a state is a crucial factor.
3. The mass media are very important for terrorists and can serve as another way to gain political support. Mass media are usually handled by a national or an international community or granted to terrorist groups by a state backer.

In examining the matter of support to terrorists, we should ask five questions, focusing especially on Palestinian terrorism: Which states support terrorism? What is the ideological motivation behind such support? What form does such support take? What benefits accrue to states that give support to Palestinian organizations? How can such support be prevented?

Turning to our first query, almost all of the Arab countries support the Palestinian terrorists. If we are to single out the more active ones, we find that the radical states—Libya, Syria, Algeria, and the People's Democratic Republic of Yemen (PDRY)—provide the greatest support. All these states have a common denominator in that they are the flagbearers of radicalism within the Arab community. All of them are also heavily supported by the USSR. It is not coincidental that all four of these countries, along with the Palestine Liberation Organization itself, constituted what they called the "steadfastness front," or the "rejection front" in 1977-78. The pretext for the establishment of this front was Anwar el-Sadat's peace initiative, but this was only the trigger. The overall strategic value of this rejection front was (and still is) rather low. Their attempt to institutionalize it failed. Though the front is not active today as such, we still find that on every political issue raised concerning the Middle East, most of these countries adopt the same position.

Important political support is given to the PLO by the oil countries, particularly Saudi Arabia. We usually think of Saudi support as only political. Recently, however, we learned that the Saudies are backing the Fatah—the main faction of the PLO—also in the military sense. Kuwait, too, has a key role in supporting the PLO, mainly because of the large Palestinian community in the Persian Gulf area.

The Arab commitment to the PLO creates an ideology and practice of supporting terrorist factions. The PLO and the Arab world have been very closely interlinked for a long time now. The PLO was founded in 1964, and within that year the Arab countries held their first summit. The Palestinians have attended all Arab summits except for the Amman summit of November 1980, which was boycotted by the PLO and the rejection front countries.

Although the PLO calls for self-reliance, advocating the promotion of the Palestinian cause by Palestinian means, in practice, Fatah stresses the Palestinians' need to rely upon various important Arab sources. The Arabs really brought the PLO to its present posture as a world terrorist power; it is mainly the Arab political support that explains the notable political achievements of the PLO.

Some of the Arab political support for the PLO is aimed at transforming larger terrorist acts into political revenues. An example can be drawn from what happened in Ankara in June 1979. Four Palestinian members of the

Eagles of the Palestinian Revolution (which is believed to be a cover name for the pro-Syrian Saiqa faction) attacked the Egyptian embassy in Ankara. The Syrian-supported Saiqa was the actual active party; the PLO, the umbrella organization. The Kuwaitis mediated in order to free the Egyptian hostages, and finally, the PLO received official recognition by the Turkish government, allowing them to open an office with diplomatic status in Turkey. This is a tangible example of the Arab political support for the PLO.

As to other forms of aid, attention must be paid to material and financial support. Since 1978, the PLO has received approximately $150-200 million per year, granted through an inter-Arab institutionalized system. Receipt of such funds from an international body of sovereign states makes the PLO unique among terrorist organizations. In addition to this continuous, institutionalized financial support, we find ad hoc support for the various terrorist factions. Muammar Qaddafi, for example, favors certain factions and thus grants them financial support. A group that achieves a spectacular feat of terror is likely to draw indirect benefits, either through such ad hoc financial support or in the form of arms delivery. There is also periodic support, meaning an on-going flow of money, delivered to the rejection front organizations by Iraq, Libya, or Algeria. This is done mainly because the institutionalized financial support goes directly to the Fatah and not to other organizations. The PLO's arsenal today contains cannons, rocket launchers, and other sophisticated weapons. The weapons are usually imported and unloaded in Arab ports. The list of suppliers is well known. They are East Germany, Czechoslovakia, Bulgaria, North Korea, and Cuba. One can predict that Hungary will join this list.

Operational support may appear in various forms. First of all, training. The type of training a PLO member gets is very important; he becomes acquainted with sophisticated technology and advanced weapons.

Additional forms of support are documentation—including false documents and diplomatic passports—and shelter. There is "night shelter" all over the world for some terrorists sought by local police. Europeans, Japanese—all may take temporary shelter in certain Arab countries.

There is also an exchange of intelligence between the terrorists and certain sovereign states. Of course, there is the access to means of communications, including provision of diplomatic pouches and other channels for transferring data or materials. The aforementioned forms of operational support given by Arab states to the PLO are duplicated by the PLO, which itself offers international terrorist groups assistance in similar fields.

Support through training, weapons, and documentation is also given to the Palestinian organizations by the Soviet Union or her proxies. Let me point out that in 1975 three Cuban diplomats were expelled from Paris after supporting the Carlos network; and in South America, in the beginning of the seventies, some Soviets were involved in a similar case.

Support for the Palestinian groups by granting them the freedom of action and development in Arab countries is, of course, very important to the terrorist community. The ability to carry arms, to wear uniforms, to have offices, and to recruit new members ensures the terrorists a firm, constant base for their existence and actions.

A unique form of support is the handing over of extraterritorial areas to the terrorists. Such is the sanctuary that existed in Jordan during the end of the 1960s and was established in Lebanon in the Fatahland. Today, between the Zaharani and the Litani rivers in Lebanon there are five thousand PLO members. Extraterritorial bases for terrorists can be found in other parts of the world as well. There are similar sanctuaries in Angola or Zambia. Terrorist groups that are active against either Namibia or other parts of the South African Republic use these sanctuaries. But the Fatahland has a unique connotation—this is also a political term because it was granted Arab legitimacy. The Fatahland is a true sanctuary, where legal permission has been granted to PLO members to have their bases and their weapons and to carry out operations against Israel. This was granted to the PLO in the 1969 Cairo agreement in general form, although the scale and dimensions of PLO presence in that area have grown far beyond the boundaries mandated by the original agreement.

Another form of support is ideological support, which I think brings about internal cohesion for the Palestinian terrorists within the PLO community and contributes to what Professor Dror called "the nation building effect." This ideological support has attracted sympathy all over the world. The revolutionary idea was taken up by various supporters, including the Arab states, superpowers, and newspapers and other mass media means. The interesting point is that the Palestinians themselves are a unique ethnic group within the Arab community, and they are a very stimulating factor in this field. They are extremely proud of being the intellectual vanguard of Arab thought and writing. Naturally, they skillfully use the mass media of various Arab countries. For example, most of the newspapers in the Persian Gulf area are being published by local Palestinians. Indeed, they have a very independent network for their writings.

To characterize the support given to the PLO, we find that at any given time there is at least one support country whose backing is vital to the PLO's existence and operation. The importance of this kind of support is exemplified by the Kurds. When their Iranian backing was cut off, their anti-Iraqi rebellion died rapidly. With regard to the Palestinian terrorist groups, we find more than one country supporting them.

From the geographic point of view, there is a great similarity between the Middle Eastern model and the South African one. Geographic propinquity can dictate the form and the level of support given to a terrorist group. This is a very important lesson to learn, mainly from the Middle Eastern example. Syria and Lebanon are potential territorial bases for Palestinian terror activity, as is Jordan, for they share the status of confrontation states in the Arab world. Examination of the loose political coalition called the "steadfastness front" shows that Syria attained its dominant posture within this coalition because it has the status of a confrontation state. This means that states such as Libya, Algeria, and the PDRY, which do not necessarily agree with the Syrian concept, submitted on various issues to Syrian conceptions concerning the question of the Israeli-Arab conflict because they acknowledged the importance of Syria as a confrontation state.

This leads us to examine the Syrian role in supporting terror. During 1978 the Syrians were very willing to take part in terror acts carried out by Palestinians. They helped Fatah prepare an "inferno ship" in Latakia port. This was a ship loaded with rocket launchers that went through the Mediterranean Sea to the Gulf of Aqaba. The Syrians were directly involved in the preparation of that attempted terror act. To that we should add the operations of the Saiqa faction outside the Middle East. This is a unique pattern in Syrian behavior. In the political field, there was rapprochement between George Habash, the leader of the Popular Front for the Liberation of Palestine (PFLP), and the Syrians. It should be mentioned here that in 1968 George Habash was held in a Syrian prison and for ten years thereafter avoided entering Syria.

One cannot overlook the fact that the Palestinians continue to act freely in Lebanon in spite of the Litani operation. Although the Syrians have had the opportunity to tighten control over the Palestinians' actions in Lebanon, they have not done so. On the contrary, the Syrians are supplying the Palestinians with heavy arms, including cannons and rocket launchers, which the terrorists use to attack Israel's northern front. It seems only natural that the party who supplies the arms or holds the ammunition has a say on the subject of whether or not terror actions should be taken.

Thus, the Syrians have used their support for the Palestinians to strengthen their own position in the Arab world, particularly during the crucial period of 1977-79.

For these reasons, it is not incidental that a country like Iraq became more involved in the Palestinian cause only in 1971-72. Iraq is not a confrontation state geographically. Likewise South Africa—Tanzania, which is not so close geographically to the area of combat, mainly supports the South African terrorist groups politically. General Harkabi said that the frontline of terrorism or guerrilla warfare is often not very clearly demarcated. In the Middle East, the proximity of the country supporting terrorist acts is of prime importance. Various examples all over the world prove the importance of physical proximity: in Greece, the ability of the rebels to cross the border to Yugoslavia and Albania; in Algiers, the ability of crossing over to Tunisia; the Kurds, crossing from Iraq into Iran.

The sanctuary not too close to the target state is used for various facets of training. We find various camps for training in Libya and in the PDRY. This is similar to what we find in countries surrounding South Africa. Within these training camps are people of various nationalities training terrorists; East Europeans, Cubans, and Palestinians work together.

It is not sufficient to discuss only Arab support to the PLO; we should also examine the benefits the PLO can offer the various Arab states. Arab countries use the PLO factions for their national policies, even where it is difficult to find a connection between these policies and PLO aims. The Iraqis operated a faction called Black June, led by Abu Nidal, for purely inter-Arab struggles. This is a classic application of a minor scale surrogate war. Abu Nidal acted against targets in Jordan, Syria, and even Egypt. To this date, the organization has rarely attacked Israeli or "imperialist" targets. In 1979, the Abu Nidal faction was pushed into a corner because of the Syrian-Iraqi rapprochement. This rapprochement has made it no longer acceptable to the Iraqis to support Abu Nidal's actions against Syria.

Another example is the Syrians' use of the Saiqa faction, which really acts as a kind of front organization for the Syrian Ba'ath party. In 1975-76 the Syrians launched the Saiqa against other Palestinian groups. This was, in fact, a preliminary stage before the heavy Syrian involvement in Lebanon using a Palestinian faction to do the dirty work for it. It caused the Saiqa such an identity crisis that the leader of this faction at that time had to flee from Lebanon, and the Saiqa was expelled for a certain period of time from PLO institutions.

On the political level, the Saiqa acts as a Syrian protegé within the PLO umbrella organization. The Syrians also used the Saiqa to attract the pro-Iraqi factions when they wanted to create a stronger coalition, perhaps against Arafat, perhaps in order to prove their strength within the PLO as part of the power struggle against Iraq. As a final development, the Syrians activated the Saiqa outside the Middle East. They have acted in France, Austria, Egypt, and lately, in Turkey. This latest act was perpetrated in order to prove that Syria is the leading Arab factor against Egypt. Syria did not deny involvement in the Saiqa when its activities were published in Syrian newspapers in April 1979. The description of this group, under the cover name of the Eagles of the Palestinian Revolution, makes it clear that it is under Syrian auspices. The Saiqa also participated in the Syrian strategic cover-up plan that took place before the October War. On that occasion, they took over a train of Jewish immigrants near Vienna. According to Syrian explanations, this was to have made the Israelis concentrate on this terror act and not on the preparations in the Golan Heights.

There are a few conclusions that might be drawn from this use of terrorist groups for aims of national policies. First, when there is a contradiction between national interests and the ideology of the terrorist group, the terrorist group may submit itself to the national interest. Second, if a country decides that it has no further use for the terrorist group, this group may vanish. Third, we can use the research of the terrorist group in order to study political intentions of various states, which is, of course, an old intelligence problem. For example, Syrian willingness to support terrorist groups and take more risks vis-à-vis Israel might be helpful in understanding Syrian policy, Syrian problems, and possible demands in the near future. If we agree that terrorism serves as a strategic tool, we may view it as a kind of laboratory, at a rather low price and with low strategic effects. Thus, for the intelligence officer, it may be regarded as a device which helps one make important predictions. Indeed, there is an Arab saying that Lebanon as a whole is a fine microcosm to understand the whole Arab system.

How can state-supported terror be combated effectively? Three factors should be taken into account: the effective use of military force to deter states from supporting terrorism, expert intelligence to aid both in fighting terrorism and in countering its political message, and the development of clear international norms condemning those states which support terrorism.

Although there are limitations on effective means to deter states from supporting terrorism, one has to set a price in terms of military retaliation. For this, target states, such as Israel, must maintain an effective intervention capability in various places around the globe. Also, in order to achieve this deterrence, it might be useful to activate the deterrence force for one specific occasion in a very calculated and controlled manner. The operations, such as Entebbe and Mogadishu, speak for themselves. Sometimes the price of terror is set by the terrorists themselves within supporting countries. This might bring the supporting country to what Professor Dror described as "second thoughts." Jordan, for example, made such a decision and expelled the Palestinian terrorists in the 1960s. It seems that now, ten years after the occasion, Jordan is still reluctant to allow the presence of the Palestinian terrorists within its boundaries. Another example is Lebanon.

The behavior of the Palestinians in Jordan and Lebanon might lead individuals or groups within these countries to have second thoughts.

At the other end of the scale, distant countries—Libya, Algeria, the PDRY—because of their geographical distance from Israel, feel that they may support terrorism with impunity. Uganda felt quite safe in cooperating with the hijackers who landed on its territory. In such cases, the price for supporting terror must be set by the target state.

The second element of deterrence is intelligence. The intelligence community has a highly important role to play in supplying their policymakers with data. Once a terrorist act occurs, intelligence must check whether or not it was carried out with any foreign state's support or permission, or whether it is just a provocation within the framework of the quarrels within rival terrorist groups or rival countries. It is of prime importance to have a daily exchange of feedback between policymakers and intelligence on the subject of terrorism, so as not to act prematurely and blindly and hit whenever terrorists strike; sometimes it is better to wait. This exchange is also valuable in order to supply information and data to policymakers that will enable them to deal with foreign involvement or Arab involvement in the terror business.

Indeed, one should not neglect the political struggle against terrorism. Rephrasing what was said here earlier, if the terrorist is the fish, then the permissiveness of liberal society and the inefficiency of the international community is the water which the terrorist needs to survive.

Israel has constrained terrorism also by explaining its positions and problems to the world. The international community may not be capable of stopping states altogether from supporting terror. But the international norms condemning terror must be common, recognized, and respected.

Discussion

PARTICIPANT: I would like to talk about the Arab world. What is the political significance of supporting political terrorism from the point of view of the Arab states? What is the depth of their commitment?

The Arab commitment to the PLO and to Palestinian nationalism is, in my view, an expression of Arab and Islamic conflict against the West. This, in turn, is some sort of substitute for the Islamic unity under the khalif, which no longer exists. Support for the PLO is an expression of Arab unity; it enables Arab states to tend to their own particular affairs while paying a sort of lip service to the pan-Arab idea and to the struggle against Israel. It helps pro-Western countries deal with the West while sustaining the general Arab and Islamic anti-Western campaign. If you are an Arab leader looking for legitimacy and for Arab status, you need to claim support for the Palestinian issue or even to be a guardian of this issue. Therefore, the commitment is deep.

Yet I question whether this deep commitment to the PLO and to Palestinian nationalism in all Arab states is the first order of priority. Is this cause of national interest in all Arab countries? Are Arab states willing to go to war with Israel for the Palestinian cause or for the PLO even if it means serious damage to any of their own national interests? Is there consensus in the Arab community as to how to support the Palestinians, how far they are willing to go on behalf of the Palestinians or the PLO?

You will find that the degree of commitment in Arab states differs according to the various circumstances. I think you can sum it up by stating that all of the Arab states, regardless of their commitment to the Palestinian issue or to the PLO, place their own national interests above those of the Palestinians. In other words, if you want to stop Arab states from supporting the PLO, you should try to hurt top priority national interests. From the Arab viewpoint, political damage caused to Israel by the PLO would not, I think, justify the price which might have to be paid as a result of damage to the national interests of Arab states. This is true in the case of Syria, in which the Palestinian cause is a top priority national interest. In other states, such as Egypt for example, the commitment to the Palestinians is less; in that case it is enough for Israel to hit lower priority national interests. The price for such retaliatory acts, however, might be too high for us in spite of the benefits which may result from forcing an Arab state to stop supporting terrorist activity by the PLO from its territory. Therefore, we should not try to learn how to pressure Arab states to stop supporting terrorism, but rather how to reach a political situation where terrorism would be eliminated or would be pushed aside because it would lose a constituency and legitimacy.

PARTICIPANT: I want to move from the Middle East to the international problem. After all, we are not focusing here on the problems of the Arab-Israeli conflict alone, but regarding it as a case in point for the broader problem. I think it is rather clear that were it not for states that support terrorism, terrorism would be much less of a problem. In other words, the amount of state support in the different functions of terrorism is a critical factor. Therefore, doing something about state support may be of critical importance in doing something about international terrorism. It may be easier than many other things. Not to grasp this as one of the main aspects of terrorism as a global phenomenon is to miss one of the most important issues. If state support were stopped, though international terrorism would not wither away it would be diminished; and the possibilities for more technological advancement in terrorism would be much reduced.

One of the most interesting things to understand is why some states support terrorism (a question which was handled to some extent) and why other states tolerate this. In order to understand this, the characteristics of the present international system as a whole must be examined. The combination of oil and terror, East-West conflict, and the tradition of Western countries—which makes it difficult to close down consulates and question diplomatic immunity—must be taken into account. One must examine the whole network of interstate relations. The question of Germany and South Yemen, for example, assuming that South Yemen provided training to terrorists operating in Germany, has to be looked at within the complete constellation of relationships. In other cases, the situation may be very delicate. The way in which the British government might convince the United States to crack down on money collection in the United States intended for the Irish Republican Army is a delicate problem.

PARTICIPANT: I would like to take up two points raised here. One deals with deterrence, particularly military operations or paramilitary operations as a form of deterrence. This cannot work in the case of the Basques or in other instances of internal political terrorism. Deterrence can work in situations such as that of the PLO, quite often due to the fact that the movement is state-supported. In other words, if the PLO were not state-supported, it would be much more difficult to find a target to strike. The obvious case is Jordan until 1970. The fact that Jordan was providing sanctuary and aid to terrorists made it vulnerable to punishment. When the punishment was stepped up, Jordan's inclination to support the PLO went down.

PARTICIPANT: I think that this is the way the Jordanians would like to project it, as a justification for the liquidation of the Palestinians. But, in my opinion, the Jordanian struggle with the Palestinians at that time was not a result of the Israeli attacks as much as the struggle concerning the representation of the Palestinian people.

PARTICIPANT: A few words concerning the degree and the various forms of commitment to the Palestinian cause. There is an inherent contradiction between the national interests of the various Arab states and the Palestinians. For example, although everybody in the Palestinian community would say that Sadat betrayed the Palestinian community, Sadat claimed that he understood its people better than they did themselves and that he would promote their interests as he deemed appropriate. For the time being, this remains a contradiction. Such was the case with Lebanon over the Saiqa issue and Syrian involvement in Lebanon and with the Palestinians in 1975-76. Under certain circumstances there might be a collision or merger of interests between the Palestinians or the PLO and various Arab countries. For example, following the Sadat initiative, the Syrians and the PLO found themselves in one camp opposing Egypt. They felt the need to act together, to create strategy, to reach an understanding on the political level. Yet basically, they have conflicting interests, as became evident in Lebanon.

From the Palestinian point of view, the same inherent contradiction exists. The Palestinians claim they are the sole legitimate representatives of their causes; thus, they will have to determine their future, what matters they want to promote and by what means. Yet they declare openly that they are very limited in resources that could promote their interests. Therefore, they call upon the Arab world for support. Philosophically, this is an inherent contradiction. Either you are an autonomous factor which can advance interests on your own or you have to rely upon other factors. In the field of political science this means that at times you have to submit to others in some interest conflicts or where there are conflicting convictions. The Arab community has a deep moral and political commitment to the Palestinian cause going back to the 1930s, long before the founding of the PLO in the 1960s. Yet along with this involvement there have always been the various changing international interests in the Arab community. The question was raised concerning Arab willingness to go to war because of the Palestinian cause. My answer would be a blunt no. The Palestinians were not in on behind-the-scenes consultations. They had no major role in the war. They did what they could from the Lebanese border. But there was no strategic plan including the Palestinians in the Arab military effort. In retrospect, in examining PLO actions in 1967, we can say that they in part caused the 1967 war. But from the PLO's side, I do not think this is a good example. We found them unprepared for something as encompassing as a war, let alone such a military defeat.

Judging by past experience, I would say that the Arabs will go to war when they are ready to confront Israel, regardless of the Palestinian problem, which seems to be just a cover-up.

PARTICIPANT: An important point has been touched upon, and that is the degree of a movement's dependence on its state backer or backers. That really affects our prediction or estimate of the degree of threat, the likely target, the impact of logistic support, and so forth. I would think that the PLO is really in a very bad position, where one has to interpret its combat in the light of the policies of the back-up powers. One wants to build up one's intelligence on the degree of exploitation involved and the degree of influence of combat cooperation, and so forth. I would think that from the Israeli point of view it is heartening that there is such a dependence on outside backing. Here is a movement that claims to be a national liberation movement, that apparently cannot get under way, cannot get reasonably organized (as the Basques organized in their own populated area), and that apparently cannot do without a vast amount of financial aid. The more it becomes identified with a foreign power and with a foreign propaganda arm, the more difficult it becomes for it to establish a really firm basis.

The ideological division found within the organization is also partly a product of the foreign support. Foreign support means, in effect, that the broad umbrella unifies under it antagonistic movements which are engaged in interfaction warfare.

PARTICIPANT: Despite the fact that the Palestinians have so much strength, they still need unity and have yet to set up common headquarters. One of the reasons for this is multiplicity of support. They are dependent on a number of Arab countries and some of the factions or organizations within the PLO represent an extension of the country which they depend on.

PARTICIPANT: A point was raised about the global atmosphere and the need for global management. In order for us to really combat terrorism on the national level, the national interests of the countries need to be very much involved. At present, there are very few countries whose national interests, as far as survival is concerned, are involved. Until we all are involved, we will find that the problems are left to groups like the one assembled here. But, as mentioned earlier, there have been instances—such as the antihijacking acts some countries signed—which prove that where national interests were involved, countries could get together and something positive could result—a reduced number of hijackings. We should, then, consider the matter from a global perspective.

From this perspective, we can all be criticized for mismanagement. Besides the oil crisis, there are other crises in the world such as hunger, overpopulation, and the socioeconomic gap between the rich and the poor. If we wish to treat not only the symptoms of our mismanagement, but also the root causes, we must involve all the nations, with the United Nations as a key. We in the academic field as well as those in the international policymaking field are very much aware of the need for a global approach in order to eradicate problems.

What is America doing about terrorism? True to the American way of attacking problems, we have formed a special committee. It is relatively new, but it is functioning and contributing. Our policies have emerged from it and the various service departments are taking action accordingly. I think most of you are aware of what forces are able to participate in counterterrorism and to what extent: primarily the air force, of course, with a special operations air unit; the army with its special forces and rangers; the navy with its Seals, other equipment, and technology. Thus, there are moves afoot; there is interest.

PARTICIPANT: I would like to discuss the effectiveness of the PLO. Has the Palestinians' terrorism really been effective? I would think that it has not been effective overall in terms of yielding political results. If you look at their position now, they appear to be more excluded from the area which they claim to be their own domestic base and their nation-state than they were when there were Palestinians living in Jordan, negotiating and organizing various resistance and guerrilla movements. I would not think they could show great political development if one is looking at their impact on the international scene, although it is true that people in countries which were previously less aware of the Arab-Israeli conflict, or perhaps not aware of it at all, might be aware of it now as a result of terrorist incidents. Still, against that you have to set the fact that there have been five major wars in the area and that anybody with any level of political information at all in countries that receive newspapers and have world news programs on radio and television was aware to some extent of these wars between Israel and her Arab neighbors. Therefore, I think the argument that terrorism was the only way in which the Palestinian problem was recognized in the world is a spurious one.

One thus has to ask, if terrorism has not been responsible for focusing world attention on the Arab-Israeli conflict, what has it achieved? I suppose the Palestinians would claim they have shown they can keep the struggle going even after the disaster of the 1967 war. But in a sense terrorism has become a fig leaf for their revolutionary virtue. They felt they had to do something, and this was it. To some extent terrorism also served internal functions of the Palestinian movement.

I think that if you look at the balance sheet regarding the longer term, you will note that the Palestinians have lost more than they have gained through the use of the terror weapon. They lost in terms of popular support in Western countries. Certainly, many people in the West did not approve of the methods used even where they shared some sympathy with the Palestinian grievances. Terrorism resulted in a loss not only in terms of mass opinion, but also in terms of the effect on world leaders in countries which could have been helpful. The PLO also lost some of its own people, for obviously many of them have been killed in attacks or have been imprisoned. With regard to their potential recruitment of activists, there is some evidence that the numbers of people coming forward for kamikaze-style or sacrificial action is dwindling. Thus, high-risk terrorist attacks helped stop the flow of recruits into the Palestinian movement and into the guerrilla movements. Also, they helped close the ranks of Israel, to unite individuals of different political affiliations in backing strong measures against the low intensity operations and in taking a much more assertive line over securing the frontiers of Israel.

PARTICIPANT: All these points are certainly open to debate.

PARTICIPANT: I accept your points concerning the effects. But I question you on the costs.

PARTICIPANT: I do not think there is clear scientific evidence regarding the costs. I think you have to make an assessment on the basis of recent history. I suggest that we must look at the overall plight of the Palestinians as well as at the PLO itself. The question is, Where are the Palestinians now?

PARTICIPANT: I agree that this is not a matter that can be subjected to strict empirical measurement. Still, we could get intelligence data on the recruitment patterns and the correlations of recruitment with the number of people killed. The usefulness of this kind of research may, however, be limited in practice. One could get public opinion on political behavior patterns in Europe, for example, but regardless of how many leaders proclaim their abhorrence of terror, they nevertheless give in to the PLO in letting them open offices and so forth.

PARTICIPANT: There is more interesting and tangible evidence since 1973, and it concerns international terrorist attacks carried out by the Palestinian movement itself. Unless you argue that the decisions concerning these attacks have been forced upon the PLO, one has to at least consider the possibility that the decreased scope is due to a change in strategy.

PARTICIPANT: The PLO has concluded that terror has served its main purpose; it is now striving for respectability. Stopping a policy does not mean that it failed. It can mean that some purposes were achieved and now the PLO is shifting to another policy. You cannot be sure that the simple fact of change of policy demonstrates that terrorism has been proven a failure. In fact, I'm sure that empirical policy studies would show that in many cases policies that have failed were used again and again by different states.

PARTICIPANT: Let us consider what the PLO has achieved. In Jordan, they apparently overreached themselves, not in terrorist activity against Israel, but in arrogance in posture vis-à-vis the Jordanian army. Hussein did not decide to act against the terrorists until he was told by the senior officers that if he did not act against the Palestinians, they would act without his approval.

Palestinian terrorism has been successful, however, vis-à-vis Israel. As far as Israeli public opinion is concerned, the PLO achieved political success.

I think that without Palestinian terrorism, the impact of the Palestinian problem on Israeli public opinion would have been much smaller.

Finally, I think that Palestinian terrorism strengthened the PLO position vis-à-vis the U.S. government, but not because the U.S. government admires terrorism. The PLO gained important points due to the continuity of terrorist activity that portrays a certain strength. Also, the fact that the Palestinians in the Gaza Strip and the West Bank have recognized the PLO as their representative has added to the PLO's prestige in the United States.

PARTICIPANT: I think the PLO accomplished two things with terrorism. First, they radicalized Arab positions in general towards Israel in ways which could be backed up by other means of terror. Also, they made other Arab groups appear moderate by contrast. States are considered moderate because they do not use the same kind of terrorist methods the PLO uses, even though they do not denounce these means. In Western eyes, the PLO and Libya are the crazy ones with whom you cannot deal; but Saudi Arabia is moderate, reasonable. This is the contribution of terrorism.

13

International Cooperation among Terrorist Groups

Z. Gad

In examining the phenomenon of international cooperation among terrorist groups, the questions that come to mind are whether cooperation among most of the terrorist organizations in the world is extensive and whether we can point out particular groups which control or guide this terrorist activity. Another question involves the bases for the cooperation among terrorist groups. Is there a common ideology which unites these groups, or is cooperation based only on pragmatism? Can the forms of cooperation be classified according to the nature of the terrorist groups? Can we say that all or most of the liberation movements are acting in some coordination, or that most of the anarchist groups work together? What reasons lie behind cooperation? We aim here to create a model for cooperation among terrorist groups, examining the roles of each of the sides and the dynamics of their interactions.

I should like to begin with a description of the connection between Palestinian and non-Arab terrorist organizations. Cooperation between Palestinian and non-Arab terrorist organizations began to develop during the late 1960s, when the Palestinians began to carry out terrorist attacks outside the Middle East. As early as 1968–69, non-Arab terrorists received training in Arab terrorist camps in Jordan. In September 1970, the first non-Arab (a Nicaraguan) joined an Arab (Leila Khaled of the Popular Front for the Liberation of Palestine [PFLP]) in a joint mission: the hijacking of an El-Al aircraft. Such cooperation is based on both ideological and pragmatic considerations. Ideology played an important but not exclusive role in George Habash's PFLP's considerations regarding the establishment of close ties with non-Arab organizations. Thus, the PFLP maintains ties only with organizations which, like itself, espouse a Marxist-Leninist ideology. On the other hand, pragmatic considerations were dominant in Fatah's decisions regarding the establishment of close ties with foreign terrorist groups; Fatah has had ties with both left-wing and right-wing organizations.

The major Palestinian organizations maintaining ties with non-Arab groups are the Fatah and the PFLP. Other organizations, such as the Popular Front for the Liberation of Palestine—General Command (PFLP-GC) of Ahmad Jibril and Abu-Abbas's Palestine Liberation Front (PLF) are also active in this sphere, although to a much lesser extent. A variety of groups have ties with the Palestinian terrorists, including national liberation movements such as the Eritrean Liberation Front (ELF) or the Polisario; anarchist organizations such as the Japanese Red Army (JRA); the German Red Army Faction (RAF); and legal organizations, especially in Europe. Committees of support are set up in order to assist the Palestinian organizations and the Palestinian cause in many parts of the world. The differences among the non-Arab groups are immense, and this determines the nature of the ties each one has with the Palestinian organizations. In general, these ties can be divided into the following categories:

1. An operational terrorist cooperation, the aim of which is to increase the terrorist potential of the group. The JRA's ties with the PFLP exemplify this sort of relationship. It is clear that this activity increases the capability of the non-Arab organizations as well as that of the Arab ones.
2. Military cooperation between terrorist organizations of national liberation movements. The aim of such cooperation is to enhance the military capability of these organizations. Cooperation involves arms supply, military training, and so forth.
3. Political and humanitarian cooperation. Many left-wing organizations maintain this level of cooperation with Palestinian terrorist organizations. Committees of support established by such organizations strive to assist the Palestinian organizations in such areas as propaganda, fund raising, and medical aid.

As to operational terrorist cooperation, at the beginning of the 1970s both Fatah and the PFLP had operational ties with non-Arab organizations. In 1971–73 Fatah operational nets in Europe maintained ties with Algerian underground movements in France, whose operatives—for example, Muhammad Boudia—helped Fatah plan and carry out attacks in Europe which included the attacks against oil and gas installations in the Netherlands in March 1971 and February 1972. After 1973, links of this nature grew weaker. The main reason for this was Fatah's decision to suspend terrorist operations abroad. The organizations' reduced operations and activities abroad naturally weakened Fatah's operational infrastructure abroad, thus weakening its ties with other terrorist groups. On the other hand, Fatah's ties with underground organizations and national liberation movements in the military, rather than terrorist, sphere expanded. Its ties with such organizations as the Montoneros of Argentina or the ELF grew closer in the years of 1975–77. However, since 1976 and especially in 1979, Fatah displayed renewed interest in operational ties with European terrorist organizations. The direct causes of this are the political developments, beginning with Anwar el-Sadat's initiative, which harmed the standing of the PLO. These developments have apparently caused Fatah to reconsider the possibility of resuming attacks abroad. Toward this end, Fatah has recently been making efforts to renew and strengthen its operational infrastructure abroad, at the same time tightening links with European terrorist organizations. The close ties between Fatah and the Irish Republican Army should be viewed in this context.

The PFLP maintained ties with non-Arab terrorist organizations until the end of 1973. These ties were promoted by two departments within the organization: the foreign operational department, headed by the late Wadi Haddad, which dealt with operational aspects; and the foreign links department, which dealt with political aspects of cooperation. When Haddad in effect left the PFLP in 1974 and began to operate independently as head of his own faction, he became the main Palestinian element cooperating with non-Arab terrorist organizations. Upon Haddad's death, and the disintegration of the faction which he headed, a vacuum was created in the sphere of non-Arab terrorist ties with Palestinian organizations. Presumably the non-Arab terrorist groups will try to find replacements to fill Haddad's place. I conjecture that George Habash's PFLP will be the one to maintain relations with those organizations.

Cooperation between Palestinian organizations and non-Arab terrorist groups has been taking place in several fields. The Palestinian organizations assist foreign terrorist groups by training their members in Palestinian terrorist camps in the Middle East, especially in Lebanon, Iraq, Syria, Algeria, Libya, and South Yemen. The members of the JRA who seized the French embassy in The Hague in 1974 had been trained in one of Haddad's camps in Aden. A group of Dutch extremists—one of whom, Ludwina Janssen, was captured in Israel—was also trained in Palestinian camps.

Non-Arab terrorists also receive weapons from the Palestinians. In 1974 members of the RAF were found to be in possession of delay devices produced by Palestinian terrorists. Fatah also sent the IRA arms at the end of 1977. I believe that Palestinian terrorists will continue to supply foreign terrorist groups with weapons, possibly including sophisticated weapons such as RPG-7 antitank rockets and SA-7 surface-to-air missiles.

In the other direction, among the weapons found in the Paris apartment where Carlos once lived were grenades belonging to the same production series of the M-26 grenades stolen from an American military depot in West Germany. The grenades were used in the takeover of the French embassy in The Hague by the JRA as well as in the September 1974 attack on a drugstore in Paris, which was carried out personally by Carlos.

A third aspect of cooperation is the forging of documentation. Palestinian organizations have an efficient apparatus for forging various types of documents, and non-Arab groups presumably receive assistance from this apparatus. Palestinian terrorists also receive false documentation from non-Arab subversive groups. As for cooperation in the field of forgery, it should be recalled that when the Carlos network was uncovered, a large quantity of forged documentation—passports, driving licences, stamps, and visas—was found. Previous incidents indicate that Palestinian and non-Arab organizations can obtain and alter documentation of almost any country in the world.

Direct operational cooperation exists in a number of spheres, including the collection of operational intelligence and the preparing of attacks. For example, the person who rented the car used in the PFLP attack on the El-Al plane at Orly Airport in January 1975 was a German leftist named Johannes Weinrich. Similarly, the PFLP assisted the JRA in preparing the takeover of the French embassy in The Hague. A second form of operational cooperation is the carrying out of attacks on behalf of each other. For example, the JRA has hijacked airplanes for the PFLP; and Wadi Haddad's group hijacked a Lufthansa plane for a group of German terrorists. Palestinian and non-Arab groups also work together, as in the attack on fuel tanks in Singapore in January 1974, when PFLP and JRA members worked together; the 1975 attack on the Organization of Petroleum Exporting Countries (OPEC), carried out by a mixed squad of Palestinians, Germans, and others; and of course, the hijacking of the Air France plane to Entebbe. The use of multinational squads has advantages both in the operational sphere, where operational experience can be shared, and in the political sphere, where the unity of the struggle against imperialism can be demonstrated.

A fourth form of cooperation concerns the escape. After carrying out attacks, members of non-Arab organizations often take refuge in Palestinian terrorist camps in the Middle East. Arab countries—mainly Algeria, Libya, Iraq, and South Yemen—are also involved in rendering this sort of safe haven. Libya granted refuge to the five Japanese terrorists who took over the American embassy in Malaysia in 1975; South Yemen granted refuge to the German terrorists who were released after the Peter Lorenz kidnaping;

and Algeria granted refuge to the JRA members who had hijacked a Japanese plane in 1977.

Cooperation in financing and in logistical support also takes place. The Palestinian terrorists give financial aid to non-Arab subversive groups. For example, some of the funds which Michel Moukharbel received from the PFLP were given to the terrorist organizations with which he was connected. Members of non-Arab organizations supply logistical support to Palestinian terrorists abroad, providing them with safe houses and getaway aid. An example is the case of the Turkish terrorists who placed their Paris safe house at the disposal of the PFLP in 1973.

In addition to cooperation among subversive groups, recruitment of non-Arabs by Palestinian organizations takes place on a personal basis, and non-Arabs are sometimes given roles in operations. At times, these non-Arabs are sent on suicide missions without knowledge of the nature of the mission.

Despite the close cooperation among the various terrorist groups, cooperation is not institutionalized in the form of a terrorist international that plans the operations of all these groups. Since cooperation exists in all spheres, there is solace to be gained by the fact that a single commanding body for all the terrorist organizations and subversive groups does not exist. Moreover, I believe that there is some bilateral or even multilateral cooperation among terrorist organizations and some local center may be controlling a given activity in a specific area. Cuba, for example, may be involved in much of the terrorist activities in Latin America. I believe that there exists some sort of dynamics of collaboration and cooperation between extremist groups and terrorist groups, the result of which is that the supported groups become more inclined to use terror actions under the influence of active terrorist groups. I think an example of this is the connection between the Red Aid in the Netherlands and the PLO and, later, the PFLP and the Haddad faction. As a result of contacts with these Palestinian terrorist groups, a group that was initially a political group became a terrorist organization. The benefit to the terrorist organization of such cooperation is the establishment of a huge political and logistical infrastructure, which enables terrorist organizations to widen the arena of terrorist activity outside their own borders, bringing it to an international level.

Discussion

PARTICIPANT: What factors can account for the cooperation between Palestinian and non-Palestinian terrorist groups, and what are the consequences of such cooperation?

GAD: There is a correlation between the level of Palestinian terrorist activity outside the Middle East and the intensity of connections with non-Arab organizations. I think the years 1971–74 were the years of the Palestinian organizations' strongest relations with most terrorist organizations. This was true with regard to German, Japanese, Turkish, and Iranian groups. The reason for this was that the Palestinians were very active on the international level. For some time afterwards there was a decrease in connections; we observed links only with German terrorists and with the JRA. Thus, if, as seems to us at present, the Palestinians—especially the Fatah—are going back to international activities abroad, it means that they are looking for new connections as well as for the renewal of connections they had in the past. Therefore, we are about to see an increase in the international links between Palestinians and non-Arab groups.

I also want to point out that Fatah remains the key organization for the terrorist activities of the Palestinians. If Fatah perpetrates terrorist activities abroad, other organizations will follow suit and therefore they, too, will look for connections abroad. This raises the question of who is seeking these connections—the Palestinians or the non-Arabs? Who is benefiting more? Obviously, the answer is somewhere in the middle, because everyone gets something from these relations. But I think it is very interesting to note that in most of the cases, at least in the past, it was not the Palestinians who were looking for connections with non-Arab groups. To non-Arab organizations, the Palestinian organizations are the center that may give them the support they need. They are trying, therefore, to bring themselves closer to the Palestinians. When the Palestinians have their own interests in such a relationship, they develop and improve it. When they are not interested, they cut it short.

The constant interest in ties with the Palestinians stems from the fact that they have the only terrorist organization that has all the infrastructure and all the freedom to maneuver in several countries. Also, their organization, unlike others, can supply such things as training in a free and open manner. The relations are very important for the non-Arab groups especially because of the military training they can get, particularly training for guerrilla warfare that they cannot get elsewhere, and because of weapons, especially sophisticated ones, that they can thus acquire. These factors make it easier for the Palestinians to rebuild relations when they so desire; the other side is always more willing and is always interested in doing so.

The Palestinians benefit from international connections mainly in terms of logistical support and infrastructure. I think that this is what they need. For when they want to act abroad—in Europe, for example—they need flats, connections, information. This is what they gain through cooperation. They also gain political support from the various organizations. This is very important, especially for the Fatah. Such political support, the solidarity it indicates, is considered the first stage. The next stage is joint political activity abroad—propaganda, demonstrations, and so forth. The third stage involves visits to the Middle East, to refugee camps, for humanitarian reasons only. Up to this point, the cooperation has nothing to do with terrorism; afterwards, however, the organizations may also cooperate in that area. There are instances in which immediately after visiting the Middle East, a non-Arab group became part of a supporting pool for terrorist activity, ready to be recruited for terrorist activities on an individual basis.

Cooperation with the PLO may develop in one of two main directions. The first is limited military cooperation, meaning mostly training and weapons, but no operational cooperation. The second is full cooperation, including direct operational cooperation in terrorist activity. I think that every extreme group in the world, especially in Europe, that started having relations with the Palestinians—even if on the political level only— constitutes a potential partner to terrorist activities on different levels.

I do not believe in the effectiveness of the reported summit conferences of the terrorist organizations, which were allegedly held in Cyprus, in Greece, in Ireland, and other such places. I do not view these summit conferences as the formation of the "united terrorists of the world." But, these events receive much publicity, and the media like them very much.

PARTICIPANT: You presented a sequence of events that begins at the initiative of the non-Arabs in an expression of solidarity, which eventually includes a trip to the Middle East on humanitarian grounds, and potentially ends in future cooperation in terrorist activities. How much of that model is specific to a certain period of time? This model was valid for the period between 1967–68 and 1972–73, but is no longer so. We do not see new groups emerging with expressions of solidarity and taking new trips to the Middle East for humanitarian reasons. My reason for asking the question is that one of the notions about Western European terrorism is that, in a sense, it was specific to a certain generation, to that generation of students who marched against the war, who fought the battles against the establishment, who revolted on the streets of Paris, at the University of Heidelberg or Frankfurt. The idea is that it was a unique generation, and from that generation there were people in the United States who went to Cuba, or people in Western Europe who visited refugee camps in Lebanon; and that provided the basis for later relations. How much of that is going on now, and how much of that has gone on since that period? Is there some continuity in this, or was it fairly unique to that moment in history?

GAD: I think that this phenomenon is still going on, and I have facts to support this notion. I have mentioned the Dutch Red Aid connection with the Palestinians, which surfaced in 1976–77. There was also a new German group, second generation of the Baader-Meinhof group, that went to Aden in 1975–76 and took part in the 1976 Kenya operation against Israeli airplanes there. There are new connections; for example, between the Montoneros and the Fatah. A visit of some Montonero leaders to the Middle East was recently publicized, and some agreements between them and the Fatah concerning weapons were made known. I think this phenomenon continues as new terrorist groups form throughout the world. There have been some developments in the relations between the non-Arab groups and the Palestinians. The relations between the PLO and German terrorists are different today from what they were in 1968–70, when the first group of Germans went to PFLP camps in Jordan to receive military training. It is true that today the German terrorists do not need the Palestinians as they needed them in the past. Nevertheless, when in trouble—as when four members of the RAF needed a safe haven—they have fled to the Middle East, waited it out there for a while, reorganized, and then returned to Germany. A group of Germans, freed in the Peter Lorenz kidnaping, went to South Yemen, stayed there for three years, and afterwards returned to Germany and organized the new generation of the RAF. This is the manner of cooperation. The same holds true for the JRA today. Although it has its own bases and its own infrastructure, safe havens are available only in the Middle East.

PARTICIPANT: If the Palestinians' talks with Willy Brandt and Bruno Kreisky are not a passing episode but a sort of signal for a trend, are we not now entering a period in which the PLO is striving for legitimacy and, thus, association with extreme groups is becoming a severe liability? Does this lead you to believe that we are about to see—at least with regard to the PLO or the Fatah—a decrease in the links with other terrorist groups?

GAD: I do not think the meeting between Yasir Arafat and Kreisky should be seen as a new phase in relations between the PLO and the West, for the PLO started seeking legitimacy several years ago. I think they achieved this legitimacy for the first time when Arafat spoke at the UN General Assembly in 1974. If I believed that the PLO plans to cease terrorist activities, I might agree with your suggestion that cooperation between the PLO and other terrorist groups might be expected to diminish. However, since terrorist activities continue to be pursued, the PLO continues to need the operational support of foreign terrorist organizations. Fatah, in particular, has a unique problem, for it is not a revolutionary organization, while the extreme left-wing organizations in Europe are. Fatah has only what you might call a pragmatic nationalistic argument; therefore, during the years that it did not maintain relations with terrorist groups or the new Left in Europe, it came to be considered a bourgeois organization. Since 1978, the Fatah has been seeking to regain the glory of being a revolutionary organization. This is one of the reasons it is looking for connections with foreign left-wing groups.

PARTICIPANT: I think it is interesting that the links among the various terrorist groups have been largely at the initiative of the local elements. It seems that the Palestinian connection has been important in accounting for certain levels of terrorism reached by domestic groups. It may be that these linkages are somewhat less striking now than in earlier periods because of the growth in the capabilities of local terrorist groups, and the concomitant weakening of the need for external help. The Palestinians themselves have ceased actively forging links with local groups. However, these links continue to exist. Indeed, if the Palestinians decide to launch another major international campaign of terrorism, they will probably again develop and exploit their links with local groups.

PARTICIPANT: The PLO has been receiving a lot of weapons from the Eastern bloc countries both directly—via planes or ships that arrive in Lebanon from the satellite countries such as Czechoslovakia or Yugoslavia—and indirectly—through Syria or Libya. Syria tries to put some limitations on the weapons it gives to the Palestinians, because of its own predicament in Lebanon. Supplies from Libya include sophisticated weapons, but it is not always clear whether it was a Libyan or a Russian decision to supply them. The Palestinians in Lebanon, especially Fatah but also other organizations, have no problems obtaining SA-7s; they receive them continuously from either Libya or the Soviet Union. They also obtain RPG-7s without any difficulty. While these weapons may not be intended for terrorist activities, once they are in the hands of the Palestinians, outside suppliers no longer control the uses to which they are put. The Palestinians thus have no problems acquiring weapons and supplying them to any non-Arab organizations with which they have close links.

With regard to the interests of the United States, as they are affected by international terrorism in general, and by Palestinian terrorism in particular, the approach of the PLO to the United States has been ambivalent. On the one hand they declare repeatedly that U.S. interests are targets. On the other hand, they have not taken any real initiative against U.S. targets, neither in the Middle East nor in Europe. I think the explanation for this lies in the political aspirations of the PLO, which include negotiations with the United States. They are therefore very careful not to make the

United States feel that the PLO is trying to blackmail them. The PLO thus prefers to perpetrate operations against Egyptian, Israeli, or even European targets rather than confront the United States directly. But the Palestinians are not represented by one organization; rather, there are seven, eight, maybe even ten groups and every day a new organization becomes active. Consequently, it may happen that while Arafat is trying to negotiate with the Americans, some other extreme Palestinian organization will act against the United States in order to prevent negotiations between the PLO and the Americans. Thus we cannot exclude the possibility of American interests being attacked. The likelihood of a Palestinian attack within the United States is very low, however. It would be very difficult for the PLO to carry out an attack in the United States, and I think they are very hesitant to act there. Only on very rare occasions has the PLO committed terrorist acts there, finding Europe and the Middle East far more convenient.

14

The Capability and Motivation
of Terrorist Organizations
to Use Mass-Destruction Weapons

B. David

The purpose of this paper is to evaluate the likelihood that terrorist groups may obtain and employ mass-destruction weapons. The possible motivation for the use of mass-destruction weapons and the constraints that apparently have prevented the execution of this threat are considered. The paper concludes with recommendations on how to improve or maintain the current safeguards against the use of such weapons.

At a symposium on international terrorism held recently in Jerusalem, several facts emerged concerning the support of terrorist groups. First, at least some groups enjoy the direct or indirect support of sovereign states. These organizations are aided by state organs such as intelligence services, which provide information about prospective targets, and foreign offices, which are instrumental in supplying equipment. Second, some state governments openly allow, and in fact encourage, terrorist groups to maintain bases on their sovereign territory. Third, close connections are maintained among various terrorist organizations throughout the world. This is manifested in the granting of mutual aid, cooperation at the operational level and, at times, the actual execution of a terrorist attack by one terrorist group on behalf of another. Fourth, at least one superpower is known to provide aid to terrorist groups.

In considering the means required to produce mass-destruction weapons, we must distinguish between chemical and biological agents, which can be obtained or produced without great difficulty, and fissionable materials or nuclear devices, the manufacture or procurement of which is much more complicated.

Chemical agents available for mass attacks can be obtained from various sources. Large quantities of insecticides can be procured for use as weapons; nerve gases can be produced under quite primitive laboratory conditions. The production patents for Vx, for example, have been openly available for some years. Chemical agents could also be stolen from military stores or from research laboratories.

The production of biological agents is also quite feasible, although the professional qualifications required for the production and storage of significant quantities of agents are more difficult to meet than in the case of chemical agents.

A major difficulty with both chemical and biological agents is the efficient dispersion of these agents. The technical problems associated with the efficient dispersion of large quantities of chemical and biological agents are complex and require considerable professional and organizational capability. Targets for chemical and biological attacks are central water systems, large central air conditioning systems, and foodstuff production facilities. Dispersal by aerial spraying may be effective, but it is difficult to conduct. One example of dispersion through foodstuffs was the poisoning of Israeli oranges with mercury in 1978. The operation, if aimed at hurting the Israeli economy by causing fear and panic among the European consumers, demonstrated both operational and strategic sophistication.

Specialists and decision makers have conflicting estimates of the likelihood that terrorist groups will acquire nuclear devices. There is even less of a consensus with regard to what such organizations might do with nuclear devices if they acquired them. Some observers dismiss both the possibility of the acquisition of nuclear devices by terrorists and the possibility that they may use them as unreal, while a small but vociferous minority views every nuclear installation as a threat to the existence of mankind.

Let us first consider the likelihood of terrorists developing and producing nuclear devices. Such a process requires a considerable amount of time and quantity of resources. Any interested group would need to obtain the fissionable material; design, produce, and assemble the bomb; deliver the bomb to the target; and finally, actually set off or threaten to set off the device. Because of the high likelihood of detection at each stage, it is unlikely that terrorists would undertake such a project. Only by being given freedom of action within the confines of a certain territory, by having available technical specialists in at least a dozen different disciplines, by being supplied with sufficient financial resources, and by having a tenacious determination to complete such a lengthy task—only then would a terrorist organization have any chance at all of success.

A simpler approach would be to seize an operating nuclear reactor and cause a severe accident. Such an operation is unlikely to cause damage to the extent that can be achieved by a nuclear blast. However, judging by the public reaction to the Three Mile Island incident, the psychological effect appears to be potentially significant. Nuclear reactors, especially those located near large population centers, may thus serve as targets for quite credible nuclear blackmail.

The highly vulnerable global network of nuclear facilities deserves particular attention. This network is composed of facilities in which fissionable material is produced, utilized, and stored. It includes uranium enrichment and fuel processing and reprocessing complexes; reactors in the service of utilities, research, or desalination; nuclear weapons production plants; and storage facilities. Within this complex of widely scattered facilities, significant quantities of fissionable material of various degrees of refinement are transported constantly. This transportation of nuclear material appears to be the most vulnerable to theft or terrorist attack.

A terrorist group might feel impelled to resort to a mass-destruction weapon theft or to the employment of a nuclear device threat in order to attract the attention of a public that has undergone a process of densensitization to terrorist incidents. The public has become so accustomed to hijackings, for example, that their occurrence no longer causes a great deal of alarm. Also due to desensitization, publics no longer presume that a government will meet terrorist demands in exchange for the release of hostages. On the contrary, over the last several years, a general consensus has been reached not to give in to such demands. It is quite possible, therefore, that in order to obtain the fulfillment of demands, a terrorist group might decide to raise the ante. This could be achieved through a drastic increase in the number of people placed under direct threat. Terrorists could present a credible threat to use mass-destruction weapons against a densely populated area. In fact, there have already been some isolated incidents that may point to a tendency to increase the scale of violence of conventional terrorist acts. An example is the recent massacre of sixty-three cadets in the Artillery Officers School in Aleppo, Syria. The cadets were targeted because they belonged to the Alawi sect, the minority sect currently in power. This incident of mass murder was carried out in the wake of a campaign of terror waged for some time by the Moslem Brotherhood against prominent members of the Alawi sect.

Should the demands of a terrorist group be of limited scope, the threat to use mass-destruction weapons may be effective for various reasons. First, in comparison to the damage threatened, the terrorists' demands may be perceived as miniscule. Second, the larger the number of hostages, the greater will be the direct involvement of the public. As a consequence, more effective public pressure on the government can be expected. In light of the threat's dimensions, the public is likely to insist that the terrorists' demands be met. Third, the element of surprise, fear, lack of preparedness, and lack of suitable methods to deal with such a situation is likely to slow down the government's reaction, possibly paralyzing it altogether. This would necessarily reduce the efficacy of the government's response. Fourth, the terrorist organization performing such an act is likely to achieve publicity much beyond what the terrorists could hope for through the "small" acts conducted until then.

A terrorist organization might also use mass-destruction weapons to topple the ruling regime, to bring about a change in the form of government. When it is demonstrated by a terrorist act that a regime is no longer capable of safeguarding the well-being of its citizens, its legitimacy can be seriously questioned. Repeated acts of this kind may precipitate the downfall of a regime. Also, a terror organization might decide to threaten to use mass-destruction weapons against major population centers in order to bring about a bloodless revolution.

Other possible terrorist motives include the desire to disrupt completely the routine life of a country in order to expose the helplessness of an existing government; the attempt to prevent the government's central organs from functioning effectively; and the attempt to bring about a general atmosphere of panic and insecurity in a campaign to create chaos as a preparatory step to mass revolution.

The actual use of mass-destruction weapons by terrorist organizations for the purpose of causing damage poses several serious questions. A wide range of possible scenarios can be imagined, beginning with an attack against limited targets which correspond to the political goals of the group and ending with a mass slaughter for its own sake. The actual employment of mass-destruction weapons against major population centers may appear to be an act of madness beyond what one expects even from terrorist organizations. Yet there are several terrorist organizations that are ideologically opposed to Western society and all it stands for. Such organizations strive to rebuild a new society on the ruins of the old. The actions of the Khmer Rouge in Cambodia, for example, illustrate superbly the almost total destruction of the existing civilization carried out as a precondition to the reconstruction of a new society.

As noted earlier, an organization that failed in its efforts to create the desired atmosphere of fear and terror by conventional means might attempt to escalate by turning to unconventional weapons. The probability of such actions increases when terrorist organizations are in conflict with the government of a nation to which they themselves do not belong, as in the cases of the Irish Republican Army and the Palestine Liberation Organization. A domestic terrorist group operating in its own country would be less likely to use such weapons, since such tactics may alienate the masses from the group and so be counterproductive. Such a possibility cannot be dismissed altogether, however.

The fact that no actual use of mass-destruction weapons by a terrorist group has so far occurred is the result of a number of factors. First, despite all their deficiencies, preventive means have presented those wishing to acquire such weapons with serious obstacles. Second, terrorist groups face serious motivational constraints concerning the use of mass-destruction weapons. Third, the use of such weapons might cause a serious deterioration in the relationship between the terrorist organization and its supporting countries or terrorist groups. Furthermore, there is the fear of retaliation. Since the use of mass-destruction weapons increases the likelihood that the supporting state will be retaliated against by target states, states are far less likely to cooperate with groups whose intent is to use mass-destruction weapons. Provision of bases to groups using mass-destruction weapons makes the identification of the supporting state easier, thus increasing the likelihood of retaliation. In addition, the use of mass-destruction weapons is likely to cause mutual dissociation among terrorist groups. Since most of these groups constantly strive for legitimacy, they are likely to separate themselves from groups using inhuman methods. Finally, there is the factor that a superpower would clearly refrain from cooperation with groups using mass-destruction weapons. Once such groups are equipped with mass-destruction weapons, they would be relatively immune to superpower influence and control. They may involve the superpower in escalation and catalytic processes in which the superpower might have no control. The risks involved would be too high. A superpower intent on making significant gains within a generally stable international system is thus unlikely to support groups that might run wild with means of mass destruction. The Soviet Union is further unlikely to aid terrorist activity with mass-destruction weapons for fear that such capabilities may be turned against her one day, thus enabling previously supported terrorist groups to blackmail the Soviet Union.

Of all the terrorist organizations, the PLO appears to be the best equipped to acquire nuclear, biological, and chemical weapons. It enjoys enormous technical support from irresponsible national governments of sovereign states, such as Libya; it enjoys much freedom of action on Lebanese territory; it can meet the financial burden through the aid it receives from Saudi Arabia, Iraq, and Libya; and it enjoys observer status at the International Atomic Energy Agency (IAEA), a position that gives the PLO direct access to material concerning the security of nuclear installations. Even in the case of the PLO, however, I believe the use of mass-destruction weapons is a high-risk but low-probability threat.

Where there is the will to do so, obvious measures can be taken to lessen the likelihood that terrorist groups may obtain and employ mass-destruction weapons. First, we can increase the physical security of source materials and facilities concerned. Second, we can prevent access to technical know-how and the acquisition of facilities necessary for the production and dissemination of mass-destruction weapons. Third, we can encourage international cooperation in the surveillance of the activities of terrorist groups and their supporting states in this area.

Discussion

PARTICIPANT: Mass-destruction weapons are by their nature nonselective. For this reason, I believe that these weapons could be used when there is a clash between two different ethnic or religious groups. For other reasons, however, using such means is counterproductive, because their use is detrimental to other goals of the group, which may include support in world opinion, support by the superpowers, and so forth.

In order to utilize mass-destruction means, a small group may rely on a larger organization. I am certain, for example, that the PLO has the ability and the facilities today to use some of the mass-destruction weapons such as chemical or perhaps biological weapons. While I do not believe that the PLO as it stands today would decide to use such means, a small group within the PLO may do so.

Smaller terrorist groups are more prone to carry out mass-killing operations. A large organization like the Fatah, for example, usually shies away from mass killing. The smaller Palestinian terrorist organizations have committed many more such acts. An exception was Fatah's attempt to launch a ship armed with forty-five Katyusha missiles, destined to explode at the Israeli city of Eilat. In this case, I think the main point is that although the operation was unselective in the sense that the individual potential victims were anonymous, the planned mission was selective in that it was aimed at an Israeli target.

PARTICIPANT: I think the nuclear problem is the most acute and the most interesting one. We overestimate the difficulties in producing such a weapon, because we tend to overlook the fact that the main obstacle is military standards, which are nonexistent for terrorists. The probability of such weapons being used increases, in my opinion, when terrorist organizations feel concerned and desperate regarding achievement of their goals. It may also increase due to internal conflicts within an organization.

PARTICIPANT: It was said that one of the constituents of terrorism is the purpose beyond the mere act of violence. Bearing this in mind, I think there is a low probability that the terrorists would employ mass-destruction weapons. I think there are certain rules of the game between terrorists and national governments. There is a lack of resolve on the part of governments, for example, to take what I would call brutal action against the terrorists. Both parties agree to certain rules, namely, not to go beyond what is acceptable to both. Once political terrorists used mass-destruction weapons, the whole conception of the rules of the game would change. A second point relates to the question of what the terrorists would achieve by use of mass destruction. I cannot see any reasonable purpose that would motivate them to employ such a threat. There is also a problem with regard to the countries willing to give such terrorists asylum after a nuclear attack. Currently, for example, Iraq and Libya grant asylum to terrorists. Would either continue to do so following the killing of, say, thousands of people? I am not certain.

PARTICIPANT: Basically, the reason for raising the threshold of threat would be the same reason you would have for raising the ante in a game of poker; that is, you raise the ante so high that it is impossible for the other side to call you. Therefore, you might imagine from the beginning that your threat will succeed because the other side is not going to put it to the test. Thus, it is not essential for the terrorist organization to have the means for mass destruction if it can act convincingly as though it has those means.

A second point is the need to distinguish between self-produced means of mass destruction and acquired mass-destruction means. The latter possibility is much more plausible. I think the idea that an organization, even with the backing of a state, could produce biological warfare material is so farfetched that it can be discounted. However, the possibility that a terrorist group could obtain such existing biological warfare material by stealing it from existing supplies is a different possibility altogether and requires a different approach for prevention.

PARTICIPANT: The use of unconventional weapons would put terrorism in an entirely new stage. Such use would create new problems of massive casualties, of qualitative changes in perceptions. New responses would be needed. While we seem to agree that the probability of use of these weapons is low, I think it is higher now than it was a few years ago.

PARTICIPANT: The only statement we could safely make about the probability of terrorist use of unconventional weapons is that it is greater the second time than the first time. In other words, I believe in a threshold concept: whatever the probability of it happening a first time, once it is done there is a higher probability of groups trying to imitate such an act, claiming—with increasing credibility—to have such capabilities. This will be a hazardous period of time, unless retaliation measures are so strong that it will be unconceivable to use it again. Therefore, I see great value in statements and arguments made in advance regarding the consequences that will follow the use of such devices or weapons.

PARTICIPANT: Terrorism is basically a form of psychological warfare which kills a few in order to inspire fear in many. Thus, we must separate the actual use of the weapon from the mere threat of using it. Although terrorism may have a declining publicity value in the world and a declining coercive value, some terrorist movements have struggled for a sufficiently long time and have gained sufficient confidence in the ultimate achievement of their goals that they no longer feel a need to escalate their terrorist acts. One example is the IRA. It can simply go on killing several soldiers a month in Northern Ireland. It realizes that by doing so, there will be several funerals every month in England. The people of the United Kingdom are becoming tired of the enormous economic burden and are becoming depressed by the constant picture of funerals. English soldiers on the first and second tours of Northern Ireland may be optimistic, but now that most of them are going back for their fourth, fifth, and sixth tours, they are becoming increasingly convinced that the violence at the current level will continue, and that ultimately London will be compelled to name a withdrawal date.

A second example is the PLO. Look at their progress over the years: they are recognized in more than fifty countries; they have observer status in many international forums. Thus, they may become convinced that by maintaining the current level of violence they have made themselves an element in any future Middle East settlement, and that perhaps by continued pressure—albeit not the threat of mass destruction—they will be able to persuade not only Western European countries but also, increasingly, the American population that concessions to the PLO are necessary in order to end the intolerable continuation of current terrorist activity. No escalation is needed, just maintenance of the struggle and hope for attrition of will on the other side.

Another constraint which may effect terrorist decision making is morality. There is some evidence that groups have stated that it is simply immoral to kill many innocent people who are not their enemies. In an interview with *Der Spiegel*, when discussing the West German terrorists' threat to down a Lufthansa airliner, Hans Joachim Klein—a former German terrorist—said that it would simply be wrong to do it. It is the "little people" on board the airplane that make it wrong to do it.

I would also emphasize that the terrorists' desire to appear legitimate, to appear as a government, might be another constraint for certain reprehensible actions. There is also their fear of alienating their perceived constituents, although, invariably, these tend to be perceived as much wider than they really are. The terrorists fear provoking widespread public revulsion and unleashing harsh crackdowns that will have popular support and threaten the organization's existence. They are concerned about retribution by the world community. They are afraid that for all the foregoing reasons, their operations will provoke considerable debate and dissension within the ranks of the terrorist organization itself. This would increase the risk not only of betrayal of the operation, but also betrayal of the organization.

Equally important to consider are several conditions under which these constraints might be eroded. For example, this could occur where the terrorists' opponents and intended victims are clearly of a different ethnic group, such as Catholics against Protestants, Moslems against infidels, or Christians against Moslems in Lebanon. We note in sectarian violence the ability to become quite cruel. One is mentally able to reduce the opponent to a subhuman status. Also, religious beliefs and fanaticism erode many of the constraints because the religious fanatics have the sanction of God. The Guyana mass murder and suicide-by-persuasion, though not an act of terrorism in the sense that we have discussed, shows us the ability of religious fanaticism to remove the ordinary human constraints against actions of this sort. Another factor to consider is that the length of the struggle itself may have a brutalizing effect. We have seen this on a smaller scale already. Certainly the acts of arson in a Frankfurt department store, which marked the beginning of the Baader-Meinhof gang, seem somehow innocent when viewed in retrospect with the perspective of the murders of Jurgen Ponto, Siegfried Buback, and Hanns-Martin Schleyer. The lengthy struggle, the loss of comrades, and the desire for immediate revenge may be significant factors. Had the surviving members of the Symbionese Liberation Army (SLA) in California possessed any type of mass-destruction weapons, surely many of their constraints against the use of such a weapon would have been seriously eroded while they watched their comrades burn to death in a televised spectacle. The perception that the terrorist cause is hopeless may provoke a doomsday finale to an episode. Certainly, some of the actions contemplated by the Organisation de l'Armée Secrète (OAS) in Algiers in 1962—although not carried out in all cases—were of a bombastic sort, like a doomsday finale. "If our cause is lost and we lose everything that we have fought for, then no one else will possess that either, we will destroy everything"—that's the attitude.

Finally, there is the bureaucratic argument. Why should a terrorist group necessarily be different in this sense from a government developing weapons capability? In other words, and this is only speculation, could it not be that the will to have this weapon—even without having a specific use for it—will drive them? But once you have one such weapon, it serves as an incentive for using it. Even for armies this holds true. If you have tanks, you use tanks; the American army in Vietnam used tanks even in the delta where tanks were totally useless. I am not arguing against the conception of low probabilities. What I am trying to do is to make a balance between the constraints and the factors which cancel out those constraints. The question in my mind is whether the probability for this is just as low now as it was five or ten years ago. What conditions change that probability and how? It is difficult to conceive of the demands one would make commensurate with the threat that the action would involve. One does not threaten to blow up a city in order to free three prisoners. Somehow there is an imbalance. But a credible claim by the Palestinians that they possessed, say, a nuclear capability would alter the equations of power in the Middle East or at least people's perceptions of those equations even if they did nothing else with it.

In a sense, just the possession of the "Islamic nuclear bomb" somehow alters things regardless of people's thoughts of how, if at all, to use it. This is particularly true with nuclear weapons, less so with chemical or biological ones. The possession of nuclear capability has become the sign of statehood. The group which possesses the nuclear capability does not have to worry about extinction; and this somehow shows statehood. If you have a nuclear weapon, even though you may not have territory that is recognized, you have entered the ranks of legitimacy. In a sense, that might make nuclear weapons more attractive than chemical or biological ones. Also, the nations of the world have renounced the use of chemical weapons and of biological warfare, yet nuclear weapons are legitimate. Therefore, one could acquire or seek to acquire nuclear capability without necessarily risking the loss of legitimacy, and maybe even seek legitimacy through nuclear weapons.

The argument of prudence when in possession of nuclear weapons rests on a very slippery word: *rationality*. People talk about governments as being rational, and they talk about terrorists as being irrational. Yet governments are quite capable of being irrational in a certain sense of the word. Many people would consider the pursuit of military success by the United States in Vietnam through the application of the levels of violence such as they were as irrational. Many people would perhaps tag as irrational many actions carried out by so-called civilized nations with modern bureaucratic structures of decision making. So without saying that terrorists are lunatics or irrational, one can conceive of circumstances in which the perceptions of the group are such that their actions are rational from their standpoint. We should expect no more and no less from terrorist groups with regard to rationality than we expect from national governments. The U.S. government, engaged in a long war and after having suffered heavy casualties and great brutality during the course of the campaign against Japan in World War II, decided rationally and appropriately, from their standpoint, to use nuclear weapons, though they knew the consequences full well. On a smaller scale with fewer people involved, is it not equally conceivable that a terrorist group that has suffered brutality and that has grievances could say that it is appropriate for them to use nuclear weapons? That is, I think, a major area of ignorance in our knowledge of the terrorist mindset and of terrorist decision making.

15

Government Response to Mass-Destruction Threats by Terrorists

Robert H. Kupperman

Let me preface the paper with some general comments on mass-destruction terror. Since I began to study terrorism in depth, I have felt that mass-destruction terrorism should be viewed as a very high-consequence, low-probability event which must be studied seriously, for it is unfortunate but true that a great deal of trouble can be created by terrorists who are sufficiently dedicated and willing to take considerable personal risks. Whether or not weapons of mass destruction are within the reach of small groups and can be employed by them depends upon a number of factors. It is important to bear in mind, however, that such weapons when constructed by a national entity for military purposes differ considerably from those likely to be constructed by a terrorist organization. To a nation, it is of utmost importance that a nuclear weapon be highly reliable and of predictable yield. These requirements are much less important to a terrorist organization. For terrorists, it is sufficient that some nuclear explosive yield be present, or that the threatened authorities not be certain that the weapon does not exist.

With regard to the assessment of credibility of a mass-destruction threat, the problem is that credibility cannot be determined absolutely, for only when it is far too late, when the weapon of mass destruction has been detonated, does the threat become clearly credible.

Were a nuclear weapon detonated, an exhaustive investigation would ensue. Many problems of unprecedented proportions would arise. For example, there would be a major political problem. A sizable number of people would demand revenge. The most immediate problem, however, would be the amelioration of the consequences of the explosion itself. That is, holes would have to be dug in the ground to bury lots of bodies. I am sorry that this is such a brutal statement, but that is exactly what would happen if a massive attack, such as the detonation of a nuclear weapon within a city, were to occur.

Bearing in mind the serious consequences of the employment of nuclear weapons, I cannot be certain—at least at this point—whether such an extortion has a high or a low probability of occurrence. The United States has received many nuclear weapons threats so far. We have also been faced with a limited number of biological and chemical threats. All of them have been hoaxes or the products of diseased minds. In fact, in some cases, the perpetrators had a difficult time spelling *plutonium*. However, it is simply foolish to claim that such extortions will not or cannot occur. In the event of a threat, it is necessary to determine policy and to take appropriate action. The threatened must first ascertain whether the threat is technically feasible. That is, have the extortionists not made such bad mistakes in the description of the weapon that the threat can be virtually dismissed? Should there be some semblance of physical reality to the threat, the people concerned must decide how to react. They must consider who is threatening them and why. What do the terrorists want? Will they actually execute the threat? These considerations then beget issues of bargaining, management, and negotiation.

Since Henry Kissinger was secretary of state, the United States has operated under the theory that it would not cave in, that it would not concede to terrorists' demands and would pay no tribute to any extortionist. Up till now, however, the United States has dealt with relatively minor incidents, such as rather routine hostage taking.* Yet, we have reached the stage at which we must seriously consider different tactical options, for terrorists are upping the ante and may potentially threaten a great many people or disrupt large communications and power systems. In cases in which whole nations could be reduced to panic, the possibility of not negotiating is, in reality, excluded. If a terrorist group in possession of an atomic bomb were to demand the release of hundreds of so-called political prisoners, we could not afford to state that no discussion is possible. On the other hand, were there time for discussion, we would have the opportunity to develop tactically significant scenarios in which tactical concessions would not necessarily be of great importance; they might merely serve to facilitate implementation of the overall strategy.

In order that the government be capable of making timely, intelligent, crisis-oriented decisions when necessary, it should begin now to classify the types of demands it might face and the analytical techniques that could

---

*It should be noted that the conference took place a few months before the takeover of the U.S. embassy in Iran in November 1979.

be used to determine tactical and strategic options that could be employed at the time of greatest stress.

Basically, it seems to me, there is a great need for a small but knowledgeable crisis staff, one operating at the highest levels of government. That staff cannot be effectively put together overnight. Unfortunately, there is a great tendency in most democracies to deal with planning horizons on the order of ten minutes. Certainly this is true of the United States, and I think that possibly other governments with which I am not as familiar suffer from similar problems. We have a tendency to believe that nothing can be done in preparation, that no prophylactic action can be taken. Where mass destruction, or even far lesser attacks, are a real possibility, I submit to you that it is depressing to believe that there are no useful options or that no contingency planning is in hand. For we find ourselves dealing with every crisis matter on an ad hoc basis. This perception must be changed. We cannot expect to go in with six-guns blazing and solve terrorist problems of mammoth proportions. A crisis team could take the time to exhaustively consider various aspects of different problems and solutions. Then, were a credible threat to arise and time be at a premium, options could be employed more quickly and efficiently to resolve the crisis. Obviously, a crisis team must consider problems of control, containment, and restoration. This means that highly sophisticated command, control, and communications systems must be planned; there must be available a core group of people who have dealt with a wide variety of crises; and the group must have immediate access to the decision-making authorities of the central government.

For the U.S president, the business of making policy decisions is a terribly difficult one. With a strong president we have a chance of taking decisive action; with a weak president, we seek political consensus. Obviously, we are limited by 535 congressmen and senators, all of whom will pretend to be crisis managers.

Another factor that must be considered in the case of the United States is the lack of control over the media. It cannot be blacked out. To deal effectively with the media, we must take its members into account from the very beginning. In fact, under some circumstances—in order to avoid chaos and, ultimately, the embarrassment of the government—we must take selected members into the government's confidence. Thus far, mass-destruction possibilities have not become a reality, though we have had a great many hostage incidents. There have been difficulties with the press, but much of it has been worked out. Certainly after receiving considerable criticism, many responsible members of the press have developed their own codes of ethics.

I fear that I have raised more problems than I can possibly solve. I can suggest, however, that we must examine the structure of crisis teams and construct them, but we should develop them to deal with a wide variety of crises, not with terrorism alone. Thus, for example, such a group could deal with natural disasters, major industrial accidents, labor sabotage, and other like issues. There is no point in developing a bureaucratic group of several hundred people in a crisis team awaiting the massive terrorist event which may never occur. Yet, should a mass-destruction threat become real, the crisis team would have varied experiences on which to draw when determining the most effective option, and it would be ready to act on short notice.

Discussion

PARTICIPANT: How would you characterize the nature of a crisis management team for handling terroristic mass-destruction threats? In such cases special expertise is needed. What kind of expertise would be needed in such a crisis management group, and what kind of means would they require? Should the decision maker be involved in the discussions or should he be removed from the debates?

KUPPERMAN: I think what is needed is a kind of chief of staff, with a regular functioning team that will meet with him periodically. At the operational level, intelligence experts, communications experts, psychologists, and people who have dealt with strategic planning systems are needed. Media and public relations experts are also required, to handle the informational aspects of a crisis team. The team should have the ability to extract vast amounts of information quickly and to display the physical aspects of the various options. All this can be simulated in exercise games and public relations.

PARTICIPANT: A crisis situation calls for certain changes to be made in the usual democratic process. It seems obvious to me that in such a case political problems would cause difficulties in the work process of such a team. Therefore, it would be necessary to call a state of emergency, which would allow the crisis management team to act unrestrainedly, accepted by all political sides. In order to activate such a body one would need to introduce laws that would formalize and insure such actions.

PARTICIPANT: In the United States we are now forming such a body, called the Federal Emergency Management Agency. Part of its job is management of terrorist incidents. In the event of a crisis, the National Security Council is the coordinating element for the operation. I think that a crisis management team, if fully exercised in advance, could prove to be a very valuable aid.

PARTICIPANT: There are a number of major barriers, in addition to those already mentioned, to the creation of a crisis management team. There is an inherent problem in that the intelligence community considers the likelihood of terrorist use of mass-destruction weapons as very low and deals with these threats accordingly. A second obstacle to the creation of a crisis management team is political. Such a team would represent an enormous concentration of power outside the circle of regular advisors to the president. The more acute the crisis, the tighter becomes the set of people the chief executive contacts. Intimate friends rather than professional advisors are often consulted. A crisis management team thus represents a bureaucratic challenge to the president's advisory staff.

PARTICIPANT: Still, there is great importance in having a team of such capability and in a government's appearance of strength regardless of its policy on the issue. Clearly, in many of these cases, governments have not given a clear indication that they are in charge. I would like to examine here the example of the Three Mile Island incident. The Nuclear Regulatory Commission, the White House, the governor of Pennsylvania, the corporation involved, and a half a dozen other entities were involved there. Yet it was never made clear who was in charge and who was making what decisions. As a result, the government, in a certain sense, came apart and did not create the impression that it was clearly in charge of the crisis situation.

PARTICIPANT: Another governmental problem that would arise in terrorist events, especially mass-destruction threats, would be that of conflict of interests. In the United States this would be expressed in a conflict between the federal and state governments. In other nations the conflict may be among the different parliamentary groups. Clear-cut legislation distinguishing boundaries of action are thus needed. In the United States, for example, the standard procedure for nuclear threats is to turn them over to federal investigation authorities. The FBI investigates the threat and decides whether or not to assemble the emergency action team. This committee then has the option to call on yet another team, the threat and assessment team, whose members are located all over the United States, and make use of sophisticated technical aids in all fields. This gives some idea of the complexity of the crisis management team and its operation. The assessments are made within one to four hours, and the results are then returned to the emergency action team which in turn decides which higher authorities shall receive information for the decision making. The system, I might add, has been exercised successfully a number of times. But we should be aware that although a fixed policy may exist, the rules for its use change depending on the event and the risks involved.

PARTICIPANT: I would like to examine these ideas with respect to the Entebbe case. There were "only" 103 Israeli hostages captured in Uganda, and it was not a question of mass destruction. Yet, the pressure on the Israeli government was tremendous, almost causing it to give up, although Israel is very committed to an uncompromising stance against terrorists. A less committed nation would indeed have given up instead of looking for other options.

PARTICIPANT: The question of policy is to a large extent a political one. A strong policy requires national consensus and a wide basis of support. Strength of policy thus depends upon the strength of the government. In the final analysis, however, the decision of the government will depend largely on the feasibility of countermeasures. In the Entebbe case, the government—although under great pressure—did not give in because it believed there was a feasible solution. If the government had come to the conclusion that there was no feasible solution, the results would have been entirely different. In another situation the conditions were such that the Israeli government yielded and exchanged seventy-six terrorists for one Israeli soldier. This exemplifies again the importance of feasible solutions.

16

Government Policy in Incidents Involving Hostages

Ariel Merari

The catalogue of extortionate terrorist acts is relatively small, but the importance of the acts is far greater than the frequency of occurrence would lead one to expect.

Three types of terrorist events compose this category: barricade-and-hostage incidents; hijacking of aircraft or other means of transportation; and kidnaping. The difference between the first two kinds and the third is that the location of the hostages is unknown in the case of kidnaping; therefore, there can be no direct military operation to release the hostages.

Together, the three kinds of extortionate terrorism have amounted to about 20 percent of all international terrorist incidents throughout the last decade. The majority of these actions were kidnaping, mostly in Latin America. Barricade-hostage incidents represented only about 3 percent of all international terrorist activity.

From the terrorist viewpoint, hostage-taking operations are the most dangerous and complex type of activity. Why, then, do terrorist organizations devote so much effort to hostage taking? The preparations necessary for the planning and execution of an operation such as the Israeli coastal highway bus hijacking are quite elaborate. They include months of specialized training of a relatively large terrorist team (thirteen persons in this particular case); the collection of intelligence on the targets; and considerable logistical efforts. Moreover, volunteers willing to risk their lives must be recruited. Despite the danger and complexity of these missions and the far greater simplicity of alternative tactics, such as bomb planting, terrorist groups continue to stage hostage-taking attacks. The reason for this preference lies in the fact that no other type of terrorist activity is as successful in achieving the terrorists' objectives.

The most important of these objectives is publicity. During the 1977 Hannafi triple barricade-hostage incident in Washington, D.C., all television networks interrupted their regular programs to report the incident. They followed with on-the-scene reporting, analyses, and interviews with the terrorists, which covered hours of prime time broadcasting. Radio stations and the written media paid no less attention to the event. It has been reported that in 1977 when *Gone with the Wind* was shown on television for the first time, the network had been paid over a quarter of a million dollars for each minute of commercials. Thus, the monetary value of publicity such as that obtained by the Hannafis exceeded a billion dollars. Indeed, there is hardly anyone in the United States today who does not know something about the Hannafis and the personal plight of their leader, whereas very few had heard of this bizarre sect prior to that event.

Terrorists are well aware of the publicity value of hostage incidents. In his memoirs, Salah Halaf (alias Abu Ayad)—one of Fatah's main leaders and the chieftain of the Black September organization which carried out the 1972 Olympic Games massacre—testifies that one of the aims of that operation was "to exploit the unusual concentration of mass-communications media in Munich in order to give our struggle international publicity—positive or negative, it does not matter!"[1]

Other major terrorist aims in hostage incidents are to humiliate the government, thus harming its credibility as a protector of law and order, and to sow dissension among the population. Whatever course of action a government adopts in the face of a hostage incident, it is always subject to criticism. Giving in to the terrorists' demands is interpreted by some as weakness and encouragement for the terrorists to repeat these feats; governmental intransigence is viewed by others as recklessness and a failure of the liberal democracy to exercise its most basic responsibility: the preservation of its citizens' lives. The disputes that arose in Germany over the handling of the Schleyer case, in Italy over Aldo Moro, or in Israel following the Ma'alot incident clearly demonstrate that terrorists indeed succeed in fomenting criticism of the government and creating division among the population.

Cases in which the hostages include foreign nationals have been a source of international friction, which is, of course, another benefit for the terrorists. A well-known example is the 1979 kidnaping of the West German ambassador to Guatemala, Count Karl von Spreti, by the Revolutionary Armed Forces (FAR). In opposition to German pressure, the Guatemalan government refused the terrorists' demands for the release of twenty-five

---

1. Abu Ayad, *Le'lo Moledet* [Without A Homeland] (Jerusalem: Mifras, 1978), p. 158.

of their jailed comrades and the payment of a $700,000 ransom. Von Spreti was killed by his abductors, and West Germany took diplomatic sanctions against Guatemala.

Governments have differed considerably in the ways in which they have handled hostage incidents. Some of the differences stem from situation-specific idiosyncrasies, such as the nature of the terrorist group, its specific demands, the identity of the hostages, and the expected internal and international repercussions of the incident. Overall, however, two basic governmental policies can be identified: the flexible policy versus the tough policy. The remainder of the discussion will examine these policies and their implications.

The essence of the flexible approach to extortionate terrorism is presented by Frederick Hacker as follows:

> Mixed strategies (delay, negotiation, promises, firmness, consistency, force) used flexibly in different, changing situations and not chained to any preconceived political or other biases produce the best results. I do not advocate softness; to yield under any circumstances is just as unprofitable and futile as to decide in advance never to yield.[2]

The most consistent and outspoken representative of the tough policy towards hostage-taking terrorists has been the U.S. government. Since 1972, American officials have reiterated this policy many times. The following statement by Secretary of State Cyrus Vance is typical of this approach: "We have made clear to all that we will reject terrorist blackmail. We have clearly and repeatedly stated our intention to reject demands for ransom or the release of prisoners."[3]

The basic justification for the flexible policy is moralistic: a government is responsible for the lives of its inhabitants and is therefore obliged to take every step necessary to protect hostages. Nevertheless, advocates of this policy also raise pragmatic arguments that cast doubt on the effectiveness of the tough line in handling terrorists. In Hacker's words:

> What is intended as toughness against the terrorists actually turns out to be toughness against the victims. Such a response requires nothing but rhetorical courage. Rigid sanctions that have not been very successful in curbing ordinary crime will not work at all against crusading terrorism; they just create a false sense of security.[4]

---

2. Hacker, Frederick J., *Crusaders, Criminals, Crazies* (New York: W.W. Norton, 1976), p. 338.

3. Testimony before the U.S. Senate Committee on Governmental Affairs, January 1978, quoted in "Terrorism: Scope of the Threat and Need for Effective Legislation," *Department of State Bulletin*, March 1978, p. 54.

4. Hacker, *Crusaders, Criminals, Crazies*, p. 270.

To the arguments which are based on philosophical beliefs or logical grounds one should add the emotional responses of decision makers under the trying circumstances of a hostage incident. Faced with the pressure of the hostage families, some of whom may be personal acquaintances, it is almost inhuman for the head of state to adopt a course of action that would jeopardize the hostages' lives, regardless of the dictates of pure logic. Former Israeli Prime Minister Yitzhak Rabin attested to this in his memoirs. Describing his meeting with a father of one of the Entebbe hostages a day before the expiration of the terrorists' first ultimatum, Rabin writes:

> He came at seven in the morning. I had known him for years. He was not one of the moderates in his political opinions. He sat in front of me, broken and bitter. I told him that the government is vexed and knows the severe meaning of giving in to the hijackers, but if necessary—it would take a decision to open negotiations the next day. "You are familiar with this kind of deliberations ... " I said. He did not let me finish: "When you are personally involved in the matter ... " He stopped for a couple of seconds. I saw the signs of internal struggle on his face. Then he said: "For how long will you play roulette with our children's lives?" The words hit my heart like heavy stones.[5]

Quite understandably, under such circumstances it is very difficult to distinguish between the philosophical-political conviction and the call of the heart.

The arguments in favor of the no-concessions policy seem more rational, although it is likely that in practice they are not free from emotion. Objection to any concessions to terrorist blackmail is based on the notion that rewards result in repetition of the behavior that produces them. The application of this elementary rule of learning theory to the subject under discussion implies that if terrorists succeed in extorting their demands, they will attempt to repeat their success over and over again.

There are two major criticisms of the no-reward reasoning. One of them argues that although this principle may be true for normal people who weigh the consequences of their actions according to some rational profit or loss calculations, it is not applicable to terrorist behavior, which is irrational, even suicidal. One should remember, however, that terrorist organizations are not a random collection of Bedlam inhabitants. They are political entities that strive to achieve political aims by extreme means and at great personal risk. Examples of true suicidal behavior by terrorists are very rare. The Japanese Red Army (JRA) suicidal attack at Ben-Gurion

5. Yitzhak Rabin, *Pinkas Sherut* (Tel-Aviv: Sifriat Ma'ariv, 1979), p. 528.

Airport in May 1972 and the suicide committed by Red Army Faction (RAF) members in German prisons are exceptions rather than the rule of terrorists' behavior.

The second criticism of the no-reward theory is better substantiated than the first. It claims that the fulfillment of their overt demands in hostage incidents is only a secondary gain for the perpetrators. The terrorists' real aims in these operations are not the release of prisoners or monetary ransom, but rather publicity, demonstration of power, and the damaging of the authorities' prestige. These results, especially publicity, are achieved by the terrorists whether or not the government yields to their nominal demands. Since the most important damage is done regardless of the government's policy (according to this reasoning), there is no sense in prolonging the drama and jeopardizing the lives of innocent hostages.

This argument ignores the human factor on the terrorists' side. Barricade-hostage operations are conducted by humans, not by robots. The perpetrators are affected by fear and concern for their own lives, and the way the government handles the incident has a huge effect on their fate, not only on the hostages'. Thus, the tough policy not only implies no reward for the terrorist organization, but also punishment—that is, personal deterrence—for the actual perpetrators.

Throughout the history of Palestinian terrorism against Israel, there have been only nine cases of barricade-hostage incidents inside Israel. Considering the fact that there are some fifteen thousand members in the various Palestinian terrorist organizations, this is a very small number of such incidents. Given that the Palestinian terrorist groups are well aware of the impact of barricade-hostage operations, why have they not carried out more operations of this kind? The main reason seems to be the extremely high risk involved in such operations in Israel. It is not easy to find volunteers for missions in which the chance of survival is less than 5 percent, and the chance of return practically zero. This personal deterrence factor may also explain the fact that all of the barricade-hostage incidents in Israel have been carried out by teams who came from across the border, although there are over 1.5 million Palestinians living in Israel and the administered territories. Apparently, it is much more difficult to convince a member of a terrorist cell to risk his life in hostage taking than to induce him to place a bomb in a marketplace.

The relative infrequency of barricade-hostage incidents, despite their great effectiveness as a terrorist method, indicates that even in the larger terrorist organizations, such as the Fatah, the number of volunteers for highly dangerous missions is rather small. This is at least a partial explanation for the repeated participation of the same terrorists in high-risk operations.

This being the case, the recommended government policy with regard to hostage taking should be not only "no concessions to terrorists' demands," but also "no safe return for the perpetrators."

The practical meaning of this principle is that wherever there is a military option, the authorities should forcefully overpower the perpetrators if they refuse to surrender.

Possible Terrorist Reactions to the Hard-Line Policy

Resort to other methods

No symptomatic treatment, including a hard-line policy regarding hostage taking, can eliminate terrorism. However, terrorist groups fight against overwhelming odds and have to use their manpower sparingly. Whenever they encounter great losses, they turn to a less risky method. This has been a simple principle of survival for guerrillas for centuries. Thus, PLO terrorists gave up attempts to hijack El-Al airliners once security measures aboard them were tightened, and turned to lower-preference but less defended targets. Consequently, it can be expected that a policy of no concessions and no safe return, which implies greater risks for the perpetrators, would lead terrorists to resort to safer methods, such as bombing. From the government's point of view, this is a positive outcome, for hostage incidents carry the greatest political damage of all terrorist assaults.

Tougher negotiations

In order to put the no-concessions policy to the test and to increase the pressure on the government, it can be expected that terrorists would conduct tougher negotiations. They would present the authorities with shorter deadlines, refuse to free wounded or sick hostages, and set interim ultimata, accompanied by the killing of some hostages as a demonstration of their determination.

Increase in the disparity between the pawn's value and the demands

In an attempt to make it difficult for the government to adhere to an announced or evident no-concessions policy, the terrorists would try, on the one hand, to increase the value of their pawn—by taking a larger number of hostages or especially sensitive ones, such as children or dignitaries—while reducing their demands on the other hand. It would be almost impossible for a government to reject the demands of terrorists who were holding a hundred children hostage and demanding only their own safe release and the release of one jailed terrorist. In fact, this terrorist tactic in the face of a hard-line governmental policy has already been evident.

Note, for example, the sequential changes in the demands that were posed in hostage incidents by one Palestinian terrorist organization, the Fatah. These are summarized in the following table.

The Number of Jailed Terrorists Whose Release Was
Demanded in Hostage Incidents Perpetrated by Fatah

DATE	INCIDENT	NUMBER OF JAILED TERRORISTS DEMANDED
May 8, 1972	Hijacking of Sabena airliner to Tel-Aviv Airport	317*
September 5, 1972	Takeover of Israeli athletes at Munich Olympic Games	200*
December 28, 1972	Takeover of the Israeli embassy in Bangkok	36*
June 24, 1974	Takeover of an apartment house in Nahariya	Demands not submitted
March 5, 1975	Takeover of the Savoy Hotel in Tel-Aviv	10
March 9, 1978	Hijacking of a bus on coast highway in Israel	5

*These operations were carried out by Fatah under the cover name Black September Organization.

The terrorists' main aim in hostage incidents is rarely practical—the actual release of jailed comrades. Their major objectives are the achievement of a symbolic victory and the humiliation of the government. These can be achieved if the government concedes to the terrorists' demands, regardless of the number of terrorists released. The breaking of the no-concession principle itself is the victory. Furthermore, once it is demonstrated that the government has yielded to the terrorists' demands—minor as they may be—and the perpetrators were granted a safe return, it would be much easier for the terrorist group to recruit more volunteers for similar operations. For these reasons, I regard the lowering of the level of terrorist demands in bargaining as much more dangerous than their increase.

Some Preparatory Steps

Tactically, hostage incidents are a struggle for the lives of the immediate persons at danger—the hostages. From a broader perspective, however, they are a struggle over the legitimacy and prestige of the government and the democratic rule of majority that it represents. It is for this broader perspective that the government must adopt an unyielding policy. Yet, choosing the right policy is not enough. The no-concessions policy may be extremely difficult to apply, especially when the hostages are numerous and sensitive (e.g., children). Part of the difficulty stems from the terrible emotional burdens on the decision makers who must, at the time of the crisis, determine the fate of known persons, not anonymous and random soldiers. The strain is greatly increased by the direct pressure exerted on the decision maker by the hostages' families and the public at large.

The decision will never be easy when human life is at stake. Yet, there are some steps that can be taken in advance to facilitate the government's ability to apply the right policy.

The first step is a governmental policy decision in advance. It is much easier to make a decision of this sort when it is impersonal, that is, when it has no immediate consequences concerning the lives of known hostages. It is also much wiser in general to make policy decisions at leisure, without the time pressure of an ongoing incident.

Furthermore, the decision must be made known to the public. Some countries have done so (the United States, for instance), but most governments, including Israel, have refrained from publicly committing themselves to a clear policy on treating hostage incidents, presumably in order to retain their freedom of action and flexibility of response. The advantage of making a public commitment to a no-concessions policy is twofold: not only does it create certain expectations on the part of the public as to the government's stance under such circumstances and prevent confusion and uncertainty at the time of actual incidents, but it also removes some of the personal burden from the shoulders of the individual decision maker, since he acts within the framework of a prestated national policy.

Making the policy known beforehand also enables the government to influence public opinion in the preferred direction through all channels of mass communication. This advantage should not be underrated, for in a democracy the government's choice of action is determined to a large extent by public opinion.

Finally, without going into details, it is important to mention the necessity of preparing a well-trained, professional crisis management team for the handling of hostage incidents. The team's role is not to make policy decisions, but to ensure the skilled and flexible use of the various means at the nation's disposal in order to achieve an inflexible result—the fulfillment of the government's policy.

Discussion

PARTICIPANT: Basically, I do not disagree with your hard-line policy. But I have a couple of comments to make. First, regarding the figure of nine barricade-hostage incidents inside Israel. While that is true, there have been many more attempted incidents of this sort, and the reason they were not successful is that Israel has a very good forward defense. Had it not had border defenses, there would have been many more than nine incidents inside Israel. Secondly, you said that there is a very small number of terrorists willing to go out on what is basically a suicide mission. However, it does not take very many to carry out this kind of mission. For example, the Ma'alot incident in 1974 was carried out by three terrorists. In terms of world opinion, I think that in Ma'alot the terrorists won, even though they were all killed.

There seems to me to be a little bit of a gray area between a hard-line and a soft-line response. This is the negotiating response, which I consider different. For example, after the first Dutch train hijacking, there were negotiations; and after twelve days the terrorists surrendered. So there is an area in between a hard and a soft policy. You lose nothing by negotiating. But, again, I do not disagree with your thesis. I think this was a unique case.

MERARI: I agree that there should be negotiations, but not at the expense of policy requirements. That is, you can negotiate, but within the limits of the no-concessions policy. I approve of negotiations for tactical gains, and I think that the Dutch gave us a beautiful example in the Moluccan incidents.

With regard to the border defense, of course you are right. There have been more attempts than successes in taking hostages in Israel. If we include the failures, the number of incidents would more than double; instead of nine, the number would reach twenty-five or thirty. But it does not really matter. The point is that the tough-line image that Israel has gained throughout the years has deterred many terrorists from trying to come here, and it has caused some terrorists who succeeded in crossing the border with the intention of taking hostages to simply wait for the first Israeli army patrol and then raise their hands and give up.

Remember, also, that all of the terrorist teams intending to carry out barricade-hostage operations came from outside Israel. Every one of them. Now, why did they not come from the very large population—about a million and a half—within Israel and the administered territories? There are no border defenses. Arabs work in Tel-Aviv hotels; Arabs work in Israeli factories; they move freely, those from the administered territories as well as those from Israel itself. I see only one reason why they have not launched barricade-hostage operations, and that is deterrence.

PARTICIPANT: It is because they have their families in an area which is under our control.

PARTICIPANT: I disagree totally. Abu-Jihad, the chief of Fatah's operations, has a family in Gaza.

PARTICIPANT: No, we do not take advantage of the families. Those who came from across the border also have families here.

PARTICIPANT: You make it sound very easy, this choice between soft and hard policies. For the sake of argument, I would like to point out that there is something in between.

However, I entirely agree with the strategy which is based on deterrence; and a publicly announced no-concession policy is a part of that. Yet I think there are equally important and in some ways more important kinds of deterrents which can be used increasingly. For example, there are physical deterrents, such as border patrols or physical protection of our embassies abroad. I venture to say that the recently attacked Egyptian embassy in Ankara had no protection at all, whereas the American embassy and Israeli embassy are very well protected.

PARTICIPANT: There is a kind of intermediate range of concessions which one at least has to be prepared to look at. These are ways of buying time, and ways of persuading the terrorists to surrender. If they surrender, they can be put behind bars, which amounts to the physical disposal that you suggested is very important, and I agree. I think we ought not eliminate the possibility that we may be forced to do some things or even consciously choose to do some things which are between your soft and hard line.

PARTICIPANT: You are saying, then, that there are two things we should not consider: safe passage and release of prisoners. There is an emerging consensus among American police forces not to give the terrorists more weapons. If someone holds hostages with a gun and asks for three more, he is not to be given them. Yet there are two things that frighten me with regard to the hostage situation. Currently, the losses are tolerable in such situations. We have agreed about that. What frightens me is escalation to mass murders, to "megaviolence," which is a possibility that Robert Kupperman repeatedly warns against. It is important that we think about it. As you pointed out, what I call the "Merari theory of inflation in extortion" has already occurred. Your policy is leading towards an inflation of taking more and more people to get less and less. We should consider why this is happening and to what extent.

The other thing that I really worry about is loss of trust in the government's ability to govern. That is what a hostage situation confronts us with, much more than the bombing, assassination, or attack on a facility. The government must try to solve problems under duress, with the whole world watching, and the possibility of the governed feeling that the government is impotent or draconian in its counterresponse. If we lose that kind of concert between governed and government in a democratic society, then we lose democratic institutions. I do not know if you all agree with what I have said, but those are the two extremes that I regard as intolerable.

Otherwise, we could get along with a certain amount of hostage taking. We certainly have it in the criminal area. I am not saying that we should change our policy totally. We have a policy which seems to be working worldwide, and yet we are considering escalating and changing our response as democratic nations to something that is currently tolerable. Why? Do we see a danger right now of biological agents, chemical agents, nuclear disaster? Do we see a breakdown of democratic institutions or of trust in democratic government because of hostage incidents? Are we not panicking to the extent of playing into the terrorists' hands by taking the next step, and finding that we can talk less and less to terrorists? I think I am overstating the case, for the sake of debate.

PARTICIPANT: Let me give two examples, showing that both the soft line and the hard line may buy peace for a country. There have been hardly any terrorist attacks within the Soviet Union or against Soviet interests elsewhere. You can say this is partly because the Soviet Union is a supporter of terrorism. Yet there is another reason. I think that if there would be a terrorist attack on a Soviet embassy for instance, the KGB would hunt the terrorists round the world and kill them, and they know it. This is the hard line. The soft-line example is Saudi Arabia; it has also rarely been a target for terrorist attacks. The reason for this relative immunity is that Saudi Arabia is buying its peace by contributing huge sums of money to the PLO.

PARTICIPANT: Would you extend the tough policy to criminals, too? If someone robs a bank and is trapped with hostages there, would you not let him go if he frees the hostages?

PARTICIPANT: It varies from place to place. But New York's policy is that we have six thousand criminals that we have not caught yet anyway. Why not let the barricaded criminals free in order to save the hostages?

PARTICIPANT: The United States has had much more experience with criminals and bank hostage incidents than with terrorists. Sometimes I feel that you draw too much on the criminal experience.

PARTICIPANT: Did the Israeli government announce publicly that it would never concede?

PARTICIPANT: No, Israel never said so.

PARTICIPANT: The United States government did formally announce a no-concessions policy, and I doubt that it should be regarded as a helpful step. The chancellor of Germany acted in a very tough way in the Schleyer and Mogadishu cases, but even if he had announced a no-concessions policy in advance, I doubt that public opinion would have regarded the government handling of these cases as a success.

PARTICIPANT: In the Netherlands we never made a formal announcement of a no-concessions policy, although one could read it between the lines, and the government's position in hostage incidents has become tougher.

PARTICIPANT: Actually, we think the tough line has worked. Since that policy was made, we have not been a target for hostage taking so often.

PARTICIPANT: Not because you said it, but because you did it.

PARTICIPANT: First of all, I want to declare myself a supporter of the tough line, if there is a tough line. But I think that the problem of handling hostage incidents should be treated as a part of the question of defensive measures in general. In this context, intelligence is of great importance for the decision maker. Furthermore, if the terrorists had no safe haven after seizing hostages, it would ease the problem considerably. So, it requires some solidarity or some coordination among nations. This problem is becoming an international one, and unfortunately there is too little coordination among nations. Some people say that it would be terrible if nations exchanged information or jointly used intelligence services. This has been interpreted as a violation of freedom and as handing over too much power to intelligence services. But I think democracy is protected by intelligence, and the democratic decision-making process needs to be based upon precise information. When a totalitarian regime makes a mistake, nobody complains. In a democratic regime, the decision makers must be much more careful; yet they cannot be careful unless they base their decisions on precise data and sound evaluation of the data.

The other point I want to make is that you have to differentiate between strategy and tactics. In tactics, you can be quite flexible. In spite of the fact that the best way of extinguishing extortionate terrorism is probably to build a wall with no cracks—that is, no exceptions—it is impossible to achieve this aim unilaterally. I would advocate such a policy if we were not the only ones adhering to it, but in our world where there is a variety of approaches, there are bound to be exceptions to the no-concessions policy. Yet I would like to emphasize that we can create an impression of a hard line on the strategic level, and act accordingly—that is, grant no concessions—in 99 percent of the cases. But on the tactical level, you can create an impression of flexibility in order to establish better conditions for your operations.

PARTICIPANT: I think we can make a critical distinction between the deterrence strategy, and an incarceration or elimination strategy. These are very different ideas. Deterring the terrorists from doing something is one thing, but Dr. Merari's initial theory was that there is only a limited number of people capable of taking hostages in a known setting. I am not so sure that this is true, yet if so, then, of course, the hard-line strategy makes sense, though not for the purpose of deterrence, but rather for the purpose of finding and capturing or neutralizing that limited supply of practitioners.

MERARI: Indeed, these are two different arguments in favor of the hard-line policy. One argument is deterrence: the hard-line policy frightens others and deters them from taking the same course of action. There are at least six thousand Fatah members in Lebanon. How many of them have actually tried to cross the border into Israel in order to perpetrate a barricade-hostage incident? Very few. We have more people here at this conference than Fatah members who ever tried to cross the border into Israel for a barricade-hostage incident, and this is a very small conference. Now deterrence in this case has been successful because only a few Fatah members have been willing to enter Israel. Why? Why is a terrorist willing to place a bomb somewhere, yet unwilling to take hostages? I suppose that 90 percent of the Palestinians in the administered territories are pro-PLO, yet so far none of them has tried to take hostages in Israel. Why? Because it is very dangerous. This is the deterrence aspect of the hard-line policy.

The other advantage of the hard-line policy is the physical disposal of the small nucleus of terrorists willing to carry out hostage-taking operations. A study conducted at the Rand Corporation, and quoted afterwards in many places, reported an alarming statistic: 79 percent of the terrorists who have participated in hostage-taking incidents succeeded in getting out alive and scot-free. At first glance, this statistic is indeed terrifying; it makes terrorism seem to be a very good occupation. However, you have to remember that most terrorist groups are very small; even in the larger groups the number of trained, indoctrinated people who are able and willing to carry out such operations is very limited. Thus, if a terrorist organization wishes to maintain a high level of activity, the same people appear again and again in different operations. Now, if a terrorist's survival probability in a single operation is 79 percent, his chance of getting out scot-free and alive from three operations is only 49 percent, and if he participates in five operations—assuming independence of events—his chance of escaping intact would be only 30 percent, which is not high. Therefore, the prospect of eliminating this hard-core element of terrorism would be much better if nations adopted a tougher policy.

PARTICIPANT: I am willing to be a convert. I will buy your policy for purposes of finding those hard-core terrorists, keeping them in prison and making no concessions regarding their freedom, but it does not make too much sense to me when you argue in favor of deterrence. The death penalty has not deterred people from engaging in criminal acts.

PARTICIPANT: Some participants seem to imply that giving in to certain terrorist demands—for example, monetary ransom or political concessions—is more tolerable than conceding to others, such as the release of prisoners. In my view, this is wrong. Monetary ransom helps finance terrorist operations and may be more harmful than the release of jailed terrorists. Political concessions are even worse. After all, the ultimate goal of terrorist groups is some political achievements. For instance, the Turkish government's agreement to open a PLO office in Ankara in exchange for the release of the hostages taken by a Palestinian terrorist group in the Egyptian embassy there was such an achievement.

PARTICIPANT: We have to differentiate between reversible and irreversible concessions. Political concessions are reversible. For example, Turkey could recognize the PLO, but withdraw this recognition later.

PARTICIPANT: Even if concessions are withdrawn after a while, they nevertheless represent a psychological victory for the terrorists.

17

Negotiating with Terrorists

Frank M. Ochberg

Negotiations with terrorists holding hostages is generally accepted practice among Western nations. Regardless of a nation's policy concerning granting concessions to terrorists, negotiation skills can and should be taught, so that governments can turn to finely skilled negotiators when necessary.

To understand the role of the negotiator, it may be helpful to set forth the decision-making hierarchy, which is certain to be present in any situation involving hostages.

At the highest level is the head of the political jurisdiction in which an incident has occurred. Under normal circumstances, this level of authority is never involved in operational command; there are simply too many examples of things going awry when the political decision maker is closely involved with operational command. Beneath the head of the political jurisdiction is the level of command responsibility. This may be a chief of police or a subordinate with operational responsibility for a section of a city; he is the individual with responsibility for the conduct of negotiations as well as deployment of lethal force. Between this individual and the negotiator, there may or may not be one or more buffering individuals. Finally, the negotiator is the one who generally speaks directly with the hostage holder and has varying degrees of authority to make decisions. It is interesting to note, however, that the Germans have developed the concept of a speaker who carries on conversations with the terrorist, but who makes no decisions at all regarding the negotiation. The negotiator heads a small group which includes the speaker (where separate), a psychologist, and an interpreter; he reports directly to the operational command.

Characteristics that are found desirable for negotiators include maturity, verbal ability, imagination, and a general fund of knowledge that can be brought to bear upon a particular case. Fluency in a foreign language used by a foreign terrorist can also be a critical factor. Midrank police detectives are generally best suited, while behavioral scientists can be useful adjuncts if they know their place.

Having seen over a hundred negotiators, I have come to recognize the difference between the outstanding negotiator and the mediocre one. The outstanding negotiator has an instinctive ability to use his wits, to exhibit some warmth, and to ask questions at the right time. There is nothing wooden about the relationship he manages to evolve over a telephone, something very important to the negotiations.

The physical layout in which the negotiation occurs is extremely important. In the management of an overt hostage incident, there is invariably an outer perimeter controlled by uniformed policemen or military personnel to keep the general public at a safe distance. An inner perimeter is accessible only to members of special weapons and tactic teams and in some cases negotiators. A forward command post is established, usually within the circle, but sometimes outside the inner perimeter. Face-to-face negotiation is preferred by some units; land-line telephones are preferred by others. The bull horn has generally been found unsuitable, except for opening moments.

The physical layout may determine the proximity of the negotiator and commander. Some units prefer to keep these two functions apart, while others argue for close physical proximity.

Most training programs for negotiators include an academic block of instruction emphasizing psychological principles, terrorist types, negotiation principles, and a review of illustrative cases. Role playing is an essential element in the course. There is often cross-training in special weapons and tactics as well as in command decision making to familiarize negotiators with various critical elements in siege management.

We have found it very difficult to train tactical people in negotiation, although at one point we did a fair amount of such training. Small forces have no choice because of manpower constraints. That is, a small force may not have the luxury of a weapons specialist and a negotiation specialist. However, where sufficient personnel are available, training of specialists appears superior. Cross-training should also be given in order to encourage empathy with the roles of others.

One of the principle techniques of negotiation is the establishment of optimum levels of authority. This means demonstrating to the hostage taker that you, as the negotiator, have enough authority to deliver to him on some lesser demands, but that you lack authority to make major decisions, which are reserved to the command level.

Although people believe you should not give something for nothing, many skilled negotiators give ground early. Good negotiators deliver on demands; they establish credibility and rapport by acceding to minor requests before asking for favors in turn.

There are specific techniques for maintaining conversation, for making small talk, for avoiding embarrassing silences, and for minimizing questions and answers. The poor negotiators I have seen—and these are in mock situations, not real ones—often end up asking a lot of questions. Frequently, they do not know how to keep a conversation going, repeating the last thing someone else said or allowing a captor to ask the question. Negotiators must be perceptive listeners, but this can be difficult when they are struggling to maintain conversation. The negotiator who misses a critical comment or misinterprets a remark is at a distinct disadvantage.

There are also specific techniques for keeping the hostage taker in a decision-making mode and techniques which can intentionally delay the entire negotiation process. Let me speak briefly about delay. You should note that there is an important distinction between delaying tactics and the strategy of delay. Delaying is one of the four strategies in siege resolution, the others being attacking, bargaining, and capitulation. The delay tactic can be used to set up an attack, to arrange a bargain, or to stall until capitulation is decided upon by a higher authority. The delay strategy is based on the observation that terrorists do tire. It is also based on the fact that sieges move through three phases: from chaos to rationality to exhaustion. At the point of exhaustion, many hostage holders simply give up.

In conjunction with the delay tactic, let us also consider the Stockholm syndrome. This syndrome refers to the set of positive feelings generated in the hostage which can be reciprocated by the terrorist. The Stockholm syndrome is enhanced with delay. It may promote affection between the captive and the captor leading to a diminished inclination on the part of the hostage holder to continue threatening assault.

Let me emphasize that I am not an advocate for choosing the delay strategy or for urging negotiation with terrorists. However, I am a strong advocate for ensuring that all governments master the skill of negotiation in order to be able to use it effectively whenever it should be used.

Discussion

PARTICIPANT: What do you mean by the Stockholm syndrome?

PARTICIPANT: I do not know why that particular phrase has caught on, but in the credit bank incident in Stockholm in 1974, a positive relationship between the terrorist and the hostage developed. This relationship became romantic and sexual and lasted for over two years. This has happened over and over again. Frequently, when a middle-aged man is held hostage by a young male, he describes his positive feelings in a fatherly or avuncular tone.

OCHBERG: We teach negotiators about this Stockholm syndrome. What it means is that the hostage cannot be trusted. You cannot say to him, if you contact him by phone, "We are coming in in ten minutes," because the hostage can have a very strong unconscious attachment to the terrorist, much stronger than his trust in the police negotiator. Thus the information can be revealed.

Also, when you successfully resolve a siege and the hostage is released, you often find that this star witness has much more sympathy with the terrorists' cause than for the government agency that freed him. This problem can be handled if there is a certain kind of debriefing which takes place first.

In addition, after a notorious incident, the whole world sympathizes with the victim and wants to hear from him. The victim can transmit a message that is, for unconscious reasons, much more positive about the terrorist.

These are three negative factors as far as we are concerned. But the positive factor is that when this occurs, the two parties inside the siege room—the hostage and the terrorist—are locked in some affective bond which promotes the survival of both. For that reason we train negotiators in how they might promote the Stockholm syndrome. There are things, for example, which can lead the hostage taker to behave like a doctor.

PARTICIPANT: Did the Stockholm syndrome develop during the most prolonged hostage incident so far: the Moluccan twenty-day capture in 1977?

PARTICIPANT: It was much stronger in the hostage case before that one: the 1975 Moluccan incident. In that case, a rather remarkable Stockholm syndrome developed. But the terrorists learned a lesson from that. The next time they took over a train again, they kept apart from the passengers. They put the passengers in some compartments, and they took another compartment for themselves. They practically did not mix, because they kept the hostages under fire. So the Stockholm syndrome did not develop.

PARTICIPANT: Would you say that one cannot trust the hostages?

OCHBERG: No. Decidedly not. I wouldn't do that.

PARTICIPANT: This is one of the problems that we have in hijacking. The principal decision maker in a hijacking is always one of the hostages. And we have yet to work out a sensible way of dealing with this problem, for the airlines operate on a very nineteenth-century view of maritime law, which dictates that the captain is the captain of his ship, regardless of his ability to perform under the duress of a terrorist incident. We have had cases where it was quite clear that the pilot had panicked or was not making very sensible judgments about the environment in which he was operating. It is a real dilemma.

PARTICIPANT: I would like to turn to the question of the negotiator. How do you rotate negotiators? Obviously in an incident of long duration one man cannot play this role. Do you have a number of people establishing this same relationship and confidence?

OCHBERG: There are two schools of thought, and I will give you an example of each as its ideas were used practically. In a certain incident, there were two negotiators, one of them superior to the other. The superior arrived at night, began the negotiation, and turned it over to his deputy at the end of his twelve-hour shift (as usual, they were on twelve-hour shifts on this case). The two men were going to be coequal: either one could make whatever breakthrough he could get. It turned out that the deputy developed the real relationship, mainly because he was the daytime negotiator.

In Holland, there were three spokesmen, all of whom were psychiatrists or psychologists. Two were on the day shift, and one was on at night. The three were not of the same rank, and this quickly became clear to all, including the terrorists, who learned to deal only with the senior negotiator.

PARTICIPANT: We are coming more or less to the point of view that we prefer midlevel policemen for the real contact. But I do not agree with you, at least not with regard to Holland, that you have a vast potential of interrogators. In my experience—and I go through all the training—there is a very small number of people who are really fit to serve as negotiators. In Holland, a vast majority of policemen are not open enough. They are selected by their commissioners first, then they go through the training program, and then we keep one or two to go on with.

PARTICIPANT: Would you change the negotiator according to the type of terrorist? That is, might you start with someone and then try to find out what type of person the negotiator for the other side is, and then pick the right person on your side to negotiate with him? For you might have a very good negotiator who, however, would get into a conflict because of a difference of personality, difference of origin, difference of thinking. If you can establish the type of negotiator on the other side as soon as possible, and accordingly find a suitable type on your side, you can choose the right person to handle the negotiations for you.

OCHBERG: It has not happened that way frequently, but it does make sense theoretically. It is usually fairly well locked in once you start. But we do train the negotiators to overcome whatever sense of pride they have, to report honestly. If they feel that they are not developing a relationship, they can suggest someone else. And certainly during the training exercises, we almost always stress how a negotiator can respond to a terrorist's statement, "I do not want to talk to you, get me anybody else, I cannot stand you."

PARTICIPANT: Have you had any experience with women as negotiators?

OCHBERG: They are being trained. But the female negotiators themselves have said that they do not think they are the best ones to negotiate with female terrorists. The original reason to involve women was the large number of female terrorists. Some women feel they make good negotiators with certain types of men, particularly the trapped robber, and sometimes the mentally disturbed, where the woman's ability to develop a certain kind of relationship—usually more maternal than flirtatious—is useful.

PARTICIPANT: Once again, I would like to refer to specific circumstances. In South Africa, for instance, there are various tribes. Suppose you have a Zulu hostage holder. Would you recommend getting another Zulu to carry on the negotiations with him, or is it possible to use a white man or someone from another tribe?

OCHBERG: I would usually not recommend that you have like dealing with like. The people holding the hostage—particularly in a criminal case—usually want to reach the symbol of some authority. They would feel, "Well, you are sending us one of our people; that shows you do not care about us." That has come out. We have dealt with this problem in training black police officers in the United States. However, it is very important to have a police officer who understands the language, the nuances, the symbolism of the hostage holders. Some British negotiators have a deep understanding of the Irish Republican Army. They know, for example, that it is all right to let them come out with their faces covered. That is part of a traditional surrender form; not to allow that would have delayed the negotiations in a particular case another couple of days, and it did not mean anything bad—that's an important bit of knowledge.

PARTICIPANT: What do you think of what is becoming an increasingly common phenomenon in America and elsewhere, that is, the involvement of people whose ideologies are similar to those of the terrorists? For example, you have a Corsican priest come to talk to a Corsican terrorist or you bring a PLO official to Ankara on the theory that these are people who are likely to have real influence.

OCHBERG: I would call that by a different label. That is a mediator. We, the authorities, do not control a mediator who is marching to a different drum. Now that is a risk, but it may be a very worthwhile risk to take. I think that the critical stage in resolving the Hannafi siege was the negotiation phase, when Rabe and Cullinane[1] were talking to Khaalis[2] and getting him to come to mediation. Finally, Khaalis came downstairs and sat at the table with the three Moslem ambassadors.[3] The siege was won. The negotiation led to mediation, and this led to a good resolution.

PARTICIPANT: Of course, you can negotiate with regard to a mediator. You first ask, "Whom do you have in mind?" Then they name somebody, and you say, "Well, we will think it over; you will hear from us tomorrow morning."

PARTICIPANT: It can be really bad to depend on your mediator, to think that your mediator is your negotiator, and to confide too much in him.

PARTICIPANT: It is vital to start the negotiations at a low level, at the police level, and not begin with negotiations with politicians.

PARTICIPANT: That is what we did in the case of the massacre in Munich. The federal minister of interior went in; that was stupid. There was no higher level left. I think it should be a rule to start at a very low level.

PARTICIPANT: Not very low; the ideal seems to be midrank. For us it would be a Scotland Yard lieutenant, a chief inspector, or a superintendent.

PARTICIPANT: What do you think of the suggestion that people who work in crisis management ought to have some training in hostage negotiations, at least in the basic principles, so they can understand what the negotiators are doing?

OCHBERG: I think that is very important. It is important because there is more tension between the negotiator and his superior than there is between the negotiator and the terrorist.

PARTICIPANT: How do negotiators such as a psychologist, psychiatrist, or captain of police work together as a unit? Do they not feel at times that their authority is threatened? Who is given the authority to make decisions?

---

1. District of Columbia Police Chief Maurice J. Cullinane and Deputy Chief Robert L. Rabe.
2. The Hannafis' leader.
3. The ambassadors of Egypt, Iran, and Pakistan.

OCHBERG: Well, I have debriefed all of them afterwards, and it has not been too bad. What causes difficulties is if afterwards they all go to the press and they all take credit for everything. Then the trust is completely removed.

PARTICIPANT: It seems to me that a psychiatrist or psychologist is most valuable when a mentally disturbed person is holding a hostage. Frequently, medical problems come up. For instance, if there is a delay of several days, women on birth control pills who do not have their pills will start menstruating at once. That is something the hostage taker has not bargained on and how that is dealt with is very important. There is an opportunity to begin to humanize the whole situation and to have the hostage holder not think of the women as targets and objects, but all of a sudden they are more like mother and sister. If you can use that correctly, that is very useful. A psychiatrist might help a negotiator see that as an opportunity and work through some strategies to exploit it.

PARTICIPANT: There is a moral dilemma that I have heard discussed, and I would like your view about it. Frequently, a decision is made to use force. Nevertheless, people are asked to continue negotiating in some kind of apparent good faith, offering the possibility of life and escape to terrorists, suggesting that their demands will be met in some way. Do you think that the negotiator should be insulated from other governmental decisions that may be taken?

OCHBERG: Yes, the answer to that is yes. The negotiator is successful if he delays and if nothing bad is happening. With regard to that twenty-day episode in Holland, I think there was excellent negotiation, although the negotiators felt a sense of loss because they did not resolve everything. It is not up to the negotiator to reach a mediated settlement. The negotiators' job is to keep things stable as long as possible. Period. If there is an assault during that time, fine. However, as you know, we have an American Psychiatric Association task force working on the ethical issues involved. It is, I think, unethical and immoral for a medical doctor to be used to set up a hit, for that would be exploitation of the credibility of doctors. The government uses the doctor as a symbol of trust.

PARTICIPANT: I could say this. I would not have a personal objection to being involved behind the scenes in a decision which would lead to the deployment of a lethal force, because ultimately you are trying to save as many lives as possible. I was asked in a case what we would do about a brain-damaged individual, and I could see no way to talk to that brain-damaged individual. The best thing was to use force to interrupt the incident. And that includes using some medical knowledge to try to resolve something to save hostages. But it is going too far to ask a doctor or a psychologist to participate in a fraud that will lead to the death of the one he has the relationship with.

PARTICIPANT: But you would do it without his knowledge? You would use him?

PARTICIPANT: Well, I think that if a psychologist or psychiatrist is going to be involved in a terrorist incident, he should understand that it is not his decision to choose between capitulation and delay. Those are strategic decisions.

PARTICIPANT: This leads to another question. What is the place of the negotiator in the crisis management team? Do you not think that the negotiator should have a very close connection with the policymaker in cases where you have to work on a very tight timetable? If you have a very tight timetable, say, of six hours, any delay in communication between the negotiator and the decision maker may be critical. That is one reason why I think that perhaps a negotiator should be in direct communication with the decision maker. Another reason is that if there is a buffer or liaison between the decision maker and the negotiator, and an operation is intended, you might be afraid that some of the rather important considerations and information will somehow be distorted on the way from the negotiator to the decision maker.

OCHBERG: If you are given a six-hour deadline, that does not mean that everything has to happen within six hours. Every case has a short deadline. Something is supposed to happen right away. Deadlines are frequently ignored.

PARTICIPANT: I would like to note the difference between your experience and our experience in Israel. We have learned from experience that Palestinian terrorists have very tight deadlines that they are very serious about. You could play with the terrorists and try to have the deadline extended, but the terrorists have been briefed and given instructions with regard to the negotiations. They are generally told that the other side is fraudulent and will play tricks and attack. They have a set of sophisticated ways of trying to avoid being tricked. Therefore, I do not think that attempts at delay can be very successful. Perhaps you can get one very limited extension of a deadline, but that is all.

PARTICIPANT: Let me, then, raise my question again concerning the conduct between the decision maker and the negotiator.

PARTICIPANT: Well, if you are not going to use the delay method at all, it is not necessary to have a hierarchy. If what is important is bargaining at the top and working out what is going to happen instantly and then making a decision to use force or to give up, you might as well use the top decision maker right away. In the case of our air force we have two different policies. One policy deals with nuclear material being compromised; the other is non-nuclear. If someone enters an area where there is nuclear material, there is no bargaining and a negotiator is not wanted. The base commander is wanted; if he says there is one minute left, then within one minute an assault is made. If you are saying that certain cases involving Palestinian terrorists are similar, then if you are not intending to use the delay method you might as well use a top decision maker.

OCHBERG: I would like to refer to earlier questions. First, let me explain about a buffer. It is usually at the negotiator's request that there is a buffer between the negotiator and the operational commander. When there is a chaotic scene with a lot of information coming in, the negotiator feels he must remain accessible to that telephone, and he wants someone sitting next to him who will talk to the captain or the commissioner. If the event is slow and there is an hour between phone conversations, of course they will be in close contact.

Secondly, I was asked about the negotiator leapfrogging over the commander and talking to the policymaker. That will take place, it should take place, at the insistence of the operational commander—the person who is being bypassed; that will take place when the operational commander has a problem with his superior and wants the negotiator to explain a point of view.

PARTICIPANT: Earlier, you spoke of tough responses. Does such a response undermine the position of the negotiator?

PARTICIPANT: Of course it does. The Palestinian terrorists have specific instructions not to believe anything that the Jews say. Still, the question is, what is more important: deterrence or prolongation of time? You cannot play it both ways. You have to decide what you prefer.

PARTICIPANT: I would like to turn to a different issue. What do you do in a case where the terrorists actually kill one hostage?

OCHBERG: Before the negotiation or during?

PARTICIPANT: During.

OCHBERG: The contingencies that will lead to a change in negotiation or a shift from a delay strategy to an attack strategy should be discussed in advance. I do not think a rule should be made to govern all cases. In a particular instance it could be decided that should one or two people be executed there will automatically be an attack. But consider the Moluccan case, with 105 schoolchildren and with an attack plan on the second day, and your military commander saying that if you attack there will be an 80 percent casualty rate. Do you attack when one person is killed on the train? These are very difficult decisions.

PARTICIPANT: Let each one here express his opinion about this.

PARTICIPANT: First, concern for the hostages should be expressed and also condemnation of the act, so that you can then get into a conversation with the terrorist, who will probably say, "I did that because you made me do that." And then you go on from there. You should not respond in an angry manner, but neither should you minimize the act.

PARTICIPANT: Why not break off the conversation by saying, "We tried to build trust. Now you did something to break it down. Maybe the conversation will continue, but not with me"? Then you break off and bring someone else, because there is no longer any confidence between the terrorist and the negotiator.

PARTICIPANT: I would not break it off as a negotiator. It is too big a decision for a negotiator to make.

PARTICIPANT: Break it off and bring in someone tougher. There is always the possibility of bringing back the first one. I am sure that you cannot continue the conversation after such an event. If you have to gain time, you must break off at this point and get somebody else to continue tactically.

PARTICIPANT: It is an option to change negotiators. But I would not teach negotiators always to end the relationship when someone is shot.

PARTICIPANT: I guess it is also important to find out why the person was killed. And if you can, that is important information. You can find that out by asking.

PARTICIPANT: Well, we had an execution while negotiations were going on; and the negotiator continued.

PARTICIPANT: What did he say?

PARTICIPANT: He reacted shocked. It was at the beginning, and he reacted completely taken aback. "What on earth did you do?" he asked. "Why?"

PARTICIPANT: Did he talk to the terrorists in a trusting manner right away?

PARTICIPANT: Yes.

PARTICIPANT: Did the negotiator take it as a personal attack?

PARTICIPANT: No, because the terrorist blamed the authorities, not the negotiator.

PARTICIPANT: When the negotiator cannot stand it, he must go out. I can very easily understand a man who says, "Well, I do not want to have anything to do with it anymore."

PARTICIPANT: Let us assume that he can stand it. Is it wise for him to continue, because he is definitely in an inferior situation?

OCHBERG: Let me point out something. There is an early stage when everyone personally is in a very chaotic situation. The adrenalin is pumping out. You cannot trust the way your brain and body are working. The negotiator's main objective is to get out of that phase and get into the next one. In the next stage you can bargain and mediate and do things rationally. Most of the unprecipitated killings that occur take place during the first stage. The important thing is to try to get into the second phase. A killing during phase two presents a different kind of a message.

PARTICIPANT: But your case was in phase two.

OCHBERG: If it is phase two, you may be right. You may feel as a commander that the time has come to change negotiators.

PARTICIPANT: It all depends on the forecast the crisis team can make regarding the continuation of the whole process. When you think there is still a chance the terrorists will surrender, then it is better to maintain relations in a way that will not make the terrorists more extreme than before. On the other hand, if you think there is no chance for surrender, it is better to take another course of action, which means preparing for an assault. However, there is still the practical question whether you should do that with the same negotiator or not. What is clear is that in any case you have to calm down the scene after the execution, whether for surrender or for assault, because it is not good to have the terrorists highly emotional. Thus your objective is to calm them down. Whether this can be done with the same negotiator depends on the specific situation.

PARTICIPANT: You also want to calm down the hostages. It's a lot better if they are calm or sleeping.

PARTICIPANT: On a different issue, what do you believe to be the optimum composition of the crisis staff?

OCHBERG: You certainly need someone who understands intelligence and can evaluate all the sources of intelligence that come in. He must understand the practice and the way the situation is being played out. It helps to have a lawyer, someone who understands what the legal implications are of any decision that is being made. It helps to have someone who is a little bit outside of the military chain of command, but can advise on what the military or the police are telling you, because in my opinion there is usually an attempt to overestimate the success of a military operation.